THE
COMPLETE
E-Commerce
Book

**Design,
Build &
Maintain a
Successful
Web-based
Business**

BY JANICE REYNOLDS

Published by CMP Books
An Imprint of CMP Media Inc.
12 West 21 Street
New York, NY 10010

ISBN 1-57820-61-X

For individual orders, and for information on special discounts for quantity orders, please contact:

CMP Books
6600 Silacci Way
Gilroy, CA 95020
Tel: 800-LIBRARY or 408-848-3854
Fax: 408-848-5784
Email: telecom@rushorder.com

Distributed to the book trade in the U.S. and Canada by
Publishers Group West
1700 Fourth St., Berkeley, CA 94710

Manufactured in the United States of America

Contents

Preface

Acknowledgements

CHAPTER 3:
Let's Build It!

CHAPTER 4:
Server Hardware

CHAPTER 5:
Redundancy

CHAPTER 6:
Connectivity

CHAPTER 7:
Security

CHAPTER 8:
Software

CHAPTER 9:
E-Commerce Software

CHAPTER 13:
Consultants and Vendors

CHAPTER 14:
Web Hosting Services

Contents

CHAPTER 18:
The Future

Preface

Unless you have been in a coma or on a desert island, you have heard about e-commerce; but do you understand it?

You have listened to and read stories about the explosive growth of e-commerce and the monstrous valuations of web-based companies. You have probably "surfed" the Web and may have made an online purchase. But, as you have picked up this book, you are probably still wondering exactly what is this thing called e-commerce and how can you get a piece of the action.

This book, *The Complete E-Commerce Book*, will provide select comparisons of various kinds of software needed by e-commerce businesses to prepare a good foundation for establishing a successful Web site. It will offer insight not only into the "how to" aspects but also the pitfalls to avoid when constructing your site.

You already know that the Web is revolutionizing the way the business world approaches buying, selling and communicating with their customers and business partners. Understanding the basics of e-commerce and its technology is a necessity for any executive in a company that is already on the Web, thinking about moving to the Web or has business partners who have moved to the Web. The reader of this book will gain the ability to understand the issues, strategies and questions that should be asked, if you or your business is to have a relationship with a Web-based operation. When you finish the last page, you should have the knowledge to make the right decisions as you journey into the e-commerce world.

After reading this book, you should be able to:

- Understand the technology necessary to construct a good Web site and make the right hardware, software and application choices.

- Choose the right Internet hosting service for your needs.

- Talk intelligently with your Web designer, Webmaster, database guru and technical personnel.

- Choose the staff, vendors, and consultants who can get the job done.

- Understand the complexity and special needs of operating an e-commerce site.

- Build a Web site with its own unique qualities — not one of the thousands of looka-like, "cookie-cutter" Web sites.

The technology that makes the Web a wonderful place to do business also makes it scary. Why? Think about it — it's unstructured, uncensored for the most part, and it speeds up the exchange of information between businesses and their customers — at a speed that most businesses are not prepared to handle. Your customers can find your business by a click of a mouse and make purchases easily; but they also expect easy access, prompt delivery, and good customer service. This book gives you the tools to understand the technology and issues involved; thus, enabling a business to adapt quickly and make the changes necessary to prosper on the Web.

An online presence gives a strong competitive edge for most brick-and-mortar busi-nesses; but it must be done right. This means bringing together product knowledge, mar-keting, distribution and other skills that may not be present in a brick-and-mortar busi-ness. This book, *The Complete E-commerce Book*, will help you ask the right questions, set realistic goals and make the right decisions as you make a move to the Web; whether it is as an entrepreneur, in a new position with a Web-based business, or moving your own brick-and-mortar to the Web.

I am also writing this book for the many non-technology executives who are lost amid the plethora of terms of the emerging technologies. When it comes to the decision of adopting new technologies, these executives rely almost entirely on their information technology (IT) department. However, executives who rely entirely on their technical gurus for significant input into their business' overall strategy are just asking for trouble. Why? While non-technology executives do need to consult with the IT managers on how technology can relate to their business' overall strategy, they must take some responsibil-ity for understanding the technologies.

Acknowledgments

The Complete E-Commerce Book was born out of my aspiration to get out the message that it takes a number of disciplines and a concerted effort to build and maintain a successful Web-based business. But also, from my awareness of the myriad of professionals whose careers touch in some way or another on e-commerce, although they don't yet fully grasp its scope and possibilities.

Researching and writing this book was no small task and there are a number of people that I want to thank for helping me along the way.

I am deeply grateful for the encouragement and support I have received from my friends and professional colleagues while working on this book.

First of all, I could have never completed this book without the support, encouragement and editing skills of Deborah Thornton.

Thanks to Richard Grigonis who provided all of the graphics for this book and gave me invaluable technical advice and support beyond belief.

Thanks to my friends who kept me going when I felt it was impossible — Cliff Perciavalle, Madeline Delrow, and Roya Mafazali.

CHAPTER I

The E-Commerce Phenomenon

It is hard to fail, but it is worse never to have tried to succeed.
In this life, we get nothing save by effort.

Theodore Roosevelt

The Internet is changing the way we do business, whether it's finding new streams of revenue, acquiring new customers, or managing a business' supply chain. E-commerce enables businesses to sell products and services to consumers on a global basis. Or, to put it another way, e-commerce is the platform on which new ways are being found to sell and distribute innovative products and services electronically.

In the 21st Century, it is important that an executive knows 1) where technology stands in the business processes of the company, 2) how technology relates to the company's strategies, 3) how rapidly technology changes and evolves, and 4) how the company and its business partners will respond to the changing technology.

As we begin the new millennium, the Web's growing influence on the world's economy is truly astonishing. The business world is realizing that the Web is one of the best ways for manufacturers to sell their products directly to the public, brick-and-mortar retailers to expand their stores into unlimited geographical locations, and for new entrepreneurs to inexpensively establish a new business.

You have probably read many highly publicized e-commerce success stories, any one of which can raise the entrepreneurial blood pressure. Just remember the old adage: If it looks too good to be true, it probably is. Use your innate intelligence and proceed with caution.

The ascendancy of e-commerce on the Web makes available an expanding business environment where even a small start-up is able to compete with the well-established business names and product brands. However, considerable effort is involved, since selling products and services on the Web presents a unique set of challenges.

THE E-COMMERCE DECISION

For the new crop of entrepreneurs and the established brick-and-mortar businesses, setting up a virtual business on the Web can be a great way to expand your market — BUT you MUST first educate yourself as to how to proceed. Extending an existing business to the Web or starting a new Web venture without understanding e-commerce is like trying to hit a baseball with one arm tied behind your back and a blindfold on. It is not simple and it is not easy to build a successful business on the Web. It takes a tremendous amount of planning. Without a clear understanding of the process and clearly defined goals, establishing a successful Web site can turn into a difficult, complicated, and costly project.

One of Tom Friedman's e-commerce columns in *The New York Times'* Op-Ed section was headlined "Amazon.You": "For about the cost of one share of Amazon.com (AMZN), you can be Amazon.com." He continues with the story of a Cedar Falls, Iowa online bookselling operation, www.positively-you.com, that costs around $150 a month to run. This bookseller uses the same wholesalers as Amazon.com, but his net on each sale is better. Friedman stated that the site "offers Millions of Books at Great Prices" including, a John Grisham book for $2.60 less than Amazon.com. Mr. Friedman's point is that for the cost of just a few shares of Amazon.com stock, and a good, clearly developed idea, a savvy small entrepreneur can compete with a "Web Giant."

THE BRICK-AND-MORTAR'S DECISION

If you are the owner of an established, traditional business, you must first determine the benefits of a Web presence. To do so, ask yourself some hard questions:

- What are your business goals and how will a Web site support them?
- What do you want to achieve with a Web site?
- Will a Web site deliver new customers or more sales from current customers?
- Will it offer better customer support?
- Will it bring good publicity?
- When is the right time to create a Web site for your business?
- Will this venture adversely affect your brick-and-mortar business?

In other words, if you build it will they come? Forget the hype and determine if and how a move to the Web can enhance the bottom line of your brick-and-mortar business. Then determine the amount of money you must invest before you turn your first profit from the Web site.

Any way you look at it, the decision to extend an already successful brick-and-mortar business onto the Web is a tough call. Before moving forward, considerable research is necessary; but, without the appropriate technical knowledge and the understanding of the ins-and-outs of e-commerce, it is easy to get lost.

On the technical side, your sequence of goals should be:

1) Learn what it takes to build various kinds of Web sites.

2) Determine what kind of Web site you want to build.

3) Build it.

4) Continue to improve and update it.

You must take care that your existing business doesn't suffer as you and your staff gain the necessary knowledge and proficiency in the technologies needed to intelligently purchase and implement the equipment and software needed for a Web site. Do you have any idea how much time, effort, and money you must invest in order to have a viable e-commerce site, one that will produce a reasonable return? It is important that you take the time to find out.

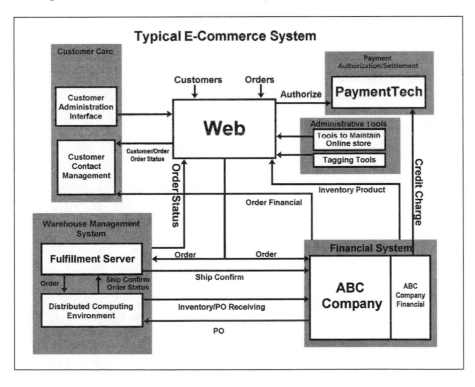

THE ENTREPRENEUR'S NEW WEB VENTURE

Most of what applies to a brick-and-mortar business will also apply to an entrepreneur's new Web venture. Additionally, a new Web-based business must leave the starting gate with an extremely high performance level if it is to effectively establish its brand name. If it stumbles, in all likelihood the Web-based business will not positively imprint its brand name on the public and therefore will not be in a position to exploit the myriad opportunities available to an innovative Web entrepreneur.

The first step for a fledgling entrepreneur is to determine your *niche market* — a defined group of potential customers sharing common characteristics that delineates their interest in specific products and/or services. This is where you should expend your efforts. A niche market makes it easier for a business to plan a credible marketing strategy. When you know your niche market, you can tailor your site's content to appeal to that market. For an example of a Web business that has found a good niche market, go to www.justballs.com.

Once you decide on your niche market and your product or service, answer the following questions:

- Is your product easy and economical to ship?

- Who are your suppliers? Can you depend on them for quality and prompt delivery?

- What is your price point (the price just above the point where lowering the price will increase your sales but not increase profits)?

- How are you going to draw customers to your Web site?

- How will you differentiate yourself from the competition?

- How are you going to accept orders and process payments?

- What type of fulfillment facilities will you use to ship products?

- How will you handle returns and warranty claims?

- How are you going to provide customer service?

- What size e-commerce site do you want to build?

- How will you build your new Web site?

- How much will it cost to build and can you afford it?

You can't just put goods up on your new Web site and expect your customers to come and shop. Find out if your niche market is one that you can reach through a Web site. How? Does your niche market have an identifiable need for your Web offering? Do they have the wherewithal to pay for it? Is the niche group sizeable, i.e., will it provide enough business to produce the income you need? If the answers are yes, you have found a good niche. Now dig deep within that niche to understand the consumer behaviors that drive it.

You should assume that your e-commerce customers are sophisticated shoppers who demand prompt delivery of a product that is exactly as portrayed on your Web site. The most common mistake that a Web entrepreneur will make is not to be diligently responsive to the order processing and fulfillment needs that are the underpinning of any successful e-commerce venture.

To help in the follow-through, you and your customer must be able to track the status of a purchase. Most new Web-based businesses do not integrate this necessary back-end support. Another "must" is to make certain that your customers know that your Web-based business will not only deliver a value online that cannot be found offline but that it is just as responsive with customer service issues as the most well-regarded, offline business. For example, on December 29, 1999, *InternetWeek* reported that Value America, an online electronics, technology and office products store issued a statement that their product fulfillment delays and system transition issues that occurred during the implementation of their new IT infrastructure hurt their sales during the 1999 holiday season.

By keeping customer service and product fulfillment as an immediate priority you can build a valuable relationship with your customer. In doing so, you earn that customer's loyalty, which can help stem the flow of attrition as they pursue the lowest price but then find that the trade-off is usually a void in the customer service department.

Another common problem for new Web-based businesses is misinterpreting the power of the Web. Yes, with your new Web site and its infrastructure, you can economically automate transactions. However, you need to understand that the real power of the Web is its role as a relationship building magnet — through its ability to provide numerous opportunities for interactivity. Therefore, if you are careless with automated processes — this very real advantage will vanish.

Use your Web site to provide not only useful and interesting information about your product/service but also about your entire niche market. The group that makes up a niche market always yearns for more information. They will return time and again to your Web site if they are being appealed to on the basis of their special interest through detailed articles and content-rich advertising specifically targeted to them.

WHY GO TO THE WEB?

It is no longer just a theory — the Web opens up a whole new market for goods and services. In addition, the Web creates opportunity for a multifaceted arena that offers new efficiencies for sales, marketing, customer service, shipment tracking, inventory monitoring, and many other aspects of the total business model.

Choice has always been the Holy Grail for consumers. Today's consumers have commerce choices of traditional businesses, catalogs or written material, and the Web. The Web, taken as a whole, is a powerful medium where consumers can browse, research, compare and then buy online or, after doing their "window shopping" online, make the purchase at a brick-and-mortar business. Businesses that keep in mind the consumers' desire for choice, and integrate into their Web site the appropriate means for customer interactions, will succeed.

This being said, the Web does not always open vast new markets for every business; but it can extend a significant degree of power to businesses that recognize how to leverage the efficiencies of this new arena. A good example is 3Com (www.3com.com) which, through its Web site:

- Provides many different technical support features online.

- Offers software downloads including drivers, updates and fixes, which prior to the Web site, would have been mailed to the customer.

- Offers an online store.

- Provides an educational center with online courses.

In short, 3Com's business and customer base didn't change — the Web changed the way 3Com services its market — it did not create a new market.

Big companies with plenty of technical expertise and buckets of money have always been able to build their own e-commerce systems, complete with a secure server, an Internet connection, and custom software. Luckily, costly e-commerce barriers are rapidly tumbling allowing any business to have a credible Web presence. What was once expensive and difficult is quickly becoming affordable and easy to use.

Look before you leap. Many companies neglect creating a business model for e-commerce. Some experiment haphazardly while others frantically rush in to stave off market incursions by Web entrepreneurs. Some businesses either wring their hands in bewilderment or bury their heads in the sand waiting for the phenomenon to pass. Some companies rashly leap to establish an on-line presence and in doing so risk losing their identities, reputations, and customers. For example, the woes of Toysrus.com with its numerous outages and complaints during the 1999 holiday shopping season were widely reported. Not to mention the 44% of shoppers surveyed by Robertson Stephens, a leader in Equity Research, Investment Banking and Sales & Trading, who said it was unlikely that they would shop on the online toy retailer KBKids.com again. Perhaps if they had scaled down their initial online effort as Bloomingdales.com did, their Web site and reputation would have fared better.

Creating a business model for e-commerce starts with the following basic challenge: Can you define your company? Next, can you state your goals for the company along with what the company needs to be? Finally — within the aforementioned context — state what role e-commerce can play in helping your company maintain or change its identity.

WEB SITE MODELS

There are typically six basic Web site models ranging from the simple static pages of a brochureware site to the richly interactive online store. Many Web sites combine several of these basic models. However, each model has its own unique characteristics that distinguish it from the others and it is important to understand these differences.

Brochureware Site

A brochureware site is a marketing site that electronically aids in the buying and selling process. A traditional business will often build and maintain a brochureware site as a marketing tool with the objective of promoting the business and its products. A brochureware site is sometimes an adjunct to a business' technical support division providing online documentation, software downloads and a Frequently Asked Question (FAQ) section. It can provide annual reports, press releases, employment opportunities as well as detailed information about the business' products/services, contact information including the business' address, telephone numbers, and e-mail addresses. Revenue from this kind of site is generated indirectly by creating an awareness of the business' products/services. The actual purchasing transaction occurs offline.

Visit www.tdiinc.com for an example of a good brochureware site. It is clean, fast loading and has all of the elements of a good Web site. Another example that demonstrates the variety of businesses that take advantage of the Web to expand their business opportunities is www.rolledsteel.com.

Online Store

An online store is a Web site where consumers can buy products or services. This type of site is most commonly referred to as an e-commerce site or a "B2C" (Business to Consumer) site. The online store displays products or services along with detailed information such as specifications and pricing, usually from a database with search features and a method for online purchase. An online store also provides most, if not all, of the content found in a brochureware site. Still and all, an online store must also provide extensive information about the products/services offered that not only aids in attracting consumers, but gives them enough confidence in the seller and the products/services to take the next step — making an online purchase.

One question I am often asked is "what should an e-commerce site offer — credit card transactions or just a toll free number or both?" The answer is: Offer both.

If you choose to take credit card transactions, you must provide a secure, reliable, cost-effective system for authorizing payment and managing transactions. A system based on the Secure Socket Layer (SSL) and/or Secure Electronic Transactions (SET) encryption technology provides the encryption of data and generates and displays a "results page" to the customer following the transaction.

Further, a successful online store must be designed with the ability to store orders in a database or as tab-delimited text files so the data can be imported into an invoicing system. Then it must be able to intelligently route encrypted e-mail to the order fulfillment division.

A good example of a large online store is www.healthtex.com. This is a great site in every respect. For an example of a small brick-and-mortar business that has designed an attractive, fully functional e-commerce site go to www.parkaveliquor.com.

Subscription Site

A subscription site targets a specific niche market that places a value on expert information, service, or a digital product delivered in a timely manner. Technical newsletters, access to research information, graphics, music and computer game downloads are examples of sites that charge a monthly or annual subscription or a small per transaction fee. With such revenue, you should be able to fund the operating costs of a subscription site, but the income will not be substantial. As the e-commerce technology of the Web becomes more sophisticated with the appearance of such things as micropayments, the e-commerce landscape will undoubtedly change. A subscription site can process payments offline and provide via e-mail a user's name and password for access, or it can provide a secure, reliable, cost-effective system for authorizing payment and managing transactions. Again, a system based on the Secure Socket Layer (SSL) and/or Secure Electronic Transactions (SET) will encrypt the data, generate, and display a "results page" to the customer following the transaction. A subscription site usually requires database-publishing capabilities.

A good example of a subscription site is www.searchenginewatch.com. Note that this site displays banner ads for additional revenue. This is a nicely designed site that provides wonderful free information (use it!). But it also has a "Subscribers-Only Area" that has detailed information about all the major search engines, including submission tips, what's considered spamming, important design issues relating to relevancy, and other topics.

Another good example of a different type of subscription site is www.iencentral.com, a worldwide game and entertainment site which offers a few free games and a variety of monthly subscription plans.

Advertising Site

The best way to describe an advertising site is: A content laden site, whose revenue base is the dollar amount derived from banners, sponsorships, ads, and other advertising methods. The traffic the site draws is the measure of its value. Recognized rating firms measure its value and then advertising rates. Important Note: Very few sites are supported entirely through advertising dollars.

A good advertising site is www.cnet.com, which has recently added an auction division to its basic site. This is a wonderful content laden advertising site that every reader should bookmark.

Another great advertising site is www.thekidzpage.com. It is designed around frames, which are a little confusing, but the content is great.

Online or Cyber Mall

A simple and easy way to sell your product/services online is to open a shop in one of many cyber malls on the Web. Most cyber malls offer a template for implementing a catalog of products, a shopping cart application and a form generator, which allow small businesses to quickly set up shop on the Web. The templated applications employed to set up a business' catalog and the ease of payment processing are tempting to a novice. These cyber malls also provide a high level of "click traffic." If you are new to the Web and would prefer to first "dip your toe in the water," a cyber mall may be the answer.

Cyber mall's biggest promise is to deliver more traffic to your "front door" than you would be able to do if you go it alone. Since you will be relying on the cyber mall's marketing savvy, make sure you check out if it can deliver. Also, note that the only "front door" which is advertised is the cyber mall's address, not your online store's address.

Most cyber malls offer a purchasing system, allowing you to avoid any up-front shopping cart software costs, but a fee is accessed on each purchase and this fee will eventually exceed the cost of the software. You need to ensure that the cyber mall you choose is one in which your online store can flourish. Consider the pros and cons of establishing your online store in a cyber mall including the restrictions and costs that some cyber malls impose. Then consider the option of setting up your own systems and independent identity. For, in reality, a cyber mall is just a list of links categorized by store and product type.

Yahoo! Store is probably the most popular site on the Web, it includes an easy tool that lets you register your own domain name (http://www.ourname.com) or, if you already have a domain name, they will help you transfer it. You are also given the option of using stores.yahoo.com/yourname, which does not require any up front registration fee.

One of the easiest cyber malls to get up and running on is icat's Web Store. If you choose icat's Web Store you will be able to use an URL such as www.icatmall.com/yourstore or use your own URL if you wish to secure your own domain name such as http://www.yourstore.com.

Business-to-Business E-Commerce Site

A Business-to-Business (B2B) e-commerce site provides products or services to another business rather than a single on-line customer. The growth of B2B e-commerce is exploding — altering how companies bring their products and services to market. For some businesses, B2B e-commerce is already influencing distribution channels, customer service, and pricing strategies. Others need to learn about B2B and look for ways to leverage this new technology to increase sales, profits, customer loyalty, and brand preference. B2B is not the focus of this book but please look for the author's upcoming book on this subject.

CHAPTER 2
Design Your Site

Paying attention to simple little things that most men neglect makes a few men rich.

Henry Ford, Sr.

Having a successful e-commerce business requires a well coordinated plan that takes into account, among many other elements, design competency, programming abilities (transactional and database), server configuration, public relations and sales and marketing abilities, implementation of a responsive customer service plan, and the technology to enable you to get the right product to the right place at the right time.

However — and even I can't quite believe I'm going to say this — *e-commerce is as much about selling as it is about technology.* So, even though I will give you tons of advice and information on technology, I haven't forgotten that, just as in a brick-and-mortar store, the selling environment, i.e., your Web pages, can make or break you. You can have the best product/service in the world; but, if you don't have a Web site that provides intuitive navigation, an easy to use process for ordering and fulfillment, along with high standards of quality control, and flawless customer service, you will never achieve consistent customer satisfaction and your Web-based business will eventually fail.

A Web site is an infinite number of Web pages connected by a common theme and purpose. A good design is important to provide your customers with easy access to all of your Web site's pages. Careful consideration of the numerous design possibilities for your Web site is essential. There are many good books and Web sites where you can find HTML and various programming information you might need, utilize them if necessary. Use this book to provide you with the tools needed to make the right decisions when it comes to designing your Web site for the e-commerce world.

FINDING YOUR NICHE

You must ask yourself if your product/service will translate to a virtual market, i.e., the Web. If the answer is no, then build a good brochureware site that will drive customers to your brick-and-mortar business. I do think that a Web site is a necessity for most businesses since, due to the growing power of the Web, customers will soon expect all brick-and-mortars to have a Web presence. If your product/service will find an eager market on the Web, you should build the site and then expend your efforts in driving customers to your Web site. If you are an entrepreneur, find your niche market, build a Web site designed for them, and then let them know you are open and ready for business.

TARGETING YOUR CUSTOMERS

After all, it's the customers for whom you are building this Web site, right? Decide who your customers are in the early design stage. For example, if your customers are located outside of North America, you will need to place a Comment Tag above the body of your Website's homepage declaring your site as a public document. If you omit the Comment Tag your site probably will not be indexed as a public document and no one outside North America will be able to find it. If you have an international customer base, you need to consider how you will provide translations and how you will handle the monetary exchange problems.

"Know your customer" is an often-used but apt phrase; however, this is just the tip of the iceberg. You also must adequately research the issues to be addressed when designing your new Web site — but only after you have determined your customer base.

Now decide which Web site model you want to build and consider what your Web site is going to offer. Will it be a brochureware site, an advertising site, a subscription site, an online store or perhaps a combination?

Who are your potential customers and what will drive them to your Web site? Your Web site must clearly describe what you are offering and why your customers would want it. Your online offering must meet the wants and needs of your customers, just like a conventional business. And like a conventional business, you must determine what price the market will bear and what your profit margin will be.

DEFINING YOUR WEB SITE'S BLUEPRINT

Now that you have determined your customer base, considered the importance of a simple, engaging and responsive Web design, and given thought to the content of your site, the next step is to develop a comprehensive e-commerce business plan — your Web site's blueprint. Successful Web sites are the ones that have managed, through the proper utilization of a blueprint, to combine content, communication and marketing features within a fast-loading, easy to use and interesting homepage that runs on a robust and scalable infrastructure that can support the back-office functions — customer service, fulfillment, financial aspects of a business, and media.

There are many e-businesses out there with ill-conceived concepts and laughable revenue models. To avoid these crippling mistakes, consider these questions:

- What are the objectives of the new Web site?

- How will the new Web site produce income?

- What makes your new Web site unique?

- If you have a brick-and-mortar business: How will you use your Web site to drive customers to your offline business and at the same time provide an e-commerce alternative?

- How can you combine your dot-com seamlessly with your traditional business (this is called "click-and-mortar")?

- How will you convey your trustworthiness and the high quality of your product/services?

- How will you manage fulfillment?

- How will you ensure on-time delivery?

- How will you respond to customer service issues?

In addition, you must establish a realistic budget and a timeline with milestones clearly defined.

One of the most difficult parts of building a Web site is deciding exactly what to build. You need a clear vision of what you want to accomplish — this is your blueprint. Use the blueprint to lay out the strategy needed to implement the technology that is necessary to gain the most leverage within your current or planned business model. Each aspect needs to be carefully coordinated — technical issues, content, marketing, front-end design, infrastructure, software, fulfillment, customer service, and, of course, sales.

This can't be stressed enough — the same principles that apply to establishing a successful business in the traditional world also apply in the 24-hours a day, 7 days a week (24 x 7) e-commerce operation. Moreover, like conventional businesses, great Web sites can take months to plan and build. Defining exactly what to build, then deciding how to build and market the site is the difference between success and failure.

As you define your site through your blueprint always be aware of the compatibility issues, which must be considered throughout the decision making process — the extendibility and scalability of all the hardware, software and connectivity decisions.

The E-Commerce Space

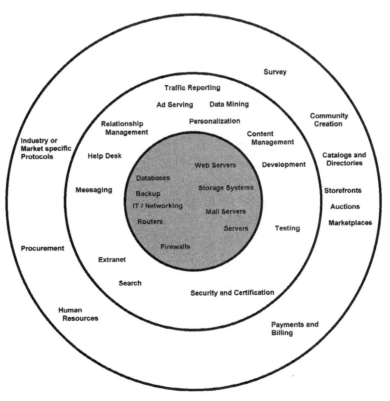

© Technology Evaluation.com

The inner circle contains your "back end" — your hardware, operating system and servers. The middle circle contains the applications and tools that give functionality to your Web site. The outer circle comprises the human element.

Design

The successful Web site starts with a homepage that is attractive, easy to understand and fast-loading. One way to put it: Your homepage should be designed like the cover of a good book — it should entice the customer to look deeper into the site (book) and return to it often as a resource. Another way to put it is that your homepage, the first page the online consumer will see, is like the window of a store. It is your showcase, storefront and calling card all rolled into one. Online, your competition is just a click away — careful design and targeted content are important guardians against customer defection.

Your Web site's design and content will have a great influence on your customers' perception of your business, which will affect their purchasing decisions. Your pages should be laid out in such a manner that navigation through your site is stress-free and enjoyable — so much so that your customers develop a comfort level in doing business on your site. How do you manage that? Read on!

When designing your site, there are certain rules or guidelines that you should follow for a successful site. The author has organized these rules into the following categories:

- Stickiness and Traffic Generation
  Content
  Search Engines

- Ease of Use
  Site Navigation

- Performance
  Speedy Downloads
  Tables
  Content Visibility
  Viewable Site
  Frames
  Java
  Plug-ins

STICKINESS & TRAFFIC GENERATION

Content

The "content" is your Web site's offering — the product, the graphics, the marketing material, banner ads, i.e., anything that will help draw traffic to your Web site. Content is what gives a Web site its "stickiness" — the ability to encourage customers to stay at the site along with getting customers to return to the site.

Independent of which Internet business model you decide to adopt, the content must be presented in such a manner as to draw a visitor's immediate interest and even more importantly, it must turn that visitor into a loyal customer. Be sure to provide all the information necessary for a customer to make intelligent purchases in an easily accessible way.

An important sales adage is — CONTENT IS KING. By keeping the content of your Web site fresh and new, your customers will be more likely to "bookmark" your Web site. Curiosity is a powerful lure and customers will come back to your site repeatedly just to see what is new. It's the useful and up-to-date information that will keep your customers coming back time and again. Your Web site has taken the first step towards being a success when you follow the Internet's golden rule — Provide Useful Content — whether it is a brochureware site, an advertising site, a subscription site or an online store.

Search Engines

Make a list of the top ten terms that your customers would use to search for your Web site when using a search engine or directory service. Then incorporate these words in your Web page content, i.e., make sure your Web pages include text relevant to those ten terms. The majority of search engines do not index by your keyword submissions alone, they send out spiders to crawl your site to check that the keywords you submitted were relevant to the content on the site. Why? Because disreputable Web site owners, especially pornographic and gambling sites, submit numerous key words that people use every day in their search criteria that have nothing to do with the content of the Web site. These same unscrupulous owners also insert into their Meta tags the same unrelated words and phrases. (See Chapter 15.) It is important that you work into your site the criteria necessary for search engines to properly index and rank your Web site, just don't let it interfere with the design process.

EASE OF USE

A simple and easy to understand navigational design ensures that your customers can quickly and effortlessly travel through the multiple pages on your Web site. If your Web site is difficult to use, it will be worthless. Your customers should never be more than three clicks away from what they are looking for. Without fast, intuitive and simple navigation capabilities, your customers will not take the time and effort to navigate your site, regardless of how good your content, product or service might be.

Site Navigation

Design your homepage to allow the customer to access all areas of your Web site from the opening page. Consider using graphics and image maps — a clickable picture (when you place your cursor on it, the cursor turns into the "link select cursor") as an attractive means of navigation. But remember the users of text-only browsers by also inserting text links (a typewritten description not dependent on an image) at the top or bottom of each Web page.

As you drill down into the site, you should continue a uniform navigation scheme, i.e., the customers can go to the same position on any page to perform a specific function. Don't forget to institute targeted text links (text that you can click on and be transported to a specific section of the Web site) in pages that are long and divided into topics or resources. By doing so you allow the customer to more easily find what they're looking for. Targeted links can be an expedient form of navigation, supplementing the scroll bar. The design should be structured to support your site as it grows in complexity. Always view your Web site's design with your customer in mind — don't make the mistake of asking your customer to remember a certain product ID or code when it comes to filling out the order form — keep it simple.

PERFORMANCE

In this age of the Internet, long download times are unnecessary and unprofitable. Making a potential customer wait for your Web site to download is a surefire way to increase your competitors' bottom line, not yours.

Speedy Downloads

There are many reasons why a page may load slowly, just make sure that your Web site's design is not a contributing factor, keep your homepage less than 100 KB in size. By doing this, your Web site will load in less than 20 seconds with a 28.8 Kbps modem.

If you display graphics, keep in mind the different graphic formats that are available, each with its own qualities and capabilities, and what is best to use in particular situations. Images on the Web consist of two basic types: those captured from nature and stored in digital format, and those created entirely on the computer.

Most images on the Web use "indexed color" which is only 8 bits (one byte) of color per pixel, which means that the image can display only 256 colors. This isn't quite as bad as it sounds since you can choose your 256 colors from a huge palette of 24-bit colors. If you pick the right colors, even a color photo can be made to look presentable on the Web.

Many programs such as PhotoShop and Paint Shop Pro will let you reduce the number of colors (color depth) in an image and will select the colors closest to the original.

GIF and JPEG (also JPG) are the most commonly supported formats throughout the world. "GIF" stands for "Graphics Interchange (or Image) Format." CompuServe developed the GIF format so that its subscribers could send image files to each other and the images could be viewed on different kinds of computers. GIFs are good for images that have solid colors, text, and line art. A GIF can be used to represent images generated by drawing programs used by computer artists. GIFs do not compress photos very well; especially images that have subtle texture or color gradations, or that are 16 or 24-bit color.

JPEG stands for "Joint Photographic Experts Group." (In the DOS world, JPEGs were called JPGs because DOS filenames were restricted to having only a three-letter extender.) It is perhaps the best format to use for photographs on the Web since it supports full 24-bit color.

To sum up, GIF is better for solid and flat colors, exact detail, sharp edges, black and white images, images with transparent areas, simple animations and small text. Use JPEG for images with continuous tones, such as photographs or images with gradient fills.

Just remember, the higher the quality/resolution of the graphics, the larger their size and the larger the size of the graphics, the longer it will take for your site to load.

One solution to the size versus resolution issue is to use thumbnail JPEG images on the homepage and then link these to corresponding full-size images on another page. This way you give the customers what they want — detail and a fast load time. A good example of an e-commerce site using this technique is www.artcut.com.

Tables

On a Web page, using an HTML table allows the organized and specific arrangement of data. The data can be text, images, links, forms, form fields, other tables, etc., arranged into rows and columns of cells (individual units). Tables let you control the look of your Web site by breaking your pages into precise segments while controlling the placement of text and graphics. You can create columns and grids, which can contain images and text. Cells can be utilized as templates or style sheets to give a uniform look and through use of color add visual contrast to your Web site. *Be careful* though, if you use colored cells in your table, then some browsers might not display the cell in color unless there is text or an image in it.

Tables can be problematic. They may load more slowly than plain text since some browsers must place the items in a table and therefore do not show a table until all the text and graphic items have downloaded. By breaking a long table into smaller tables and specifying the height and width for all the images, the browser can size the table before the images resulting in a faster download. Also, if you use a series of smaller tables instead of one long table it makes it easier to change the page's design in the future.

Then there is the *fixed-width* problem. When you add a variable width table, the horizontal dimensions readjust with the browser width. A fixed width guarantees the final appearance. But the variable width can take better advantage of the situation if the browser has a larger width setting to begin with. You must use trial and error testing to find the optimal combination of fixed and variable widths for the different parts of the table.

Some of the WYSIWYG (what you see is what you get) Web page editors (this is software) have problems with tables. Be careful, if you are doing your own design work — what your editor displays on the screen may vary greatly from what you see in a browser. Remember to test your table-based pages with a variety of browsers and don't forget to use different browser widths. Test the page scrolling function by using your mouse to pull down the arrow on the bar (which your browser automatically brings up on its far right side of your page) to see if the page jumps rather than scrolls smoothly.

Content Visibility
Design your Web site so that it is technically accessible to the greatest number of people. Just as customers come in all shapes and sizes so does the equipment and software they use to access the Web.

Viewable Site
Test your design with as many browsers (including their various versions) as you can find; Netscape, Microsoft Internet Explorer, Macintosh, AOL and CompuServe browsers, Opera, and a text-only browser such as Lynx. Don't forget the customers that surf with their browser's "turn off graphics" option activated. Make sure the technologies you are selecting can accommodate the many browsing options your customers will be using.

Frames
Also called framesets, frames are a programming device that divides Web pages into multiple, scrollable regions. This allows you to present information in a more flexible and useful fashion. Of course, frames have their own set of problems. A browser's back button can produce unexpected results, particularly if the user is working with an old browser, such as Netscape prior to version 3.0.

Visitors who have problems with their sight or are otherwise physically impaired may be using text-to-speech software that reads aloud Web pages. Frames confuse such software.

Even for the non-physically challenged, a cursor won't work with a framed site unless you actually click in the frame you want to scroll.

In addition, printing and bookmarking can be problematic with frames. If your entire site uses frames, a visitor often can't bookmark any pages within the site except the first one (the home page). Attempts at bookmarking any framed page usually defaults the bookmark to the home page, or just one section of the frame will be bookmarked and that will be the only section loaded, devoid of the frameset.

Even worse, framed Web sites can be invisible to certain search engines and directories (such as Yahoo!) and frames increase the file size and the number of total words that make up the Web site, thereby decreasing keyword weight (affecting your search engine listing). Also, when customers are brought to your Web site via a search engine, they sometimes won't enter through the front door, i.e., home page, and therefore can't see the frame that would normally be holding the page.

Exercise caution if you choose to offer links to other Web pages within a framed page. The linked page can accidentally load within the framed page on your Web site; particularly if the correct code is not inserted (such as _blank, top, parent, self, or your own designated frame) to keep external sites from loading within your frameset. This can be confusing to the visitor as well as raising the possibility of copyright infringement, since the user may think that the information appearing in your frame is your information.

When advertising one particular aspect of your site in other media, simply providing a main URL address is no longer good enough. In the case of a framed site you must give the public additional instructions about how to find the frame and page that they want. If you give out that page's address alone, the rest of the frameset becomes inaccessible.

Conversely, if another site wants to link to a particular page on your site, they're out of luck. Frames generally restrict external-to-internal links only to the home page, unless you once again want to find yourself on a page minus the rest of the frameset. In other words, if a Web site wished to link to an internal page of your Web site (like your FAQ section) it couldn't — it would only be able to link to your homepage.

Creating a non-frame site is the best approach to make it accessible to the largest number of users. All things considered, I recommend designing your Web site using tables, which offer some of the same functionality as frames with few of the limitations.

Java

A high-level programming language that is all of the following:

- simple

- architecture-neutral

- object-oriented

- portable

- distributed

- high-performance

- interpreted

- multithreaded

- robust

- dynamic

- secure

Each of the preceding buzzwords is explained in "The Java Language Environment," a white paper written by James Gosling and Henry McGilton. You can download a PDF version of the paper from http://java.sun.com/docs/white.

What are Java applets? Probably the most well known Java programs are Java applets. An applet is a program written in the Java programming language that can be included in an HTML page, much in the same way an image is included. When you use a Java technology-enabled browser to view a page that contains an applet, the applet's code is transferred to your system and executed by the browser's Java Virtual Machine (JVM).

Java applets are used to add anything from a small animation to sophisticated programs to the Web site. The applets can either run in the same HTML page or in a pop-up window that opens on the screen. To see an example of a sophisticated applet, which runs in a pop-up window, go to LandRover's site, http://best4x4.landrover.com/features/outfit/index.html. There you can see how a new vehicle will look with steel running boards... or a roof rack... or a different interior or exterior color... or a host of other options that now can be previewed over the

Web using Adjacency's Land Rover applet.

To see an example of an applet that runs inside an HTML page, you can go to Quote.com, http://www.quote.com, and click on LiveCharts to view dynamic, real-time charts of stocks.

Although Java applets, if built correctly, can enhance the functionality of your Web site, they could become a crippling factor if used extensively. Furthermore, if you are trying to reach as many people as possible, keep in mind that not everyone viewing your site will have Java enabled browser. So, if you would like to use applets, use them only when it is not important that everyone coming to your site have the ability to view the information contained in the applet. Another suggestion — if possible, never use them in your home page. Also, don't design your entire Web site so that it can only be viewed with Java enabled browsers. Why? Because, when customers who have browsers that don't support Java, come to your site, they see — instead of your Web site — an irritating message stating that the site requires a Java enabled browser.

Also, when deciding on whether or not to use a pop-up window, keep in mind that some customers find a pop-up window disconcerting.

Plug-Ins

Generally, plug-ins are software modules that run on the viewers' local machine and add to the functionality of an application. Typically, Web browsers do use plug-ins so that they can display a wider range of formats. For example, an Acrobat plug-in is used to view documents in Acrobat format (PDF documents). Most video and audio formats require a plug-in to be viewed or heard. For example, a QuickTime plug-in is needed to view movies in QuickTime format. When a customer tries to view something that requires a plug-in, which their browser does not support or they have not previously installed, they will get a message asking them whether they would like to install the plug-in.

Plug-ins are free for the most part, but downloading and installing them requires some sacrifice on the part of the customer. Some plug-ins are quite large taking a considerable amount of time to download on a 28.8 Kbps modem, and space availability may become an issue — a minimum of 3MB is usually required for a plug-in. One more consideration is that they are not backwards compatible with previous versions. This means that even if a user has previously installed the plug-in, there is no assurance that it is the correct version. For example, if a customer has the Macromedia Flash 3.0 plug-in and you use Flash 4.0 on your Web site, the customer will need the Flash 4.0 plug-in to view your site, since the 3.0 version will not work.

Plug-ins create a great barrier between the user and the content. Recent studies show that less then 10% of the Web population uses plug-ins and people are largely driven away by plug-in based content.

So, if you have a document that is important for your customers to see and you want to put it in Acrobat format, it would be advisable to also provide a text only version on the site. Also, if you build your site with Macromedia technology, it will be viewable only if the customer's browser supports the exact version your Web site is using, or the customer has the plug-in already installed. Therefore, it is *strongly* recommended that you also provide an HTML version so all of your customers can view some version of your Web site. I agree Macromedia technology allows Web-based businesses to build a great looking site, but what good does that do if your target audience cannot access it.

STORYBOARD

You must map out the progression and relationship between individual Web pages. Look at how they will work within your Web site before you start building it. I call this type of "map" a storyboard and, although, it is a tedious chore, a storyboard will save time, money, and many sleepless nights. It is imperative that you map out every step of your design process so that each detail can be tested, measured, and validated. A storyboard is a tool used in the production of multimedia, video, and film projects to show a frame-by-frame picture sequence of the action. Here I use the term to mean the pictorial representation of the screen elements and their operations for every page, which taken as a whole, constitute the Web site.

Just as an outline helps to organize your thoughts before you write a paper or report, storyboards help to organize a visual production such as a Web site. Using the storyboard process allows you to design your Web site so that you can clearly envision all the possible paths that a customer might take.

To create your storyboard I have suggested a set of guidelines to get you started.

The storyboard should be readable. It can be created using pen and paper and does not have to be precise, but it does have to be clearly understood by people who have to implement it.

The storyboard must be complete. Every page should be represented and every element on the page should be explained before actual design work is started or any of it programmed into HTML.

Every design and layout element to be included on each page should be noted in the storyboard.

Headings
Text Objects/Blocks
Links/Buttons
Graphics Images (Photos and Other Arts)

The typeface and print size of the headings should be exactly as they will appear on the final Web pages.

The number and the function of the buttons should be clearly indicated on each page.

Links between pages should be clearly indicated using arrows.

Graphic images should be noted with a box identifying it as a graphic image with a short note describing the content.

Web pages should be numbered for easy reference.

The best way to lay out your storyboard is to track the path of a hypothetical customer, with branches at every decision point — including those made by the customers and those made by the system. Have a meeting with all of your staff — marketing, customer service, Web architect, advertising, designers, programmers, etc. — think of all the possibilities. For example, in the purchasing process:

- Does the site require registration before final purchasing process?

- Is there an option to skip registration but allow the purchasing process to continue?

- If a customer wants to change or remove an item from the shopping cart, is it easily done?

- At what point does the credit card authorization take place?

- Is there a confirmation page with tracking number?

Decisions made at this point must not be rushed. Time is needed to study, absorb, and totally understand what's required to implement the most creative ideas — the ideas that will make your Web site stand out from the crowd.

The last thing you want to do is to just slap your content together — use your storyboard. I realize that both layout and design (the pretty pictures) are subjective topics but to make the best first impression possible, design a stylish page with your content laid out in a logical manner. As in decorating your home or office, use a consistent theme in the colors, styles and fonts throughout your site.

You can design a Web site that is brilliantly complex, employing all the latest technology or you can choose to design a simple site without sacrificing attractiveness or efficiency. If you keep your customers in mind and design you site to accommodate the lowest denominator (technologically speaking) in your customer base, you will have a fighting chance of being a success on the World Wide Web.

Your Web site must provide an easy way for your customers to contact you and an easy purchase and payment method. Every decision you make now regarding hardware, software and connectivity will define and can limit the future growth and evolution of your Web site.

Chapter 3
Let's Build It!

One never notices what has been done;
one can only see what remains to be done.

Marie Curie, letter (1894)

You've chosen your e-commerce model, found the perfect products/services for e-commerce sales, know your niche market, set forth the blueprint necessary to build your Web site, and designed the site using a storyboard, it is now time to extend it to the Web.

The basic e-commerce Web site should have a system that can:

- Store any number of products that have been selected by the customer prior to the actual processing of the purchase. This system is normally referred to as "a shopping cart" and processing is usually referred to as "check out."

- Provide a secure server with SSL encryption for transactions and e-mail transmission and storage.

- Accept credit cards and offer automatic, real-time processing; but offline processing via an encrypted e-mail form is also a viable option if you choose to forego the following option.

- Allow the customer to leave the site, return at a later time, and still find past items in their "shopping cart."

- Allow cross-selling, i.e., offer a similar product to the one that the customer is interested in, if the chosen product is unavailable.

- Put in place a process in which customers' orders are picked, packed and shipped quickly and accurately.

- Provide processing status though a numbered tracking system.

- Respond to customer inquiries within 24 hours.

Add to this list: acquiring a domain name, a merchant account and a digital certificate and you are in the e-commerce business.

DOMAIN NAME

The first step is to choose a Web address a/k/a domain name. A domain name is the unique address of your Web site. It's also known as your site's Uniform Resource Locator (URL). You've no doubt seen the many "dot-com" advertisements — www.[name].com (or .org or .net). That is a domain name, also known as "Web address." It's how the public will find your site unless you have opted for the cyber mall concept.

While you can choose just about any combination of words or numbers for your domain name, we recommend a catchy, easy to remember name that easily evokes your product or service. Come up with several options.

In your quest for the perfect domain name remember:

Your online business depends on the customer correctly typing your URL. Therefore, the shorter the better. And please, don't put your entire name or your company's name in the address. No one wants to input www.the-one-and-only-genuine-original-widget-company.com. Find something simple.

If your brick-and-mortar business has a well-known name that is already branded, re-enforce that brand online, don't create an entirely new "Web name." Brands are expensive to promote particularly new ones.

Think twice before you use "Web" or ".com" in your name. Yes, I know .com is probably part of your URL but it is not necessarily part of your name, which you will, by necessity, be branding. Why? Because in this day and age, technology and the growth of the Internet are moving at a breakneck speed and "Web" and ".com" will, in the future, appear stale and dated, like the old two letter prefixes on telephone numbers. In the new world of fast moving technology your business should always present the image of being on the cutting edge.

Competition for rights to domain names has exploded, many people and companies have registered not only domain names they use, but names they think may be valuable in the future. You can check the Network Solutions' WhoIs directory (www.networksolutions.com/cgi-bin/whois/whois) to see if your chosen domain name is available. If your ideal domain name isn't available, you might consider contacting the owner of your chosen domain name to try to purchase the rights from that owner.

Once you have chosen your domain name / Web address / URL, the next step is to register it. The process itself is easy, but there is much you need to know.

In 1997 the International Internet community banded together with other international organizations to establish rules for the introduction of generic Top Level Domains ("gTLDs") thereby moving the registry of domain names into a competitive business. This move was necessary due to the growth of registered domains under the existing Top Level Domains ("TLDs") of which .com, .net and .org are the most widely used.

The first seven new gTLDs are:

.firm for firms or businesses

.shop for entities who offer goods to purchase

.Web for entities whose emphasis is on Web-related activities

.arts for entities whose emphasis is on cultural activities

.rec for entities whose emphasis is on recreation and entertainment

.info for entities whose emphasis is on providing information services

.nom for those who want an individual or personal nomenclature

Anyone interested in registering under one of these gTLDs may have to wait until at least the 1st Quarter of 2000. You can visit www.gtld-mou.org to find the latest news on the availability of these new gTLDs.

There are numerous Web sites that offer to register a new domain name for a fee or you may be able to turn the registration process over to your Web Hosting Service. Here are some official registrar Web sites you might want to visit prior to registering a domain name:

ICANN   www.icann.org

CORE   www.corenic.org/comnetorg.htm

Your first stop in your search for the perfect domain name should be www.internic.net, which is hosted by Network Solutions, Inc. on behalf of the U.S. Department of Commerce. The Web site was established to provide the information regarding Internet domain name registration services. The site provides a link to the Accredited Registrar Directory that provides a listing of the Internet Corporation for Assigned Names and

Numbers (ICANN) accredited domain name registrars that are currently taking domain name registrations since numerous domain name registration service providers from around the world are providing .com, .net and .org domain name registration services.

DIGITAL CERTIFICATE

A Digital Certificate (a small piece of very unique data used by encryption and authentication software), which is also known as a SSL Server Certificate, enables SSL (Secure Socket Layer) encryption on a Web server. This allows a Web site to accept credit card orders securely; in addition, it helps to keep hackers at bay. An e-commerce Web site is required to have a Digital Certificate before a Commerce Hosting Service will allow the Web site to use their services.

To put it in layman's language, Digital Certificates are digital-based IDs that contain the user's information. It accomplishes this by attaching a small file — containing the certificate owner's name, the name of its issuer and a public encryption key — to the information that is transmitted over the Internet.

Note that Digital Certificates are not the same as the X.509 certificate generated by a browser in your typical e-commerce transaction, then sent via SSL to a Web server via a secure pipe. These do not require authentication.

There are two ways to obtain a digital certificate: Your hosting company owns a digital certificate that you might be able to use for a fee. The best way, though, is to purchase your own digital certificate which costs around $125.00; since, if you decide to change your Web hosting service provider, it is one less detail you must deal with.

Obtain your digital certificate from:

BelSign at www.belsign.com is the digital certificate authority for Europe and issues certificates to individuals and to Web servers.

Thawte (which was acquired by Verisign in late 1999) at www.thawt.com gives users a full range of certification services including issuing digital certificates for individuals and servers.

Wells Fargo gives digital certificates to online merchants that are issued by GTE CyberTrust but have a Wells Fargo Brand. Wells Fargo is one of the first banks in the U.S. to help merchants offer secured online credit card payments. Online shoppers and businesses can use Wells Fargo's Sure-Server certificates to authenticate their identity when making online purchases. Web-based businesses that use this method hope that online customers will feel that the Wells Fargo SureServer seal on a Web site assures a secure environment. If customers click on the Wells Fargo SureServer seal displayed on a Web site, they will see a copy of the digital certificate.

Among others, two public-key infrastructure (PKI) vendors offer reliable products and services that enable secure management of e-business transactions.

Entrust.Net, founded by Entrust Technologies, provides services for issuing one-year and two-year digital certificates to Web servers including full life-cycle monitoring services. Certificates issued by Entrust.net will be immediately trusted by the majority of Microsoft, America Online and Netscape Web browsers as it has a root key embedded in these browsers. The Web server certificates can be obtained from the Entrust.net Web site for the cost of $299 per 1 year and $499 per 2-year certificate.

GTE CyberTrust offers certification authority (CA) services that enable customers to issue their own branded certificates, making it easier for companies to issue digital certificates under their own brand name. GTE's OmniRoot gives companies the ability to improve Web site security as they launch new e-commerce products and services by enabling companies to create certificates and electronic credentials for verifying IDs, that are interoperable and easy to distribute. The certificates issued will be immediately trusted by the majority of Microsoft and Netscape Web browsers because they are based on CyberTrust's root key embedded in these browsers.

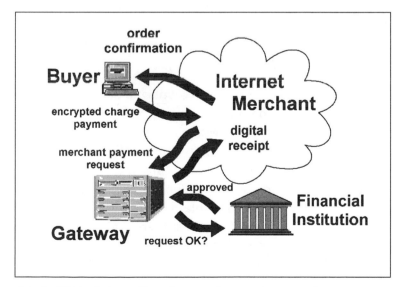

A typical Web site's credit card payment processing scenario.

MERCHANT ACCOUNT

An e-commerce site should include the ability to accept credit card payments from customers. While there are many different payment methods, the most popular include the processing of credit cards either offline or online requiring a credit card terminal and a merchant account. A merchant account is a business account at a financial institution that functions as a clearing account for credit card transactions.

If you have a brick-and-mortar business, it is likely that you already have an existing merchant account as well as a credit card terminal. You can use your existing merchant account for your e-commerce site and enter the credit card information offline. This can be achieved by including a form on your Web site so that after the customers type in their billing and shipping information, the information is relayed to you through encrypted e-mail. You then manually process the information using your existing credit card terminal.

Setting up a merchant account is a bit more complicated than opening a checking account. The gold rush mentality means that there are a plethora of businesses in addition to traditional financial institutions setting up merchant accounts. However, there is an enormous variety in the deals offered. Just make sure you do your homework, learn about the process, talk to others who have existing accounts regarding their experience with their provider and you will make out okay.

REAL-TIME CREDIT CARD AUTHORIZATION

Does your current software allow integration with real-time credit card authorization systems? Do you process credit card transactions prior to product fulfillment? If the answer to both of these questions is yes, then you might need real-time authorization capability.

With a real-time credit card authorization account, you don't need to lease or purchase equipment or install software on your computer. After your merchant account is approved, you simply open an account with a real-time Internet processing company such as AuthorizeNet (www.authorizenet.com). But note that a merchant credit card account is required to use the AuthorizeNet real-time credit card processing service. Or you might want to check with RealTime Commerce Solutions, Inc. at www.realtimecommerce.com, a complete, real-time Internet solution. With a real-time credit card authorization account, your customers' credit cards are processed instantly on your Web Site 24 hours a day, 7 days a week. Funds are deposited into your existing business checking account within 48 - 72 hours.

CHECK PROCESSING

Remember the more payment options you can provide to your customers, the more competitive your site will be. Some of your customers will prefer to pay by a check, which has its own inherent problems. Purchasing products/services by check negates the instantaneous nature of e-commerce if you wait for a check to clear before shipping. To speed things along, some businesses will ship on the receipt of a check — at least until they are burned once too often by a bounced check.

One solution is Intell-A-Check 6.0, an application suite that facilitates the processing of checks. When customers want to pay by check, they provide information about their checking account by filling out a form on the Web site. Intell-A-Check uses this information to automatically create a check or automated clearinghouse transfer that can be deposited immediately into your bank account and immediately credited against a customer's account. You don't need to worry about not being paid because Equifax, the leading provider of consumer information in the United States, guarantees Intell-A-Check checks. Intell-A-Check provides another benefit — the customer and the Web site avoids credit card fees. This application currently works only with Microsoft Site Server 3.0, Commerce Edition. You can find further information about Intell-A-Check at www.icheck.com.

OTHER PAYMENT OPTIONS

If you don't have a merchant's account you can still open an e-commerce site and your customers can still use a credit card to buy your products. How? Use an online escrow service that assumes the role of the middleman in a transaction. The escrow service holds a buyer's payment in trust, awaiting confirmation that the goods are as expected. Through the escrow service, the buyer and seller agree in advance on how the goods and funds will be exchanged, along with a return policy. Escrow service providers allow payments to be made with a credit card. The escrow service acts as an impartial third party that facilitates online buying and selling by providing both parties with trust, security and convenience. Here's how it works: the escrow service holds the buyer's money in trust. The seller ships the merchandise directly to the buyer. If the buyer accepts the merchandise, the escrow service pays the seller. Otherwise, the buyer returns the merchandise to the seller in its original condition and receives a refund from the escrow service. It's that simple. One such service is i-Escrow which charges a $5 minimum fee per order. To learn more about i-Escrow go to www.iescrow.com. Another is Tradesafe, which charges a small percentage of the dollar amount of the sale plus the shipping. To learn more about Tradesafe go to www.tradesafe.com.

Another option might be PayPal, an e-mail payment service. PayPal makes sending and collecting money as easy as e-mail. PayPal integrates seamlessly with existing financial networks, allowing anyone to send money from their credit card or bank account. Equally important, you can now accept credit card payments from anyone. For more information, visit the Web site at www.paypal.com.

HOW COMPUTERS WORK

Before you can understand the interrelations of the components needed to build a Web site, you must understand the basic terms and workings of a computer. The capabilities of your CPU, bus systems, power supplies, hardware and software are all part of the foundation upon which the Web site is built. If you are well versed in this technology read on. However, if you feel you need a refresher course on the inner workings of a computer, check out Appendix A "What is a computer."

CHAPTER 4
Server Hardware

If only foresight were as good as our hindsight!

Server hardware is the backbone of any good Web site. It is a computer on "steroids" with a very fast permanent connection to the Internet and subsystems to protect against power outages, hackers and system crashes.

Unless you have a specific reason for running your own server, it is strongly suggested that you outsource to a hosting service through a co-location arrangement, an enterprise contract (leasing servers, applications and technical service), or rental of server space (virtual hosting). (See Chapter 14 for a complete discussion on hosting solutions.) However, it is advisable to learn about the necessary hardware requirements even if you plan to use a hosting company for your Web site.

HOME-BASED WEB SITE

For many small entrepreneurs and brick-and-mortar businesses, the main barrier to building their own Web site is the cost. The good news is that the hardware necessary for hosting your own Web site is no longer expensive or difficult to set up.

Server Needs

Before you make your server decision you should determine your hardware needs. This section lays out the *bare-bones* server specifications for a Web site that will be hosted on premises by a business with a limited budget. A normal "server" whether a Web server or otherwise, consists of a computer (the hardware), an operating system (some flavor of Unix or Windows) and one or more pieces of software (the applications). The software can be Web server software, e-mail server software, commerce server software, etc. The combination of hardware, operating system and server software constitutes a "server." It is recommended that you build a Web server with components that are in excess of the barebones recommendations. For security reasons, your Web server should be exclusive, i.e., stand alone. If the Web server is tied to your business' internal network, install another computer to house a firewall.

Memory is important: 64 MB of RAM is sufficient for a small static Web server that does not house a database, but always install as much memory as your budget will allow. If you anticipate more than moderate traffic from the get-go or expect to use a lot of graphics or sound, load up on memory.

Consider how much hard drive space your software and Web pages will need. For the scenario set out above — running an operating system, Web server software and traffic analysis software — a 1 GB hard drive will be sufficient. But we suggest that you install the largest drive your budget will allow.

A Web server running a 233 MHz Pentium with MMX should work just fine. We hope you opt for a faster processor, but don't use a slower one — doing so will limit the number of simultaneous connections your Web server can handle, and it will take a longer time to load each page. To handle more than moderate traffic, choose a Pentium II or III with as much memory as possible. You will also need an uninterruptible power supply (UPS) and some kind of backup, which can be as simple as floppy disks, a Zip drive (an inexpensive external drive) or a read/write CD drive.

To sum it up, it is possible to start with a computer running a 233 MHz Pentium CPU with MMX, 64 MB of RAM and a 1 GB EIDE drive, if that is all your budget will allow. However, to grow, your Web site will eventually need a computer on "steroids." So, while working within the constraints of your budget, go for the fastest processor, the most memory the computer can take, the largest SCSI drive with a RAID set-up and backup protection such as a read/write CD or tape backup system.

ROBUST SERVER SPECIFICATIONS

Deciding upon the server hardware to run your Web site will probably engender a hard fought battle among your entire technical team — designers, programmers and IT staff. The final server hardware configuration will be based on a "best guess" in that no one will be able to reliably predict the data traffic load that the hardware will ultimately carry. Keep in mind that as your Web site grows your server configuration will need to adapt to your evolving business and whatever new technology comes along.

In the server world there is a saying: "You can never have too much capacity." In other words, the demand for disk space, memory, and available processing power seems to max out faster than anyone can predict. Web servers and other applications, such as database servers, can quickly expand beyond the limits of the Intel platform or any single platform.

Processor Architecture

"Processor Architecture" pertains to the overall organizational structure of the processor (CPU). The main elements of any processor architecture are the selection and behavior of the structural elements and the selected collaborations that form larger subsystems that guide the workings of the entire processor.

The microprocessor industry is highly competitive. Consider many factors when selecting your processor architecture including performance, scalability, open/proprietary architectures, on-chip functions, advanced functionality, software availability and, of course, cost.

The Athlon (K7) is a Pentium III-class CPU from AMD with clock speeds ranging from 500MHz to 650MHz. Using a 200MHz system bus, the chip contains the MMX multimedia instructions and an enhanced version of AMD's 3DNow 3-D instruction set. The Athlon plugs into a slot, known as Slot A, which is similar to the elongated slot used by Pentium IIs and IIIs.

The Hewlett Packard PA-8000 is based upon the older PA 2.0 architecture. This 64-bit processor with a superscalar architecture can execute four instructions per cycle with its two integer ALUs (arithmetic logic units), two shift/merge units, two floating-point units, two divide/square root units, and two load/store units.

The Intel Xeon is a Pentium CPU chip designed for server and high-end workstation use. The Xeon plugs into Slot 2 on the motherboard and its L2 cache runs at the same speed as the CPU. Xeon introduced the System Management Bus (SMBus) interface, which includes a Processor Information ROM (PIROM) that contains data about the processor and an empty EEPROM that can be used by manufacturers to track their own information such as usage and service information. Xeon chips can address 64GB of memory.

The MIPS Technologies R10000 Microprocessor is a four-way superscalar architecture capable of executing four instructions per cycle, which are then appended to one of three instruction queues — integer, floating-point, or address. Each queue can perform dynamic scheduling of instructions. Although instructions are executed in order, they don't need to be, which allows the R10000 to maintain up to 32 active instructions at a time that are in the process of being executed. It has five independently operating execution units (two integer ALUs, two floating-point units, and a load store unit for generating addresses).

The Sun Technologies' UltraSPARC is an open reduced instruction set computer (RISC) specification to which anyone can build compatible chips and in which a micro-processor is designed for very efficient handling of a small set of instructions. The UltraSPARC architecture scales very well, ranging from low power notebooks and porta-bles to multi-million dollar Cray scientific research supercomputers. UltraSPARC-based systems dominate the UNIX server market and provide the processing power behind many of today's robust ISP sites.

Clusters

One way to surpass the limitations of a single server is clustering. Clusters are essential-ly multiple servers that are used as a single unified resource through the use of software, switches and routers. The inter-connection of multiple servers sharing resources results in greater availability due to the ability of the other systems in a cluster to assume the workload of a failing resource.

Maintaining access to data is a key element of the concept of high availability and if your server is running but can't reach critical data, your Web-based business can come to a standstill. Clusters depend on strong data sharing models, the ability to have systems co-exist at different software release levels and to dynamically vary systems off-line, as well as robust recovery models that keep everything up and running.

A cluster performs load balancing to allow processing to be evenly distributed among the various machines that comprise the cluster, and, in extreme cases, the software will automatically exclude a failed server from the cluster, allowing the working servers to take up the slack. To the network's devices and the administrator the cluster appears as a sin-gle server, which streamlines management efforts.

Load Balancing Switches and Routers

Other load bearing solutions include load balancing switches and routers that distribute traffic to a group of servers, sharing the load among them.

The first versions of load balancing routers were specifically designed to support Internet traffic, especially Web servers. They used a round-robin algorithm, distributing requests to each server in sequence. The newer load balancing router algorithms provide a more even load distribution across a group of Web servers. They can react to the traffic coming through the load balancer and distribute the traffic according to the load on each server. Some balancers check to see if a system request is for data that is residing in a server's cache, thus making it easier for that server to respond quickly. They also provide monitoring of the actual load level on each server in real-time, allowing each server's load to be kept perfectly balanced.

Web server load balancing produces a cost-effective way for Web sites to respond to growth spurts without the need to replace equipment every few months with a new, higher-capacity system.

Rack Units

A rack unit is a vertical shelving system to mount servers. Racks can be freestanding or else bolted into the floor or wall. Racks generally hold rackmountable computers that are 19 inches wide and have faceplates that allow the computer to be affixed to the rack's frame via screws. Two or more rackmount servers can comprise a high-availability groupware (sharing data across a distributed system) and Web server system. Mounting servers in racks helps with space problems and allows for ease of management when it comes to the formulation and assignment of security measures and redundant power supplies.

Generally each "layer" of a rack holds one 19 inch rackmount computer, but smaller computers from companies such as Crystal Group, Swemco and APPRO allow for up to four or more PCs to share a shelf on a rack.

Multiple-CPU Servers

A multiple-CPU unit is a good choice for Web sites that demand high-end computing environments. It is a viable option used to satisfy the server consolidation requirements of very large Web sites that offer, in addition to products and e-commerce options, services such as free e-mail, chat rooms, streaming video, etc. The choice of a multiple-CPU unit should take into consideration the need for the flexibility in mixing and matching components in a rack. Choose multiple-CPU units if you are unsure of exactly what your needs are now or what they might be in the future. Another plus is that redundant power supplies are among the basic requirements (not an added feature) for an enterprise class system such as the 8-CPU Intel Servers. Consider, however, that these multiple-CPU units can cost in excess of $20,000.

Server Cabinet

A server cabinet is a metal cabinet designed to house rack-mounted servers (some also house tower configured systems). A good server cabinet will usually have a slotted front door, a perforated steel rear door and a perforated top panel to assure maximum airflow(servers throw off a lot of heat). There is room for fans or blowers to be added, which are usually necessary. The side panels usually lift off for easy and quick component accessibility.

Some examples of real life configurations that could be found in a large Web site:

- 1 Sun E450, 250 MB RAM, three 400 MHz UltraSPARC II processors with 4 MB cache, eight 9 GB (10,000 RPM) hard drives with backup plan, running Veritas' Volume Manager RAID solution, Solaris operating system, Apache Web server, F-Secure ssh 2.0, and WebTrends Enterprise Reporting Server for Solaris.

- 1 Sun E250, 128 MB RAM with one 400MHz UltraSPARC II Processors with 2 MB cache, five 9 GB (10,000 RPM) hard drives with backup plan, running Veritas' Volume Manager RAID solution, Solaris operating system, Apache Web server, F-Secure ssh 2.0, and WebTrends Enterprise Reporting Server for Solaris.

- 1 Sun E250, 128 MB RAM with two 400MHz UltraSPARC II Processors with 2 MB cache, five 9 GB (10,000 RPM) hard drives with backup plan, running Veritas Volume Manager RAID solution, Oracle Database Server Enterprise Server for 2x400 MHz CPUs

- 1 Compaq ProLiant 1850R, 128 MB RAM 1 500 MHz Pentium III Processor with two 512 K caches, 4x1 inch Hot Plug Drive Cage and 2x1 Hot Plug Drive Cage, three 9 GB (10,000 RPM) Hard Drives with backup plan, SMART Array 3200 Controller running Microsoft Windows NT Server 4.0, Microsoft IIS 4.0, Symantic PCAnywhere 8.0 Server

- Everything must have a redundant power supply and hooked up with multiple network cards.

An enterprise Web site might run a very expensive, but necessary, high-end configuration such as:

- Clustered Sun E450s with multiple processors and 1 GB RAM with the Solaris operating system and Apache Web server.

- A database server with the same configuration except running Oracle 8.1 in place of Apache.

- An E-Commerce server running two Dell 450s with 1 GB RAM and the Windows NT operating system and Microsoft IIS 4.0.

- A staging server running two Dell 450s with 1 GB RAM.

- Moreover, the system would use a terabyte (TB) of external disk packs and a RAID 5 disk array. Once again, all configurations should be powered by redundant power supplies and have multiple network cards to support High Availability.

Web Server Farms

In a Server Farm configuration, the servers are usually identical computers that are large enough to handle only a fraction of a Web site's total traffic. The number of servers needed varies. Some Web operators opt for a few large servers and others choose several smaller, cheaper servers. With either option, the load-balancing algorithm can be a simple round robin, or may be more sophisticated, taking into account each server's current load as discussed previously in this chapter.

A server farm configuration provides high availability since there are multiple machines that can take on additional processing in the event of the failure of any single server. This type of server configuration is cheaper and easier to implement than a high availability cluster since the servers don't need to be aware of each other. Only the load-balancing component is aware of all of the servers. In the event of a failure, there is no complex failover process. Instead, the system just stops sending requests to the failed server and routes traffic to the remaining servers. In this way, you get both availability and scalability.

CHAPTER 5
Redundancy

Caution, though often wasted, is a good risk to take.

Josh Billings

Redundancy is a safety measure where you install multiple units of all critical hardware devices. Redundancy of two, three, or more times may be used to support the operations of a Web site including its switches, routers, and other components.

BACKUP

Server crashes and hard drive failures are inevitable due to such things as equipment failure, lightning, power outages, simple age or defect-related failures, bugs, hackers, viruses, and, of course, human error. The most basic method of saving your data is to "Backup." All backup solutions have one thing in common — they involve copying data from your hard drive(s) to a second media, from which you can restore your data in the event that your hard drive(s) or server fail.

If you create and maintain your own Web site, keep local and up-to-date backups of all files. At a minimum, a daily backup should be made of all the data on your server, so that if the data is erased or modified in error, much of it can be restored. Backup should be a ritual and scripted so it becomes a part of your daily routine.

So what do you do? Institute a backup plan that includes a plan to get your Web site up and running in seconds. Meeting your Web site's backup needs requires:

• a secure place to keep your backed-up files that is accessible at all times

• a combination of software and hardware to handle the backups

• a tape backup on your server, allowing you to perform your own data backups remotely

- an online backup service (if you don't use a tape backup) where you transfer your data electronically to a secure location. Or you can use the service to schedule automatic backups of selected files to be backed up at each session.

The general idea in all cases is to fully backup of all your data to tape every week or two. Every other day you perform a modified backup, on a new set of tapes each day. At the end of each week you take the set of tapes from the previous week and move them to off-site storage.

There are two kinds of modified backups, each with significant differences:

1) *Differential Method* (1 full backup + several differential backups): With this method, you back up the data that has been modified since the last full backup. This is done by setting the backup software to leave a file's "archive flag" unchanged after it is backed up. This method gives you redundancy — the original full backup and the most current differential backup. Using the full backup and the latest differential backup, one can safely restore an entire hard drive. This method requires a lot of tape space, however.

2) *Incremental Method* (1 full backup + several incremental backups): This method backs up only the files that have been modified since the last backup, either full or incremental. Setting the backup software to clear the file's "archive flag" after it is backed up does this. This requires minimum tape space but may require several tape backup sets to find a lost file. To restore an entire hard drive you must restore the full backup and then restore each incremental backup in the cycle.

Get the biggest and fastest backup system you can afford.

When mapping out a backup plan, consider all the costs of hardware, software and staff time. It usually takes at least an hour to back up a single server. Manually backing up several servers weekly, semi-weekly, or daily would obviously represent a considerable amount of staff time resulting in lost productivity.

One good reason for using a reliable Internet Hosting Service is that it will provide and perform planned scheduled backup services. A good Web hosting service will have a backup system that is designed to prevent the loss of data that a Web site might experience due to server crashes, hard drive problems and hackers.

UNINTERRUPTIBLE POWER SUPPLY

An uninterruptible power supply (UPS) is a device with a built-in battery that sits between the power supply and the server. It protects the equipment from power outages, brownouts, sags, surges, bad harmonics, etc., which can adversely affect the performance of the system. UPSs are available in numerous configurations. A UPS that can protect a single Web server will cost around $250. If you have a network of servers, UPS costs can run into thousands of dollars and require a special build out to handle the weight of the UPS.

There are two types of Web site — the ones that have had a power problem and the ones that will have a power problem. Even though you think you might never need it, a UPS will be one of the most important pieces of equipment you will install to help ensure the reliable operation of your Web Site.

Standby Power Supply

There are many UPSs with varying capabilities. A "standby power supply" or "offline UPS" is not a true UPS. It won't protect your Web server. This standby power supply's power comes directly from the power line, until the power fails, then a battery-powered inverter takes over. The time required for the inverter to start providing electricity to your server varies greatly. Some servers might tolerate the quirks of a standby power supply, but don't chance it.

Hybrid UPS

A "hybrid UPS" is a device that uses a ferroresonant transformer to maintain a constant output voltage between the power source and your server, protecting against line noise. It can maintain output relying on its battery (a secondary power source) for a limited period of time. If power is not reinstated, a total outage occurs. It is questionable whether this type of device can actually respond when needed without an accompanying interruption in power. There is some debate as to whether a UPS's ferroresonant transformer will interact with the ferroresonant transformers in your equipment, producing unexpected results. The hybrid UPS system is comparatively cheap, but, if you choose it, be sure to thoroughly test it with all of your equipment before going on-line.

True UPS

My best recommendation is for you to use a true UPS. While these systems are more expensive to purchase and maintain than the others we have examined thus far, this system continuously operates from an inverter with no switchover time and offers good protection from power problems.

A true UPS has internal batteries and can absorb small power surges, continues to provide power during line sags, negates noisy power sources, and provides power for a set length of time during a power loss. It provides continuous power independent of the outside power supply. The *minimum* support you want from any UPS system is 10 to 30 minutes, enough to survive short outages and other power inconsistencies. Keep in mind though, as you design your server system that a true UPS does generate quite a bit of heat; so don't put it in a closed space.

In the next level of UPSs, the systems provide:

- automatic shutdown and restart of your Web site's equipment during long power outages

- monitoring and logging of the status of the power supply

- a display showing the voltage/current draw of the equipment and the voltage currently on the line

How to Assess Your UPS Requirements

How much are you going to pay for the reliability of a true UPS? To find the answer, decide the minimum and maximum amount of time you want to keep your equipment running after the power goes down. To assess the amount of time your system might need supplemental power support — which can be considerable with tape back-up and CD burners — add up the power requirements of the hardware you are running by using the equipment manuals (not the rating plates on the equipment). If power is stated in Watts, then multiply that figure by 1.5 or perhaps even 2.0 to get the VA rating, which is the maximum number of Volts Amps the piece of equipment can deliver.

The energy delivering capacity of a power system is measured in these Volt-Amps (VA). In the U.S., a standard electrical system outlet for the home is rated at 120 Volts of Alternating Current (120 VAC) and 15 amps (depending upon the thickness of the wire), and thus has a rated VA capacity of 120V x 15A = 1800VA. Exceed that limit and you'll trip a circuit breaker or cause a fire.

Similarly, for a UPS, an expensive, heavy-duty 300VA device has a lot more capacity than an inexpensive 100VA device. If you use a 100VA rated device anyway and exceed its rating you could blow its fuse or it will not work correctly when called upon during a power failure.

In high school you may have been taught that Watts = Volts x Amps, so you might jump to the conclusion that VA = Watts. It isn't quite that simple.

Transformer and capacitor operated devices have a spec called the Power Factor, which is a number between zero and one. The Power Factor represents the ratio of the energy used by the system to the energy required by the system to make it operate properly. Light bulbs, space heaters, toaster ovens, etc., use all of the raw energy put into them and so have a Power Factor of one. Devices based upon more del-

- alarms on certain error conditions

- short circuit protection

Although the cost of such a unit can be quite high, if your Web site is not attended 24 hours a day, 7 days a week, the true UPS may be your best power solution.

How to Rate the Various UPSs

When researching your UPS requirements and the various brands and configurations available, make certain that the UPS vendor offers a support and/or maintenance contract. If not, go to another vendor. There are many options you may wish to consider before purchasing your UPS. A manual bypass switch is helpful so that when the UPS is out of oper-

icate and complicated electronic components do not necessarily use all their power rating all the time and have a Power Factor of less than one, generally 0.5 or 0.6. Thus, a computer may need 160VA to run correctly but it actually only uses 80 Watts so the Power Factor is 80 / 160 = 0.5. Another way to find the VA is to remember that VA = Watts / Power Factor.

This also means that Watts = VA x Power Factor. You might be tempted to look at your computer, see the Watt rating of 80 Watts, then run to your friendly neighborhood computer store and buy an 80 Watt UPS. Bad idea! Things are not that simple, since Watts = VA x Power Factor, so 80 Watts = 160VA x 0.5 for our imaginary computer. This means that we need a 160VA unit to protect and supply power for an 80 Watt computer. Unfortunately many UPS manufacturers use a generous Power Factor of 1.0 when they advertise the ratings of their VA devices and are thus listing the rating in Watts instead of in VA capacity. They figure that "Watts" is a more familiar electrical term to non-techies than VA and, besides, a Power Factor of 1.0 gives the largest value for the Watt rating, so 80VA x 1.0 = 80 Watts. This causes the unsuspecting consumer to buy an underpowered UPS. An "80 Watt" UPS may really be an 80VA unit that can actually only handle a 40 Watt computer! To protect a 160 Watt computer, you would have to buy a 320VA UPS.

And even if you think you've "figured out" what the right size is for your UPS, be sure to add another 20% capacity for good measure.

What this all comes down to is that, if you want your Web site to be up and running during a blackout, then you will need a very robust UPS. Your UPS will rely on its battery (DC) to AC converter, which means an expenditure of power. Just to give you an idea at what you are looking at, we will hazard a guess that a 1,250 VA UPS could probably operate during a blackout for around 5 hours and a 2,000 VA UPS could operate during a blackout about 8 hours. Be sure to ask your UPS vendor about guarantees.

ation, power can pass through it to your Web server. You also should know how close the AC output of the UPS is to a sine wave.

An inverter is an electronic device that converts a battery's DC output to AC through a switching process, producing a "synthesized" AC, which can be charted as a waveform on an oscilloscope or graph paper. Inverters produce two types of waveforms: The so-called "modified sine wave" and the "true sine wave".

True sine waves, or sinusoidal signals, are the most common waves that exist. They're called sine waves because they have the same shape as the graph of the sine function used in trigonometry. Sine waves look the way they do because they are produced by rotating electrical machines such as generators and, indeed, a sine wave's intensity (amplitude) at any given instant can be represented by a point on a wheel rotating at a uniform speed. Since waves are perfectly "balanced" over successive time intervals (see diagram).

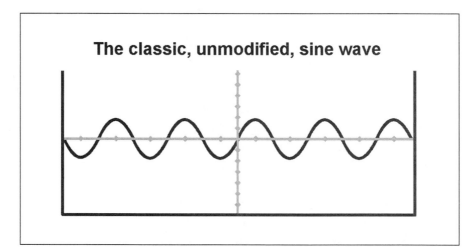

The classic, unmodified, sine wave

A "modified sine wave" is not actually a sine wave, but a stepped wave, which is the kind of wave a pendulum produces, and is not as smooth as a sine wave. But "mod sine" inverters cost half the price of sine wave inverters, thus lowering the cost of a UPS. However, they can cause electrical noise on a circuit, and digital clocks and timing circuits can be confused or even be occasionally damaged.

Sine wave inverters in a good UPS deliver true sine wave AC output power with high efficiencies from storage batteries. They have high surge ability and low idle current draw. Because of the pure sine wave, the expense is greater than a modified sine wave inverter.

If your UPS does not output a pure sinusoidal waveform, do not put a surge protector between the UPS and the server since a surge protector can mistake the non-sine waveform as a power surge and send it to ground which will damage the UPS. Some experts think that most computers use a switching-type power supply that only draws power at or near the peak of the waveform, therefore the shape of the input power waveform is not important. It is worth spending a little more for a UPS with pure sinusoidal output especially for a UPS that must continually provide a waveform to the computer.

Next, check what useful operational information the UPS itself provides via displays, etc., such as the power or percentage load the unit is drawing, the battery level and power quality. Most UPSs use lead-acid batteries with a life span of only a few years but no battery memory. Therefore they should be run "dry" as few times as possible.

Maintenance

As your UPS ages, its battery life will become shorter. Be vigilant in monitoring the active support time. When your Web site has no one accessing it (or you can take it off the Internet for a few minutes) and you've completely backed up you hard drive(s), test your UPS and its failure modes. Simulate a power outage by throwing the circuit breaker that has the UPS on it (don't pull the plug from the wall) to check the UPS. If you don't have your UPS-protected Web site on an isolated circuit, you could install a Ground Fault Interrupter (GFI) socket. (GFI sockets are the electrical switches with a red and a black button you see in houses and offices.)

Power problems are inevitable and beyond your control. Therefore, a UPS is one of the most crucial items you can purchase to keep your Web site up and ready for action.

RAID

RAID is an acronym for "redundant array of independent (or inexpensive) disks" and is a system designed to link the capacity of two or more hard drives that are then viewed as a single large virtual drive by the RAID management software. By doing this it is possible to improve data storage reliability and thereby achieve fault tolerance.

RAID *must* be a part of any Web site. By purchasing a good UPS you've protected your site against power problems. Now you need to protect your Web site against data problems and drive failure. That's where RAID comes in.

A basic RAID system includes RAID functionality built into a controller and two or more hard drives. There is also RAID software that can implement RAID in a server without a special drive controller, but the efficiency and performance leaves much to be desired. Don't use it.

RAID can be found in many different configurations and in as many price ranges:

- A floor-standing cabinet.

- A complete system in one full-size drive bay.

- A self-contained system which can have its own redundant power supplies, etc.

- In RAID Levels 3 and 5, drives can be hot swapped (you can change drives without shutting down the server) and the RAID controller and reconstruction software will automatically rebuild any lost data.

RAID Levels

Although there are many different RAID levels, we are only going to discuss the most common ones that would be used for Web site operation.

RAID-O divides each data file into blocks and distributes these among multiple disks in a process called disk striping. This provides high performance since more than one disk is read and/or written to simultaneously. A file can now be input with one revolution of four disks as opposed to four revolutions of one disk. Unfortunately RAID-O doesn't have the one key feature you expect from a RAID subsystem: Data redundancy, hence no fault tolerance. When you read that a system supports RAID-O it really means that although the system has disk striping, it isn't actually RAID at all. RAID-O is used for high performance situations such as video editing and is generally not used for Web servers, unless some kind of high performance database must be put online.

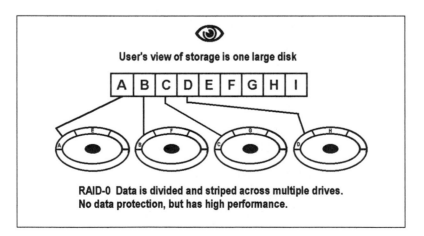

User's view of storage is one large disk

| A | B | C | D | E | F | G | H | I |

RAID-0 Data is divided and striped across multiple drives. No data protection, but has high performance.

RAID-1 is the easiest and, for a small Web site, can be one of the least expensive ways to protect your Web site's data from a hard drive failure. With RAID-1, as the data is being written it is simultaneously being copied or mirrored onto a second disk which is connected to a common disk controller and, voila! You have data redundancy. RAID-1 is considered to be the most common, secure and reliable form of RAID. However, as your need for data storage increases, your costs can become considerable. At such a point you would go looking for another storage method such as RAID-3 or -5.

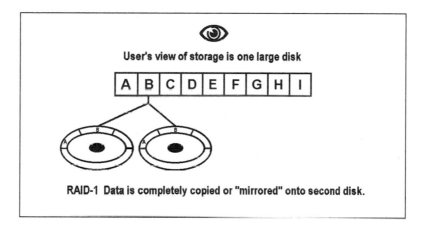

User's view of storage is one large disk

| A | B | C | D | E | F | G | H | I |

RAID-1 Data is completely copied or "mirrored" onto second disk.

Before I go further into RAID technology I should explain parity data in the form of a type of Error Correcting Code (ECC) which avoids the cost of duplicating disk drives in their entirety. There is a method of transmitting binary data where an extra bit (the "parity bit") is added to each group of bits. If parity is to be odd then the extra or parity bit is assigned either a one or zero so the total number of ones in the character will be odd. If the parity is even, the parity bit is assigned a value so that the total number of ones in the character is even. In this way errors can be detected.

I know this explanation probably appears as clear as mud but stick around and hopefully it will become clearer.

By using RAID with parity, when a drive fails the ECCs and binary value of the striped bytes or sectors can be used to recover data from a failed drive by comparing data on the still-functioning drives to the parity data which sits on a special parity data drive. The RAID system then can re-create the data on the failed drive.

This is similar to how one solves a missing variable in an equation. For example, 3+5=8, where "3" is a bit on one drive, "5" is a bit on another drive, and "8" is the data's parity information stored on a third drive. If the drive storing "3" fails, you could recalculate it by solving for X in the equation X+5=8, so X=3.

Or, to state it in very simple terms, parity-based systems calculate the data in two drives and stores the result on a third drive. Those results can be later used to reconstruct what was on the other two drives. Now we can continue with our RAID discussion.

RAID-3 stripes data across multiple disks one byte at a time. Parity is also calculated bit-by-bit and stored on an extra "parity drive." All drives have synchronized rotation. When a drive fails, data is rebuilt transparently in the background from the remaining functioning drives as the system continues to operate.

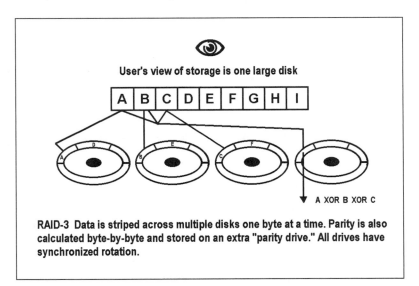

User's view of storage is one large disk

A XOR B XOR C

RAID-3 Data is striped across multiple disks one byte at a time. Parity is also calculated byte-by-byte and stored on an extra "parity drive." All drives have synchronized rotation.

RAID-5 is the most popular high-end RAID technique used today. RAID-5 stripes data at the sector or block level across a minimum of three drives. It also provides stripe error correction information by striping it along with the data evenly over the drive set. This results in excellent performance and good fault tolerance but it still lags behind the performance found with RAID-1 disk mirroring. Most of the high-end pre-configured RAID set-ups are RAID-5. A RAID-5 system with preconfigured drives, RAID-5 software and adapter cards, and the necessary cables is easy to purchase and set up.

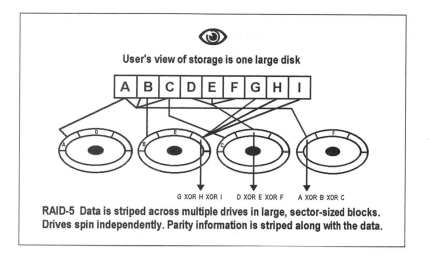

User's view of storage is one large disk

| A | B | C | D | E | F | G | H | I |

G XOR H XOR I   D XOR E XOR F   A XOR B XOR C

RAID-5 Data is striped across multiple drives in large, sector-sized blocks. Drives spin independently. Parity information is striped along with the data.

RAID-10 is really just RAID-1 and RAID-0, used in combination, i.e., mirroring and disk striping. It's a very reliable, comprehensive RAID set-up for a large, full-blown e-commerce Web site.

Some kind of RAID storage is necessary for your Web site and there are certainly all types and levels available. To learn more about RAID systems, read Richard Grigonis' book, *Fault Resilient PCs*.

MIRRORING

Mirroring of a Web site is the creation of multiple Web sites that are exact duplicates of an existing Web site. A Web site can use mirrored sites in many ways:

- To improve the download speed to your customer by providing more than one server in more than one location with the identical information. Therefore, when traffic becomes too heavy for one geographical site (or one server) to handle, your system can hand off the additional traffic to the mirrored site.

- Live standby servers where data contained on the primary servers are seamlessly mirrored on the standby servers. In the event of an unplanned outage, such an infrastructure can keep a Web site running efficiently, including both hardware and software.

- When a Web site uses a system that generates dynamic HTML, it can create a mirror of the site with fixed HTML for search engine indexing purposes, along with special scripting that can automatically direct customers to the "real site."

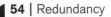

Since you are creating a duplicate of your site in every way, even software and hardware, the costs can be astronomical, depending on the size of your Web site. However, before deciding against a mirror site, consider the costs that come with a site being down because of a natural disaster at the servers' location or a hacker attack.

CHAPTER 6
Connectivity

Take care of the minutes and the hours will take care of themselves.

Connectivity is a buzzword used in Internet circles that refers to the ability of computers to link to networks and therefore the Internet. This chapter deals with the bandwidth aspect of connectivity, i.e., the amount of data that can be transmitted in a fixed amount of time. Although I do not provide a complete education on connectivity and bandwidth here, I do provide the information you will need to make an intelligent connectivity decision.

The first step is to estimate the amount of bandwidth you need to feed data from your Web server to your customers.

Bandwidth (in the Internet context) is the number of bits per unit time that can be carried across a communications line. The basic unit of bandwidth measurement is bits per second (bps), but most commonly you'll see it expressed Kbps or Mbps, which stand for kilo-bits per second and mega-bits per second, respectively. The rate at which your connection transfers data is measured in the same bits per second. This bandwidth determines how fast data is transmitted to and from your Web server and also how many requests can be serviced simultaneously. Even with a robust server, if you do not have sufficient bandwidth for the number of customers coming to your Web site, delays or failures will occur.

Select a way of delivering bandwidth that is scalable to meet your Web site's future needs while at the same time limiting additional costs and frustration. For example, a burstable or fractional T-1, a full-rate T-1, or (for an enterprise-size site) some flavor of T-3 might be the connectivity of choice. Since your Web site should be accessible to everyone on the Web, and you hope to have many visitors to your site, plan for lots of bandwidth. Note that a very small Web site can get by with a DSL connection, although this does not have much scalability. We advise that, if you can afford it, you should choose, at a minimum, a burstable or fractional T-1 line. A Web site offering streaming video, lots of audio or one which receives a large amount of traffic would need a T-1 connection all to itself. An enterprise Web site might need a T-3 (45 Mbps).

In addition to the number of simultaneous customers, think about the speed at which data is sent to your customers. This is determined by connection speed and data size. It should take less than five seconds to send a page of type. Even with the additional bandwidth demands of graphics, audio, or video, there should be sufficient bandwidth for a page should load in less than 30 seconds.

Once you've determined the amount of bandwidth needed for your Web server, consider whether your Web site will be offering other services that require increased bandwidth such as e-mail, chat rooms, streaming audio or video. Be sure to include enough bandwidth to cover these services.

The Internet connection comes through a router. A network interface card connects your Web server to the router. A high-performance network card will prevent a bottleneck between your Internet connection and your Web server.

Whatever size bandwidth you end up using, your Web hosting service should take care of most of the details of getting the line installed. Your local telephone company will provide the piece of the connection (the "local loop") that brings the Internet to your door. If your Web hosting service has a point of presence (POP) co-located with your telephone company's central office (practically all do), you'll be able to connect with them using just a local loop. Otherwise you'll have to rent a dedicated line to wherever the "on ramp" happens to be.

Web hosting services must also ensure that their POPs are capable of delivering the bandwidth and response times that their customers need to use all critical Internet applications. Ultimately, Web hosting services must be able to expand their POP as they increase their customer base and add new services.

ISDN

ISDN (Integrated Services Digital Network) is an access technology that uses digital transmission with a bandwidth of up to 128 Kbps over your local telephone company's ordinary copper wire lines. However, unlike your local telephone service, which transmits analog signals, ISDN can, over these same wires, transmit multiple digital signals simultaneously. One ISDN line transmits three separate channels — two 64Kbps Bearer or "B" channels, and a little 16Kbps Delta or "D" channel that you normally don't deal with directly. Through a process called BONDING, the two B channels can be combined into a single 128Kbps channel.

A terminal adapter (TA) is the final piece of equipment you install at the end of an ISDN line in your home or business — it can be an ISDN phone, a fax machine, or an ISDN "modem."

There are two kinds of ISDN TAs, internal and external. TAs can look like modems, computer bus cards, or interface cards for PBXs or routers. Many ISDN phones and modems have analog jacks on the back that allow you to connect ordinary phones, fax machines, and other analog, non-ISDN devices.

External ISDN TAs are easier to install (they plug into your PC's serial or USB port) but won't give you maximum performance. Some, like the Motorola Bitsurfr Pro or the 3COM Courier, actually look like modems and are often called "ISDN modems."

So, you can replace your regular analog modem with an external ISDN modem, but remember that ISDN is not scalable — you get 128 Kbps, which is a little over twice the speed of a 56k modem, and that's it. There is no upgrade available. Your data is routed from your ISDN modem to your Web hosting service over the same copper wire pair that you may have previously used for ordinary analog phone service, then out to the Internet.

ISDN is available from the local telephone company in most areas in the United States and Europe for around $150 for installation, $300 for the external adapter/modem and a $50 to $100 monthly line fee. But if you have another, faster option where you are located (such as any form of DSL) avoid using the ISDN line.

DSL

DSL (Digital Subscriber Line) technology brings high-bandwidth transmission to homes and small businesses over ordinary copper telephone lines. xDSL refers to different variations of DSL, such as Assymmetric DSL (ADSL), HDSL, and RADSL which provides high-bandwidth transmission up to 10 Mbps over your local telephone company's ordinary copper wire lines. Installation of ADSL, a popular version of xDSL, appeared in 1998 and soon exploded offering service throughout the United States and elsewhere. It is predicted to replace ISDN.

DSL works by placing special line conditioning and transmission equipment on both ends of an ordinary copper line from your location to the local telephone company's central office. Because this connection uses a much broader range of frequencies to transmit digital data than a standard analog phone line, higher speeds are possible. Your data is then routed from the telephone company's central office to your Web hosting service over high-speed trunk lines, then out to the Internet.

DSL offers several advantages over an ISDN connection. Even a "lite" ADSL connection offers from 384 Kbps to 1.5 Mbps of Internet bandwidth as opposed to 128 Kbps with ISDN, i.e., DSL is at least 6 times faster. Full-rate ADSL can move 8 Mbps, thus having the bandwidth of several 1.5 Mbps T-1s.

DSL is hundreds of dollars per month cheaper than a burstable or fractional T-1 connection. A DSL connection gives you acceptable bandwidth to your Web server at a fraction of the cost, but it, too, is not very scalable.

Since xDSL requires installation of a signal splitter there is an up-front installation expense of about $100.00. You should install a DSL router that is connected to your Web Server's network hub, which will cost around $150.00. Your monthly costs should be between $40.00 and $180.00.

T-1

A T-1 line's data-carrying capacity is 1.5 Mbps within 24 channels, each channel having a 64 Kbps data transfer capacity. For a small business this is definitely overkill and possibly too expensive.

A fractional T-1 line is less expensive than a full T-1 and is scalable. A fractional T-1 is a T-1 line that is channelized or partitioned and is referred to as a "fractional configuration." If a business does not need a full T-1 line it can lease any portion of the 24 64 Kbps channels, with the transmission method and rate of transfer remaining the same. This service is most preferable for a Web site that expects its traffic to be higher than 1 Mbps 50% of the time.

A burstable T-1 is a cost-effective Internet access solution for Web sites to receive direct, reliable, high-speed Internet connectivity. You only pay for the bandwidth that is used rather than for the total size of the circuit and bandwidth, much of which is often unused.

Access to the Internet is set at a minimum of 128 Kbps with burstability to a full T-1 of 1.5 Mbps. Although a monthly minimum is based on sustained usage of 128 Kbps, burstable T-1 service always provides the availability of the full T-1 bandwidth. An unshared, point-to-point, non-fractional 1.54 Mbps digital leased line costs around $800.00 per month, and burstable T-1 is somewhat less. Here's how the cost is calcuated: Usage is usually monitored every day with SNMP (a network monitoring and control protocol) to create an end-of-month usage report. Rates are then averaged based on the middle 90% of reported usage for the monthly basis. The reports should be included in your monthly billing. The burstable T-1 is a viable option for most small Web sites since it is scalable to a full T-1.

Any T-1 installation will come with a set-up fee of approximately $5,000 (although the cost does vary) that includes:

- all the local telephone company loop charges and carrier fees

- full 1.54 Mbps Availability

- Cisco router or other certified network equipment

- T-1 CSU/DSU

- all T-1 Installation Charges

- T-1 Set-up Fees

- as many IP addresses as can be justified

T-3

A T-3's (also known as DS3 lines) data carrying capacity is about 45 Mbps within 672 channels, each channel having a 64 Kbps transfer capacity. Note that T-3 lines are used mainly by Internet Service Providers (ISPs) connecting to the Internet backbone and for the backbone itself.

OPTICAL CARRIER (OC)

Optical Carrier (OC) is the term used for fiber optic networks conforming to the Synchronous Optical Network, a standard for connecting fiber-optic transmission systems (the "SONET standard"). Fiber Optics is a technology that uses glass or plastic fibers or threads to transmit data. A fiber optic cable consists of a bundle of fibers or threads, each of which is capable of transmitting messages modulated onto light waves.

The standard defines a hierarchy of interface rates that allow data streams at different rates to be multiplexed. SONET establishes OC levels from 51.85 Mbps to 2.488 Gbps. Below are the standard OC levels:

OC-1 = 51.85 Mbps

OC-3 = 155.52 Mbps

OC-12 = 622.08 Mbps

OC-24 = 1.244 Gbps

OC-48 = 2.488 Gbps

CHAPTER 7
Security

Even the lion must defend himself against gnats.

The Internet's openness makes it the perfect platform for e-commerce while providing inexpensive mass communication and economies of scale for low-cost distribution. However, the security of Web-based transactions and the ease with which the privacy of online communications can be violated are e-commerce's main stumbling blocks. The problem is that since the Internet is open, any type of communication traveling over it is inherently difficult to secure. There is no mechanism that guarantees the integrity of the information or provides relationships of trust between senders and receivers.

If you are building a Web site you must recognize and appreciate that you are building in a domain that is, at least in principle, fraught with danger. Therefore you need to ensure that adequate levels of security are in place, including firewalls and monitoring software to protect Web pages, and an encryption method to protect consumer transactions. Supplement the above with constant monitoring, reporting and analyzing of the security of the entire infrastructure of your Web-based business. A good monitoring system will allow you to analyze internal and external firewall activity and identify attempted security breaches.

There are high-end security analysis solutions available that can detect and resolve security vulnerabilities in your Web-based business' systems either on demand or at regularly scheduled intervals. Look at www.webtrends.com and www.pgp.com to give you an idea of what is available in the way of security suites. Some other Web sites you might want to examine and bookmark are: www.technotronic.com, www.sun.com/sunsoft/solstice/Networkingproducts/networksec.html, www.sun.com/sunsoft/solaris/security/security.html, and java.sun.com/commerce.

Web site security is an extensive subject and well beyond the scope of this book. Nonetheless, it is important to review the main points of good Web security as a piece of your site's overall reliability architecture.

With an effective security system a Web site can create an environment that promotes e-commerce and private communications by establishing a climate that is safe from robbery and fraud.

The author has noticed that security is a subject most business executives try to avoid since they feel that discussing their business' security procedures and policies might add to the risk of an attack. However, without such a discussion, these same executives will not be aware of the constantly evolving technology that can help a business make a smooth, secure move to the Web.

A secure e-commerce environment requires:

- access control, usually managed by a firewall, which regulates the data flow

- authentication, which binds the identity of an individual to a specific message or transaction

- data privacy and integrity which ensures that communications and transactions remain confidential, accurate and have not been modified

There are a number of security concerns that must be addressed by any Web-based business. E-commerce necessitates the opening of a business' systems to third parties that require access to specific data, but the business must restrict that same data from other parties. One example is that a customer might need to know how much a widget attachment will cost as the order is being entered, but that same customer should not be allowed to see the cost of another customer's order. Also, everyone agrees it is necessary to let a customer view an order while on a Web site, but it is not acceptable for that same customer to copy the entire database in which the order is stored. Many of the systems online today are not ready to handle the level of security needed to support e-commerce.

DENIAL OF SERVICE ATTACK

A "denial-of-service" attack is when an attacker or attackers attempt to prevent legitimate Web site users from accessing a site. These attacks will become more common as other types of security attacks are made more difficult.

Examples include:

- The "Ping of Death" that uses a test packet larger than allowed, which can cause a system crash or problems with network programs running on the targeted computer. Ping is the acronym for Packet Internet Groper, a program that tests a TCP network by sending a packet with an echo request to a designated host's IP address and then waits for a reply.

- Attempts to "flood" a network, thereby preventing legitimate network traffic and attempts to disrupt connections between two machines, thereby preventing access to a service.

- The Mail Bomb that sends a flood of mail to a mail server, sometimes overloading it, thus causing legitimate users to not only be denied service but to also lose mail that had been sent to their mailbox.

- Host System Hogging, where a program is actually run on the system of the Web site that is under attack causing a domino effect. It ties up the system's CPUs, the operating system crashes, the site goes down and, finally, customers can't access the site.

Not all service outages are outright denial-of-service attacks. For example, some denial-of-service attacks might be controlled so as only to cause degradation in network traffic. This in turn slows down the Web site, but does not block it completely. Your Web site could also be the victim of other types of attack such as an attacker using your anonymous FTP storage area as a place to store illegal copies of commercial software, consuming disk space and generating network traffic.

The problem is that the latest forms of denial of service attacks are difficult to counter since they can happen at any given time and, at the moment, there isn't any general solution to the problem. A Web site operator must address each attack as it occurs.

DEFENDING YOUR WEB SITE

1. The first line of defense for a Web site is to limit the access to the site by outsiders. Some methods for accomplishing this are:
    - firewalls
    - user account security
    - software security
    - additional protection for sensitive data

2. The second line of defense is setting into place a routine monitoring system so that you know what is going on with your Internet traffic and servers. With Log Analysis

Software (see Chapter 8) you can monitor the system logs and network traffic for anomalies, thereby allowing you to identify attempted security breaches and possibly track where they come from. You can also install high-end security analysis solutions that can detect and resolve security vulnerabilities on the site's systems on demand or at regularly scheduled intervals.

3. The third line of defense is encryption. What is encryption? It is a system of using encoding algorithms to construct an overall mechanism for sharing sensitive data. This is the security cornerstone for most e-commerce sites.

Encryption cannot be a Web site's only form of security. A Web site needs a total security architecture — security that exists in numerous layers to be effective — from the Web server to the application to the database to extensions to other subsystems. The brick-and-mortar businesses may have some kind of security program already installed, but, in all probability, it is not up to date. And if any part of the security architecture is not working as planned, then your whole security set-up is vulnerable.

Many Web-based businesses use security tools, techniques, and strategies that could not withstand a sophisticated security attack. This is a needless risk, especially when there are many security solutions available that can provide efficient data sharing without compromising the confidentiality, availability, and integrity of the data.

Security is another good reason for placing your Web servers within the confines of a reliable Web hosting service. A good hosting service will have the financial means to provide the resources for effective Web site security. Their professional staff will have the wherewithal to keep abreast of the latest news and technology updates as well as the ability to implement fixes and upgrades at a moment's notice.

Routers

A router is an electronic device or, in some cases, software in a computer, that forwards traffic (or data) between networks. The forwarding is based on network layer information and routing tables. Routers spend all their time looking at the destination addresses of the packets passing through them and deciding which route to send them on. A router is like a trip planner. Tell the planner where you want to go and it directs you via the shortest route. If you are a brick-and-mortar business running a network of computers, you probably already have routers for your network, but know that the considerations are different when designing a configuration for your new Web site.

Firewalls

A firewall is a device that controls the flow of communication between internal networks and external networks, such as the Internet. It controls "port-level" access to a network and a Web site. A "port" is like a doorway into the server. For example, your Internet request isn't just immediately sent to a server; instead there is a port number on the server that is the actual destination of a request. It's like sending a message to the server on Main Street in Elmville, New York, USA but forgetting to provide the specific "building" number. For example, http://www.yourname.com by default uses port 80 (the building number) on the www.yourname.com server. If a request arrives at the wrong server or the wrong port, the service handling requests on that port will ignore the request.

A firewall is technically software, although it is often installed on its own server. It can offer security, flexibility and provide a wide range of protection. Costs can range from a $10,000 router software package firewall system to a $100,000+ system consisting of routers and proxy servers. If you want to ensure that you have an efficient firewall system, hire an expert in data security.

It is agreed that firewalls are an important component of network security, and many businesses take the position of "we already have a firewall therefore we are adequately protected." It's more complicated than that. A firewall must be correctly configured to provide effective protection. A router running firewall software will probably not provide all of a Web-based business' security needs — it depends on the Web site and the applications it is running.

A *properly* configured firewall can also act as a filter to prevent suspicious requests from ever arriving at the server or can be configured to drop any request that tries to address a server or server port that has not been specifically enabled by the policy of the firewall. More importantly, firewalls can verify that the request matches the kind of protocol (e.g., HTTP, FTP) that is expected on a particular port.

Firewalls can be used in various places. For example:

- a firewall between the Internet and the Web server limits the number of ports and protocols open for use by outsiders

- firewalls between the Web site and the Web-based business's internal network protects back-end servers and data by isolating public servers from the rest of the internal network, somewhat like a high fence

- a firewall can isolate sensitive Web site data from other servers through a configuration that allows access only from the Web site application servers. This type of set-up is used to safeguard critical data such as credit card numbers

Although you should use firewalls as the first line of defense, they are only part of a good comprehensive security solution. You must also shut down all nonessential ports and services on production servers. Some of the services, like FTP, are inherently insecure because they send their password without any type of encryption. Other services such as netstat and systat actually put forth information that can assist nefarious individuals with certain types of attacks on your Web site. Although I am not providing a complete list, some of the services you should disable on your Web site's servers are:

- Mail (SMTP)
- Finger
- Netstat, systat
- Chargen, echo
- FTP
- Telnet
- Berkeley UNIX "r" commands such as rlogin,rsh, rdist etc.
- SNMP

User Account Security

One of the most common types of attacks is for hackers to gain access to a Web server by stealing a user's account. Restricting a user's access to only the needed resources limits the amount of damage hackers can do. Authentication and authorization are the two best general ways of restricting access.

Authentication verifies that you are who you claim to be. An authentication system can use login-passwords, digital signatures, and a one-time password (single sign-on). An example of usage is the need to authenticate a user in order to login to a Web server from a Web browser.

Authorization defines what a user is allowed to do. It is typically used with an access control list service (ACLS) or policy that restricts access to computer resources. Authorization may be attributed to users, user groups, or user profiles.

User IDs and passwords are the most common means of providing authentication services with authorization to access specific resources such as file directories, read/write permission, database access. User IDs are usually easy to figure out, since many are based on a user's name. So, make the passwords harder to guess. Still, this won't solve all of your problems because there are a number of tools and techniques available that can be used to decipher a password.

Some of the things you can do to improve password security are:

- Never transmit user IDs and passwords in the clear.

- Make the passwords a combination of mixed-case letters and numbers.

- Test your passwords by using a tool like password+ or Password Appraiser v3.20.

- Keep the number of accounts on production servers to a minimum.

- Use techniques for encrypting transmissions and certificates for authentication such as Kerberos (a security system that authenticates users but doesn't provide authorization to services or databases, although it does establish identity at log-on) and SSL for the administrator accounts.

- Never grant more access to resources than is needed. For example, if an application server running your product catalog needs to read its information from a database, it will need a database user account, but this account must not be authorized to read from other parts of the database (where credit cards are stored), or be allowed write privileges.

Data Confidentiality

Confidentiality ensures that only authorized people can view data transferred in networks or stored in databases. Protecting sensitive data like credit card numbers, inventory, etc. is a difficult problem for Web-based businesses. The first step is to take the time to identify the information that is sensitive. The second step is to make the data harder to retrieve by using any or all of the following:

- Put the data on a separate server behind a firewall.

- Separate the data. For example, give a database its own security subsystem and user authentication process.

- Restrict the number of user accounts that can read/write the data.

- Separate write access from read access.

- Encrypt the data and control access to the encryption key.

Software Security

Internet applications often require security services such as authentication, data confidentiality, data integrity, and nonrepudiation. The major Web server applications install their own security implementations on top of the operating system.

Any application that processes requests from a user is seen as a separate component in a Web site's architecture. Applications do handle incoming requests and therefore need to ensure that requests stay within permitted boundaries. The first step in providing some kind of security for these applications is to not trust the correctness of user input — whenever input is received it is validated. Why? Because it is possible to "piggyback" a second command onto an input request to a Unix shell by separating the two commands by an ampersand (&) or semicolon (;). Therefore, every input request should be parsed for validity or filtered for suspect content. A second step is to use separate security subsystems to control access to an application's resources where users are authorized and authenticated. This way, the application administrator, not the system administrator, controls the application's security system. As such, normally there is no one person who can control all of the information relating to a Web site. Also, e-commerce packages usually come with security subsystems to control their particular resources.

However, security methods in a Web-based business should be centralized to the largest degree possible. In this manner, you can limit accessibility to security information and the need to extend trust to many administrators is eliminated. Finally, every application running on a Web site must consistently apply a clear security architecture (and must consistently fit within your site's overall security architecture), making explicit its operational requirements.

Another step is to keep abreast of all security alerts for threats against your type of systems. Once alerted to a new technique for breaking into your type of system, counterattack with a plug and keep repeating the scenario — plug a leak, the hackers come up with a new way to break in, plug it, the hackers formulate a new break in, plug it, and on and on.

I know that UNIX with all of its good features isn't the easiest system to make secure but it can be done if you know where all the leaks are. The same situation exists with a Windows system — if you know where the holes are, you can plug them. Keeping on top of the operating system weaknesses being exploited by hackers will allow you to keep (hopefully) one step ahead of them.

Firewall applications remove unnecessary, resource-hogging services and at the same time plug potential security holes. This is easier to do with Unix-based firewalls than with Windows-based systems since developers have easier access to the Unix code. Microsoft is much more protective of its code and therefore is not as cooperative with developers.

Monitoring your Web Site

Finally, you need to monitor your Web site's usage and take a proactive stance on security holes. To ensure a high level of security, you should:

- Monitor for any break-ins. Use a user account change report or a sophisticated network monitoring system.

- Back up your Web site on a regular, scheduled basis so that, if needed, you can recover damaged data and programs.

- Monitor your logs after an attack, they can tell you how the attack occurred and might even give you a clue as to the identity of the attacker.

- Run a security analysis program that can take a snapshot of your site and then analyze for any potential weaknesses in your site.

- Perform security audits with outside auditors to check for potential security holes that you might have missed.

There are Web sites with good, reliable security information which you should visit:

- Cisco Systems Security Products and Technologies (www.cisco.com/warp/public/cc/cisco/mkt/security)

- Microsoft Security Advisor (www.microsoft.com/security)

- Sun Microsystems Software and Networking Security (www.sun.com/security)

Bookmark the following Web sites to aid you in keeping up with the latest security threats to computer systems.

- Computer Incident Advisory Capability at http://ciac.llnl.gov/

- Federal Computer Incident Response Capability at http://fedcirc.llnl.gov/

- Advanced Laboratory Workstation System at http://www.alw.nih.gov/Security/security-docs.html

Digital Certificates

Most Web-based businesses go further than the security provided at the router and fire-wall level. They incorporate such features as encryption of credit card information and other personal data, digital signatures and trust of identity of network users, hosts, applications, services, and resources.

Internet trust services, including authentication, validation and payment are needed by Web sites to conduct trusted and secure electronic commerce and communications. Digital Certificates provide trust of identity, which enables a Web site to conduct online business securely, with authentication, message privacy, and message integrity, all helping to minimize risk and win customer confidence.

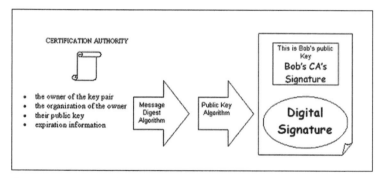

Generating a digital Certificate.

Digital Certificates (DC) can be compared to a driver's license. It is an electronic way to prove the identity of the entity/person that owns/operates the computer. For the driver's license, there has to be a credible organization (the DMV) that tries to assure that the driver license is issued to the correct person. The same is true for a certification authority (CA) that issues digital certificates to verify the identity of the entity/person before issuing a DC. The DC contains the name of a entity/person, the entity/person's public key, serial number, other information, and signature of the CA. CA signed its signature using its own private key.

Credit Card Security

With the proper precautions, online purchases are no more dangerous than credit card purchases made in the physical world. E-commerce systems keep credit card information secure by encrypting the information. Most online purchase transactions are encrypted using the Secure Sockets Layer (SSL). SSL is a standard protocol that creates a secure connection to the server using a public key encryption, protecting the information as it travels over the Internet.

There is also a security standard called Secure Electronic Transactions (SET). SET encrypts a credit card number so that only designated banks and credit card companies can read the information. SET requires you to obtain a special certificate from your bank, and then your customers must install special software on their computer. The software is supplied by various vendors, most of whom seem to have the word "wallet" somewhere in the name. The "e-wallet" software allows your customer to input all of their purchasing information (credit card, address, shipping address, etc.) once and then move merrily through numerous Web sites that accept that e-wallet, doing "one-click" shopping and avoiding the task of filling out individual Web sites' purchase forms.

So far, U.S. consumers have had little incentive to use the e-wallet applications that SET requires, and because the SET systems are costly and complex to set up, the SET standard, although readily accepted outside the U.S., is not widely used by U.S. web merchants and banks. The main barrier has been that each e-wallet provider has established its own unique technical specifications, so many U.S. Web sites have adopted a wait and see attitude with regards to SET.

As we enter the 21st Century, most of the e-commerce sites protect credit card data using SSL encryption and do not validate users' identities with digital certificates. However, SET isn't dead. Trintech's PayGate software supports both SSL and SET allowing an e-commerce site to accept SSL-based payments now and migrate to SET payments later, if necessary. And MasterCard believes that the Visa Payment Gateway will provide a bridge between SSL and SET by allowing e-commerce sites to support current transactions using SSL with the added attraction of supporting international transactions based on SET.

Alternative options are emerging for handling credit card transactions over the Web that are easier and cheaper than SET. The next-generation e-wallets are using a new standard — the Electronic Commerce Modeling Language (ECML) — that works with any Web security software and allows e-wallets to automatically feed customer information into the payment forms of participating Web sites. Implementation of the ECML standard was led by Visa, MasterCard, and American Express, with support from America Online, CyberCash, IBM, Microsoft and Sun, as well as numerous Web-based businesses.

ECML can be used with any security protocol, including SSL, and Visa and MasterCard's own version of SET. Therefore, ECML is changing the landscape for e-wallet companies and Web sites — increasingly you will find e-wallet services offered by financial institutions and credit-card companies.

For more information on e-wallets visit:

- www.passport.com (e-wallet from Microsoft Passport)
- www.instabuy.com (e-wallet from CyberCash)
- www.ewallet.com (e-wallet from Launchpad Technologies, Inc.)

A good Web site to bookmark for Internet trust issues is www.verisign.com. There you will find free seminars, white papers covering trust and security issues and other resources.

Security Audit

I strongly suggest that you retain a security expert to perform a detailed review of your Web-based business' internal procedures, network topology and permissions, access controls, hardware, software and utilities that could possibly compromise your Web site.

Finally, please note that even if you set up intricate levels of security, your Web site is never completely safe from a determined and skilled attacker. E-commerce operations are particularly hard to protect since they must be able to interact with their customers. Therefore, at the very least, build and maintain a good, state-of-the-art firewall and be sure to encrypt sensitive data, such as credit card information. There are numerous security consultants who can help you protect your Web site. And don't forget to institute an on-going program of security maintenance, monitoring and schedule an annual security audit.

CHAPTER 8
Software

If you do not think about the future you cannot have one.

If your Web-based business is to cross the finish line (in the money) of the "race for success" you must choose the right software. Software can be defined at its most basic as computer instructions or data — anything that can be stored electronically is software. When making your software choices you must consider ease of integration, scalability and robustness, i.e., does it work well with other software and hardware, can it scale as your business grows and as technology changes, and can it handle large amounts of traffic.

The basic software, after you have chosen your operating system, include Web server, log analysis, database, and e-commerce (this last is so important that it rates is own chapter — see Chapter 9).

THE OPERATING SYSTEM

An operating system (OS) acts as the CEO of your computer whether it operates on a server or a desktop computer. Just as a CEO controls all of the operations of a corporation, the OS controls all of a computer's operations, such as allocating memory, accessing disk drives and calling applications, to name just a few. The software applications that provide the bulk of an OS's services run on top of the OS. The most popular operating systems for a Web server are UNIX, Linux (a freeware version of UNIX), Windows NT and Windows 2000.

UNIX

UNIX is an interactive time-sharing OS that comes in many variations or "flavors". UNIX is not a single operating system, it is a family of operating systems with each vendor providing its own version of UNIX. The various versions of UNIX are similar, but there are enough differences that you might have problems if you decided to move (or "port") your application from one version of UNIX to another.

Some examples of the various manufacturers' UNIX versions are:

IBM's AIX 4.3 is an integrated UNIX operating environment that provides full interoperability and coexistence between 32- and 64-bit applications with processes that may run concurrently or cooperatively, sharing access to files, memory, and other system services. The inclusion of Java as part of the base operating system enables AIX to be Java-ready for both Java client and Java server applications.

Silicon Graphics (SGI) IRIX is a scalable UNIX operating system for high-performance graphics and scalable server systems.

Compaq Tru64 UNIX V5.0, is a 64-bit operating system offering a choice of management interfaces, including Web-based operations. This system reduces the complexity of installation, setup, and management compared to other UNIX systems. It supports multiple terabytes of data, increases performance in file system, storage management, and system networking and delivers very high integration between UNIX and Windows NT.

NetBSD is a free, highly portable UNIX-like operating system available for many platforms, from 64-bit AlphaServers to Macintoshes and handheld Windows CE devices. Its clean design and advanced features make it excellent in both production and research environments, and it is user-supported with complete source. Many applications are easily available.

Santa Cruz Operation (SCO) OpenServer systems are among the most popular of operating system platforms for small and medium sized businesses. The latest generation of SCO OpenServer systems allows you to quickly expand your computing environment as your business computing needs grow. SCO's integrated support for e-mail and Internet services ensures that your business can leverage the Web to give your company the exposure it deserves and communicate more efficiently with customers and prospects. Aside from critical business applications, SCO OpenServer Enterprise System provides various network services including file and print services for both UNIX and Windows systems, E-mail services, Web services, Internet connectivity, and calendar services. Built-in support for Windows File/Print services means that a single multi-functional server platform can be utilized to run your entire operation, while the field-proven reliability of SCO OpenServer keeps you in business.

Sun Microsystems (Sun) Solaris 7 is another UNIX operating system. There are various flavors of Solaris 7 including a SPARC version and an Intel version. Its 64-bit kernel supports as much as 64GB of RAM and increases maximum file sizes to 1 terabyte on SPARC servers. The Solaris 7 operating system's strength is its enterprise-class reliability and scalability and its mature networking kernel. Solaris 7 supports hot-swapping of processors and has a management console which provides a simple, customizable utility for maintaining and monitoring Solaris 7 servers along with wizards for installation of applications.

Linux

Linux (which is a variant of UNIX) is a free operating system and therefore can be copied and redistributed without paying a fee or royalty. It is a multi-user, multi-tasking operating system that runs on many platforms, including Intel processors. Linux interoperates well with other operating systems, including those from Apple, Microsoft and Novell. There are many Linux packages offering a full and rich set of utilities, connectivity tools and a development environment. There is even free software available that turns Linux into a very nice Web server. The main drawback is that there is no formal technical support for Linux.

Most programs written for either Linux or UNIX can be recompiled to run on the other system with little reconfiguration. Linux in most situations will run faster than UNIX on the same equipment. You can download a copy of Linux from the Internet or purchase an inexpensive CD set. You'll find Linux is a first rate operating system with capabilities beyond what you expect from more expensive products.

The author believes that a crucial issue to consider when making your operating system decision is that UNIX (and Linux) are inherently more secure than Windows NT and possibly Windows 2000 (its too soon to tell). Since UNIX was designed as a multi-user multi-process platform for interconnected computers, guaranteeing security has been an issue ever since the beginning. All UNIX vendors publish fixes for their software whenever a security problem is found. Microsoft is still secretive about security problems and many times don't tell you when a problem is found.

Windows NT

Microsoft's Windows NT 4.0 is one of the most well documented OS out there and with a lot of tweaking NT is a viable operating system for a Web site. Implement Microsoft's IIS Web server on top of your NT operating system and your Web site will have a robust foundation. Through third-party software it is possible to monitor NT's various functions — from NT's log files to disk usage. NT 4.0 has many shortcomings including reliability, which is why you don't find it as the OS of choice for a majority of the larger Web sites. That being said, Windows NT is a viable option for a small to mid-size Web site especially since it is easier for the novice to learn to use.

Windows 2000

Windows 2000 is essentially an upgrade of Windows NT. The Windows 2000 Server option includes a bundled Web server — Microsoft's Internet Information Server IIS 5.0 Web Server. It does offer a great array of innovative network tools and business features; however these features can cause it to be a challenging operating system to install and maintain, especially if you are unfamiliar with Windows NT.

Nonetheless, if you feel you are up to the technical challenges of Windows 2000 and/or Windows 2000 Server, it does offer features that make building and maintaining a Web site easier and more productive. For example, there are numerous ways to access the administrative functions: the "old" Control Panel; an Explorer-like Computer Management, and a wizard-like Configure Your Server which has ample help and support information. Another real nice feature is the Microsoft Management Console (MMC) which makes it easy to access options.

Windows 2000 Server OS includes Advanced Server and Datacenter, and is faster, more reliable, heavier-duty, and easier to use than Windows NT 4.0. As such, the complete set-up seems to provide added performance, stability, and reliability. Most of its more important server functions, such as, network, storage, and security have been centralized; however, TCP/IP and other Internet features are not as organized. The author notes that Windows 2000 is beginning to make inroads in the Internet environment.

WEB SERVER

The Web server is the software that serves your Web site's content to your customer's browser (Netscape, Internet Explorer, Opera, etc.). The Web server software's basic functionality is quite simple — it takes a file name passed through a command, gets the file and sends it across the Internet so it can be viewed on the requesting computer's browser software. The Web server software also tracks hits to the site, records and reports error messages, etc. Server-side technology is used to increase the functionality of a Web server beyond its ability to deliver standard HTML pages — for example, CGI scripts, SSL security, and Active Server Pages (ASPs).

Today's Web servers are used in such a variety of situations that it is necessary for the tools used to administer them to be quite sophisticated. More and more add-on options are available for Web-related software development tools.

All of the major Web servers such as AOLserver, Apache, Microsoft IIS, and Netscape Enterprise Server have comparable functionality. In spite of this, your choice of the Web server software may be based more on personal preference than actual hard core functionality considerations.

AOLserver is a solid freeware solution for any Web site but it isn't in the same league as Apache and Netscape Enterprise. The author notes that with the 2.1 release, it ended support for the Windows NT platform. This leaves it currently supporting the UNIX family — Digital UNIX, HP/UX, SGI IRIX, Sparc Solaris (v3.0) and Linux. What AOLserver does well is Secure Sockets Layer (SSL) support (40-bit encryption), multithreading and multihoming capabilities allowing the configuration of numerous virtual servers in a single process, and it has an integrated search engine. You also get hierarchical access control that allows you to restrict access to parts of your Web site. There's also built-in Tcl scripting language capabilities enabling you to quickly build custom Web applications. Other great features are internal image map support, SQL database services, and a complete C language API for writing your own custom functions, drivers, and applications along with HTML forms-based configuration, remote site and page administration, etc. Technical support for AOLserver is limited; although comprehensive documentation is available at the AOLserver support Web site, www.aolserver.com, and hard copies are available for purchase. Technical support contracts are available from Arsdigita www.arsdigita.com, though somewhat expensive, about $5,000 per year.

Apache is the most widely used Web server. It is released as "open source" with no fee for usage, plus there are a lot of modifications and modules made for it. The source code for most operating systems is available for download — Windows (all versions), Solaris, Linux, OS/2, freeBSD, etc. Apache 1.3.0 is probably the most stable and fastest of the Web servers available. However, Apache isn't for everyone — setup and maintenance of the server requires familiarity with command-line scripting tools. Also, Apache lacks browser-based maintenance capabilities or GUI configuration / administration tools. Some users will be unhappy with the lack of visuals, wizards, and browser-based administration tools.

Although there is no official support for Apache, a very useful Web site is www.apache.org. Bug reports and suggestions are sent via the bug report page on that Web site. Other questions can be directed to the comp.infosystems.www.servers.UNIX or comp.infosystems.www.servers.ms-windowsnewsgroup (as appropriate for the platform used), where some of the Apache gurus can usually be found lurking about. You can also find third-party companies that offer full commercial support for a fee.

Microsoft's Personal Web Server (PWS) is a freeware lightweight version of the Information Internet Server (IIS). Designed for Windows 95 and Windows NT Workstation users (it cannot be used with UNIX-based systems or MacOS), PWS is an entry-level Web server that provides a good option for small self-hosted Web sites. The biggest advantage to using PWS instead of a more robust Web server are the wizards that walk you through the set up of your home page and designate what files to share. Also, the PWS administrator simplifies the actual operation of the Web server. Microsoft provides free online support through its knowledge database at www.microsoft.com as well as a fee-based per incident service through its Microsoft Certified Support Center. You can also purchase "support incidents" and receive help through an 800 number.

Microsoft Internet Information Server (IIS) (See Windows 2000 section) receives high marks for superior installation, performance and maintenance. IIS scores high for its ease of installation and the quality of its management interface, which is provided separately from other interfaces. Another good feature is that IIS can be managed remotely via a Web browser. Technical support is the same as outlined for the PWS.

Netscape Enterprise Server (NES) is a "complete" Web server package for any Web site. It provides support for the HTTP 1.1 protocol plus security enhancements in PKCS #11, FIPS-140 compliance, 128-Bit Step-Up Certificates, and Fortezza support. (Fortezza, Italian for "fortress," is a family of security products — PCMCIA cards, serial port devices, server boards, etc. - that are trademarked by the U.S. National Security Agency and used extensively by the military). It also comes with a built-in search engine, log analysis tools, advanced content publishing, server clustering and administrative rights delegation. It supports Windows NT and the UNIX family — Digital UNIX, SGI IRIX, Sun Solaris, HP-UX and IBM AIX. NES is a good Web server for a traffic intensive Web site since it has features such as SSL 3.0 support with client-side certificate authentication, SNMP and SMTP support and centralized server management. Technical support is free only for the first 90 days, then it gets a little pricey; you can opt for "per incident" based support or an annual subscription based support that ranges from $400 to $600. However, Netscape does offer decent support on its Web site (http://help.netscape.com).

Xitami is a freeware, robust, entry-level server for Windows 95/NT/3.x, UNIX, OpenVMS, and OS/2 platforms. This Web server is perfect for someone operating on a tight budget, especially if the hardware used for the Web server is an older Pentium.

Installation is simple. There are no wizards but there is a browser-based interface and command-line support that is efficient and intuitive. Documentation is thorough and makes the process of getting up and running a system understandable for both novices and pros. The Web site www.imatix.com/html/xitami/ provides extensive online documentation, help via e-mail and a link to a discussion group. Third-party support is available for a fee.

Log Files

Okay, you've installed your Web server software and even remembered to put in and configure a firewall. It's now time for you to understand your Web server log files. Your Web server log files are important to the effective management of your Web site in three different ways. First, there's the overall "load" placed on the Web server. For example, at any time did the site's activity exceed the capacity of the hardware and/or software? If so, you have been provided with a "heads up" that you need to improve your site's ability to handle the traffic peaks. Perhaps you need to upgrade the server hardware or install a higher-capacity Web server software package.

Second, there's the measurement of the traffic or number of visitors that come to your Web site, what they look at and how long they stay. This gives you good insight into what is succeeding or not succeeding on your Web pages and in your marketing campaigns.

Third is security. Since vigilant monitoring of your log files will immediately alert you to any suspicious activity, the first line of defense against hackers is your log files. How? By monitoring your log files on a regular basis, you can spot any suspect goings-on. You should also install some trap macros (macros are small simple programs written to automate specific tasks) to watch for attacks on the server and create macros that run every hour or so that check the integrity of "passwd" and other critical files. Note that the macros should be programmed to send e-mail to the system manager if a change is detected.

As stated previously, a Web server creates records — called log files — of everything that happens on the server. Log files are actually huge files that contain a record of each and every activity that occurred on your Web server. When I say "everything" I mean "everything" — every request for an HTML page, every graphic file requested, every request to have an active page executed, and every CGI script that ran. The Web server considers each of these events a "hit." When the e-commerce industry first started ballyhooing the amount of traffic a certain site received, it was referring to the number of hits as tracked by the Web server log files. Therefore, the definition of a hit, as far as Web server log files are concerned is: Anything the Web server is asked to do when servicing the demands created by the traffic flowing through its content, i.e., your Web site. Please note that the number of "hits" is not an accurate indicator of the number of people that are actually visiting your site. For the all-important "people count" or "unique visitor" statistics you need some kind of Log Analysis Software to interpret Web site activity data, as discussed later in the chapter.

As long as your Web server has its logging feature activated, all of the activity on your Web site is stored in records. These records keep the details of which pages were requested, when they were requested and even information, such as, who initiated the request, the initiator's IP address and the type of browser used, along with how the initiator found your Web site. All of this information is stored in files named Access Log, Error Log (such as a page that no longer exists) and Referer Log. By providing an instant, ongoing, fairly exact and specific snapshot of the Web site's traffic patterns, these log files provide Web site owners with a plethora of raw data concerning their customers.

Using the Log files you have a record of all user activity. You will find this historical information useful, and you should maintain these logs either in an encrypted form on the Web server or store them on a separate machine offline.

Log files expand very fast. If you are using a Web hosting company to host your site, it will schedule these files to be rotated in such a way that older log files are regularly deleted. Believe me when I say you want to preserve these files. The easiest way is to institute a system and schedule wherein the log files are automatically e-mailed to you for organization and storage. This will guarantee that you will have immediate access to your data. However, this "raw" data is merely the tip of the iceberg and to be of any real use it needs to be analyzed — that's where log analysis software steps in.

LOG ANALYSIS SOFTWARE

Web server log files provide Web sites with a profusion of raw data concerning visitors to the site. Log files are a potential treasure trove of information. Historically they've mostly been used for a quick overview of bandwidth problems and basic tracking information. Although these logs contain an ongoing and accurate snapshot of your Web site's traffic patterns, they are somewhat difficult to read and understand. This is where log analysis software is of help. Such software can take this raw data and tell you if pages are frequently or rarely visited. It documents how the data is flowing back and forth between your Web server and your users, and gives information about IP traffic, e-commerce, cookies and browsers (vital if you're using Java or Active X). Log analysis software crunches the data to show how well your Web site is working, the origin and number of visitors, where they are going and how they found you in the first place. In addition a detailed click stream analysis tracks every single click a user makes on your Web site. Such data is essential for auditing a specific user's activity. The more expensive software can even offer historical and e-commerce reports reflecting time online and an authenticated user history.

The proper use of log analysis software data gives you valuable insight into how your Web site is being used. With some of the log analysis software available today, the easy-to-get-at statistics can be translated into slick graphs and bar charts for the non-technical crowd. However, unless taught otherwise, most Web site operators merely concentrate on figures such as the total of visitors to the site as a whole or to a particular page, and the number of click-throughs on banners.

But log analysis software is also very useful for finding problems with your site. For example you can track "error messages" that cause people to leave a site, if you see many of them in a day's report, you know you have a problem. You might see an error message and realize that the message only occurs with a certain browser version. Another example is security. See Chapter 7 on Security for some useful ways you can use this software to monitor your site and to help find culprits after a nefarious attack.

Large Web-based businesses have astute marketing and advertising departments that apply the logs for trend analysis and use extensive user demographics that can be obtained from the log, i.e., how are users using the site. If you add to that user-registration and a responsible use of cookies, then the collected data can be transformed into a powerful customer intelligence tool.

Traffic Reporting
The traffic report segment of your log analysis software provides data on how much user traffic your Web site attracts, who's visiting the site, where the visitors are coming from, and how your Web traffic changes on a hourly, daily, weekly, or monthly basis. A Web site traffic report is the simplest way to find out what works and what doesn't work. It can provide you with the information necessary to determine which Web pages are not selected or show one that is immensely popular. Such reports could be compiled from the Web server logs but it wouldn't be easy. In fact, without Web analysis software it would be almost impossible to decipher details such as:

- How many unique visitors visited your site, when, from which countries, from which referring sites (what search engine are users using to find your site)?

- Which pages were accessed?

- How long did the visitor stay?

- What key words were used to find your Web site?

Knowing and understanding which outside sources generate page views can give you the opportunity to execute increasingly effective marketing strategies.

Usually your homepage will be the number one visited page on your site. By analyzing the traffic you can ascertain how your site design is succeeding. If you have a *brochureware* site, you'll now be able to tell if your potential customers are going to the target pages. If you're running an *advertising* site, you'll see if the Web pages with a lot of banners gets the same traffic as a page with fewer banners. If you're running a *subscription* site, you'll understand what content is the most examined. If you're running an *online store*, you'll know what products are the most scrutinized by browsing customers. If the sales figures don't reflect the same pattern, you now have a starting point in trying to figure out why.

But, if you find that a certain page is one of your least popular pages via the traffic logs, analyze why. Traffic to an individual page may be influenced by your site design. Therefore, if it is the "About Us" page or "Investor Relations" page, don't sweat it. But if it's an important page that offers a new product or service, rethink the design. If traffic numbers to a specific area of your site disappoints you, study and look for the possible reasons, such as technical problems. Perhaps you should provide a link on the homepage or on a related content page. If you have an advertising site and you have a page that stands out as one your visitors often use to exit your site, figure out why and fix it. Maybe there's a banner on the page that that causes a slow load time or an ad that is particularly irritating. The logs may show that you have traffic on the page but visitors come, see and leave. They don't stay around and explore. Why?

After analyzing the traffic logs, doing your homework and making necessary adjustments in your Web site, wait a month or so and see if the changes helped. If not, try something else. It could be that your site is just fine but you need more P.R., advertising or some other type of promotion such as a give-away. Again, after each little tweak, wait a month and analyze the logs. You'll gradually find what works and what doesn't.

Browsers and Operating Systems: Another aspect of log analysis software is that it can give you statistics on your customers' browsers and operating systems, usually found in your Web server's referer log files. Take the lead from this data to ascertain if your customers are using browsers sufficiently advanced so that you can add more bells and whistles to your site. If the majority of your customers are using the latest technology, you know you will lose little in traffic if you implement a Java application or a Flash plug-in.

How are Your Customers Finding Your Site: This is important. You must know where your customers are coming from. Most should be referred to your Web site from search engines and directories. The second largest referral should come from linked sites. Look at this data very carefully, if your top referrers are not AOL or Yahoo!, find out why not. Is it something you can address? If so, do it. Read Chapter 15 on listing your site with search engines and directories for suggestions.

Some Log Analysis software even provide advanced reporting solutions such as monitoring Web, ad and streaming media servers, testing and checking broken links and gauging page download times along with the ability to monitor, alert and recover server and network devices. So-called "packet sniffing" technology has recently been introduced into the traffic analysis market which eliminates the need to collect and centralize log file data entirely. This technology gets its information directly from the TCP/IP packets that are sent to and from the Web server.

The products available to help you analyze your Web site's usage vary as widely as the information various businesses request. The "basics" might be able to provide you with the information you need without the sticker shock if you are willing to work with limited options and don't mind that the presentation of data is "plain vanilla." The pros will offer you a variety of in-depth features and can give you many customization options, including great reports with color graphs and bars.

The cost of the Log Analysis Software begins at "free" for AXS 2.0 (www.xav.com/scripts/axs/), which helps you to analyze the visits to a Web page. AXS 2.0 determines where visitors are coming from, charts their flow through your site, and informs you as to which links they follow when leaving. Also, you can analyze other information such as the referrer (AOL, MSN, Alta Vista, etc.), IP addresses, types of Web browser, and dates and times of each visit. AXS 2.0 then processes the records into meaningful graphs and database listings.

Another free tool is 3Dstats (www.cs.sunyit.edu/stats/3Dstats), which works with all Web servers that use the common log file format. It can create a 3D bar chart showing the daily number of total HTTP requests (hits), the number of files sent (documents actually transmitted on behalf of requests), the number of "304's" (Not Modified responses caused by various caching mechanisms), and the number of all other responses (redirections, not found responses, server errors).

Low-cost options to consider are Virtual Webtrends (www.webtrends.com), a traffic analysis tool specifically designed to work with virtual servers, and which only costs about $80; or WebManage Technologies' NetIntellect (www.webmanage.com), which is designed for the smaller Web sites, and costs around $200.

Then there are other software packages such as:

Aquas Bazaar Analyzer Pro 2.0 (www.bazaarsuite.com) costs between $300 to $1,000 but runs on any server that supports Java and provides real-time (as it is happening) traffic monitoring.

Sane Solutions's NetTracker (www.sane.com/products/NetTracker/) costs between $500 and $6,000 and runs on Windows 95/NT and most UNIX platforms.

Andromedia Aria 2.0 (www.andromedia.com) costs more than $9,800 but provides live HTTP tracking, uses the ObjectStore object-oriented database and runs on Solaris, SGI, HP, and Windows NT.

Accrue Insight (www.accrue.com) costs more than $15,000 but tracks IP traffic (not just server hits) and runs on Solaris and Irix but can be ported to HP and Windows NT.

WebTrends Professional Suite (www.webtrends.com) combines Web site traffic analysis, proxy server analysis, link analysis and quality control and monitoring, content management and visualization, alerting and recovery of Internet servers. The cost begins at around $800.

Another option is to use a service such as WatchWise (www.watchwise.com), a real-time monitoring and statistical reporting system. Each access to a registered Web site is automatically stored in real-time on the WatchWise server. It also monitors files that are downloaded from a registered Web site. Statistical reports are then generated in real-time, so you can determine who has downloaded your files. You can view these reports whenever you wish.

DATABASES

A database is software that gives you the ability to store data, retrieve it, or change it when necessary. With the appropriate database this is done easily and efficiently regardless of what the data consists of, and the amount of data you are manipulating.

A database is *integral* to the design, development, and services offered by most e-commerce sites. To allow your customers to search your site for a specific product, you need a database. A database is necessary to collect information about your customers. A mailing list is fed from a database. Another example is that of Web publishers who post up-to-the-minute information that is retrieved from a database. Get the picture?

Don't think you can build an efficient, productive Web site with its predestined multitude of Web pages, without a database. If you try, your site will quickly become unwieldy. Templates, file systems and cut-and-paste will take you only so far. The simplest tasks, such as updating your product catalog, adding editorial content, and even maintaining simple links will overwhelm you. But don't be careless in trying to implement a database — first, you must figure out a strategy for feeding information into your Web pages. Look at the informational content of your Web pages and decide how you can implement more efficient ways of managing the content. Figure out how your data is currently being stored and what tools are available that will move it to the Web.

How can you create Web pages for every single item in your inventory and keep each and every page current? The easiest way is to create your Web pages on-the-fly (or "on demand") with a program that "queries" a database for inventory items and produces an HTML page based on the results of that query.

That's just a tip of the iceberg. A database can do more than simply provide users with access to information; it can be used to manage the Web site, keep links intact, and enhance the security of the site. One big advantage is that it's actually much easier to maintain a database (once it's up and running) than it is to maintain a static Web site, with its many individual pages.

From the get-go, create a database for your site, you won't regret the decision. Keep in mind that it is important that the database interface be designed so that an employee can easily update the information with only cursory training.

Database Management Systems

Technically, a database management system (DBMS) is a software program designed to store and access information used to support the workings of a Web site. A database can gather, handle and process information in an organizational structure to facilitate storage and retrieval of information. Once information is entered into a database, a DBMS can manipulate the information so that you can easily analyze it. There are many different types of database structures, but the majority of them organize information in the form of "records" and "columns," or "entries" and "fields." On a basic level, a database is somewhat like a set of spreadsheets with rows and columns.

A database will give you the ability to separate your content (your catalog offerings) from your HTML Web page (the graphical design). It typically stores your catalog items in separate fields and tables as plain text with no formatting. An HTML template is then designed to provide a structure for the data as it is called from the database so it will be delivered to the Web site in a consistent layout every time. Databases allow your customers to quickly and accurately search for what they want since the search is limited to named fields rather than a more expansive, full-text search.

Most brick-and-mortar businesses use databases, so, your IT department should already have experienced database managers. Still, database integration will present special challenges as you design your site. Web sites demand that the information that's fed into its page forms must be extracted from the database (or moved from the user into the database) in ways that aren't necessarily a good fit for most brick-and-mortar relational databases. Also, the rate at which a Web site's database receives hits usually far exceeds the norm found in traditional business applications.

Types of Databases

Before we get into the nitty gritty of how a database models the data, we need to talk for just a minute about the major differences between databases, differentiating between analytical databases and operational databases — since you'll often hear these terms bandied about whenever the topic of databases are discussed.

Analytical Databases: An analytical database (which is also referred to as On Line Analytical Processing - OLAP) is a static, read-only database, which stores archived, historical data used for analysis. On the Web, you will often find OLAPs used for inventory catalogs that hold descriptive information about all available products in the inventory. Web pages are generated dynamically (with the help of an HTML template) by querying the list of available products in the inventory. The end product is a dynamically generated page displaying the requested information that had been pulled from the database.

Operational Databases: An operational database (which is an integral part of what's called On Line Transaction Processing - OLTP) is used to manage more dynamic data. An OLTP database allows you to do more than simply view archived data — you can also modify that data (add, change or delete data).

Typically you will find OLTPs used when it is essential to track real-time information, such as the current quantity and availability of an item. As a customer places an order for a product from an online Web store, an OLTP is used to keep track of how many items have been sold and when you need to reorder the items.

Database Models

A good way to conceptualize a database model is both as the "container" for the data as well as the "methodology" for storing and retrieving the data from the container.

There are basically three database models used today: Text file, relational and object. From the standpoint of simple information retrieval, virtually any kind of information can be plugged into a database (text, images, sound files, movies), but not all databases fit every business situation.

Text File Database: Although it's debatable whether a text file database is a true database, it is clear that it's definitely not "relational." The best attribute of a text file database is its simplicity. Because of its simplicity and ease of use for the novice, you might be tempted to use this type of database for your Web site, but don't do it. Text file databases are not scalable and there is generally no concurrent access ability, i.e., two people can't use the database at the same time. For those with pre-existing text file databases, the most economical approach is to bite the bullet now and move the data to a relational or object-oriented database.

Relational Database: A relational database is a collection of "data items" that are organized as a set of linked tables from which data can be accessed or reassembled in many different ways without need to reorganize the database tables (a table is referred to as a "relation"). This type of database looks like a set of interlocking spreadsheets, with each table in the database being one spreadsheet. Relational databases allow simultaneous updates by numerous individuals. However, there are crucial differences — for example, all the data in a database column must be of the same type and the database rows are not ordered. Some of the best-known relational database packages include Microsoft's Access and Microsoft SQL Server (www.microsoft.com), Oracle (www.oracle.com), Sybase (www.sybase.com), Informix, (www.informix.com) DB2 (www-4.ibm.com/software/data/db2/), and Computer Associates' CA-OpenIngres (www.ca.com).

When designing a relational database, great care is given to "normalize" the structure of the data. The normalization process is performed by applying a series of rules to eliminate redundancy and inconsistency. The columns in all of the tables must depend upon a single key column with values that don't repeat.

A Relational Database Management System (RDBMS) is a program that enables you to create, update, and administer a relational database. Generally you are referring to a RDBMS when you are talking about relational databases. An RDBMS typically takes statements written in the extremely popular Structured Query Language (SQL) (entered by a user or put forth by an application program) and creates, updates, or provides access to the relational database. SQL is a "declarative" query language, which means that the user specifies what he or she wants and then the RDBMS query planner figures out how to get it. The RDBMS is allowed to store the data in whatever manner it "wishes."

You need an RDBMS if you have data that changes frequently. Relational databases have *concurrency control* to ensure that the tables won't get corrupted even if many people are simultaneously writing to and reading from the database.

The term "client/server" was first devised to describe how users work with relational databases.

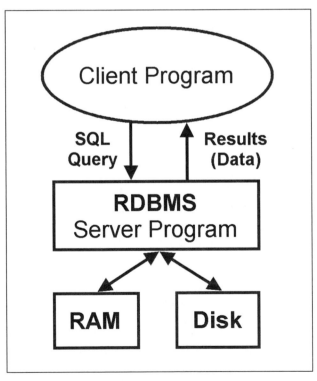

A typical client/server scenario.

In the days before client/server software, while the database may have resided on the central server, the software that read or wrote to each database record ran on the desktop client software, not the server. So when you made a query, each record of the database had to travel over the LAN or WAN to the user's desktop PC. If the record matched the criteria of the search, it was displayed with other matching records and another record was retrieved. Sending so many records across a LAN or WAN was a slow process and caused network congestion.

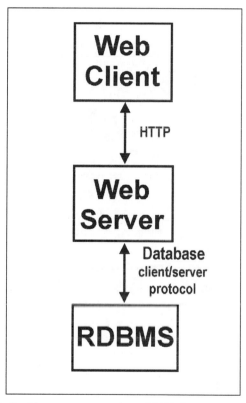

A typical client/server scenario for a RDBMS-backed Web site.

If you choose to backup your Web site with an RDBMS, make sure your Web server software can connect easily and deal efficiently with an RDBMS. The Web server software mentioned in this chapter are all multithreaded, Tcl-enabled dynamic Web servers designed to handle large scale, dynamic Web sites, i.e., they can deal efficiently with any RDBMS.

Object-Oriented Database: Generally, when talking about Object-oriented Databases, most people are in reality talking about an object-oriented database management system

(OODBMS), which is a data-management product that is specifically designed for use with an object programming language and/or is closely coupled with one or more object programming languages (C++ or Smalltalk). An object database, therefore, provides database management system functionality to object oriented programming languages and to the objects that have been created using those programming languages. In theory this approach unifies both application and database development into one seamless data model and language environment. Object-oriented databases have long tantalized the business world with the promise of less application code, more natural data modeling and easier-to-maintain code, but they have taken a considerable amount of time to catch on in terms of customer acceptance. While OODBMSs have slowly begun to move into mainstream Web site development, they still lack scalability and there is limited availability of options to access legacy relational databases. Object-oriented databases may improve both programming time and response time but you must be willing to go for a whole package — to write in an object-oriented language, to switch to a new database, and to accept the inherent risk of doing things in a new way.

Object-oriented databases include: GemStone (www.gemstone.com), Itasca (www.ibex.ch), Jasmine (www.cai.com/products/jasmine.htm), MATISSE (www.adb.com), NeoAccess (www.neologic.com), O2 from Ardent Software (www.ardentsoftware.fr), ObjectStore (www.exceloncorp.com), POET (www.poet.com), to name just a few.

Differences between Relational and Object-Oriented Databases:

Relational databases had a monopoly on the business world until the coming of the object-oriented databases. The primary differentiation between relational and object databases is that relational databases are built on a row/column paradigm - like a spreadsheet, while object databases treat every item on the Web site, from the graphics to the audio files to the URLs, as separate objects. While rows of text might map well into a relational database structure, images and sounds do not.

Relational databases are terrific for storing data that can easily be converted into a two-dimensional representation. Not all objects found on the Web are amenable to such structuring. Indeed, "flattening out" complex data structures to fit into tables sometimes resembles fitting square pegs into round holes. To use a relational database backend for storing images and sounds, you need special coding that allows the object to be mapped into the entries of the relational database. This extra coding has the potential of producing problems, plus it is a drain on your site's processing power (speed).

Also, an RDBMS uses the intersection of rows and columns for every instance of an entity in the database, regardless of whether a particular cell is needed in a particular instance, while an OODBMS only stores the particular parts of the data actually used in any specific instance.

Unlike a relational DBMS, object DBMSs have no performance overhead to store or retrieve a Web of interrelated objects, such as a set of interlocking tables. A natural one-to-one mapping of object programming language objects to database objects allows for higher performance management of objects as well as better management of the complex interrelationships between objects. This makes OODBMSs better suited than RDBMSs to support Web site document structures, which have complex relationships between data. When everything is working correctly, object databases can operate on complex data, such as images, multimedia, and audio, as efficiently as a relational database operates on simple text or data.

Final notes: If you are offering images or sounds as a main feature of your Web site, you might seriously consider using an object-oriented database. Relational databases generally store all of the data on a single server, while object databases can call upon multiple servers. It is possible to build a Web site that uses both relational and object databases in a hybrid system. The relational database can store data such as text and software downloads and the object database can be used for sound, video or images offered up by the Web site.

Desktop Database Software

While not a viable solution for most Web businesses, if you are willing to tolerate limited capabilities and performance and are operating on a shoestring budget, you can build a small Web site using a desktop database software offering. There are three desktop relational database solutions that have some built-in Web capabilities, although none come near the quality and performance of a high-end solution. These three products will, with varying degrees of success, let you get your data up on the Web quickly and inexpensively - allow for some tweaking here and there.

- Microsoft's Access (www.microsoft.com) allows you to create a database with its wizards. It is adequate when it's enveloped by and communicates only with other Microsoft products; but it isn't happy when forced to interact with other manufacturers' software.

- Corel's Paradox (www.corel.com/products/paradox) works smoothly with Corel Web Server and allows you to create a database with its "experts" (which are similar to Microsoft's wizards). But it too requires much effort to interact with other manufacturers' software.

- FileMaker Pro (www.filemakerworld.com) is the best of these three products. It is easy to use and has good documentation and templates that will allow you to build basic databases. It is one of the simplest and least expensive relational databases you can buy.

Overview of Robust Database Management Systems

There are many database management systems available for the Web site operator, each with its own strengths, capabilities and challenges. Here are just a few:

- Jasmine (www.cai.com) was the first "pure" production-oriented object database management system (ODBMS). It has a completely integrated development system, called Jasmine Studio. Indeed, the Jasmine package is a jack-of-all-trades: It has an object database engine, it can act as an Internet development platform as well as a client/server development environment or just as a multimedia content authoring tool. Jasmine offers good application development tool integration and allows multiple programming languages to use the same data simultaneously. In some ways this puts Jasmine a step up on its competitors that are programming language-dependent. Jasmine allows you to deploy and control the latest Internet applications where complex data content and interaction is commonplace.

  Jasmine also connects to and works with many other brands of databases: CA-Datacom, CA-IDMS, DB2, Informix, Microsoft SQL, OpenIngres, RMS, Sybase, and VSAM.

- MS-SQL 7.0 (www.microsoft.com) is a DBMS that is fast, scalable and free. It offers ease of administration along with numerous automated features (available only for the Windows NT platform), but there is a trade-off — much of the SQL Server is not user definable with most everything decided automatically by the system. In cases where the system makes the right choice, this feature works transparently and saves time, however, in cases where the system makes the wrong decision or choice, it can be a nightmare. Following along the automatic configuration idea, Microsoft has tried to create a self-teaching database that examines and adjusts itself to satisfy whatever requirements are being placed on it at a given time.

- ObjectStore Enterprise Edition (www.exceloncorp.com), is a reliable ODBMS for high-performance applications built for delivery of high-speed, complex Web transactions and dynamic content needed by today's Web-based businesses. ObjectStore can shorten development time by dramatically reducing the amount of complex code required.

- The Oracle8i DBMS (www.oracle.com) provides a wealth of application possibilities along with increased manageability and improved security. With the JServer option Oracle can provide a run-time environment for Java objects and with the WebDB option you can manage the content-creation process while also distributing creation tasks to reduce resource bottlenecks. Oracle addresses the security issue through its "virtual private database" support that allows the attachment of security policies directly to tables and views, thus the same security policy is in place regardless of which application is accessing the data.

Static vs. Dynamic Web Pages

I realize that you might be feeling a little overwhelmed by now. Still, setting up your Web site with a database is a big step towards building a flexible, scalable site.

Stay with me as I try to simplify things a bit. Both static Web pages and dynamic Web pages have the same goals in mind — the use of information stored in databases.

The static Web site has already prepared the information in the desired format for use by the customer while a dynamic Web site takes a "two-step" approach. Step One is to use certain parameters or keys to search a database in real-time. Then when the desired data is found (Step Two) a Web page is created for the customer's use.

If you want to take a cautious first step, use your database to create a simple "static" database site. A visitor won't be able to search through the database on demand, nor perform many of the fancier dynamic-site tricks. Rather, such a minimal database will ease the burden of data management. And it lets you move to a full-blown dynamic database-driven site later on.

A static Web site displays infrequently changing information or data. It's like putting a snapshot of your business' information onto your Web site. The contents of a static site can be marketing brochures, white papers, monthly newsletters, software, or even a small product catalog, etc. This information is not interactive, nor does it change very often. There are numerous products available for the database publishing of static Web pages. Check out Librios at www.librios.com, Showbase Extra at www.showbase.com and Whizbase at www.whizbase.com, to just name just a few.

A dynamic Web site instantly reflects changes in the underlying database and reduces or eliminates the need for page maintenance. However, it does require Java scripts, CGI programming and all that that implies. To achieve this outcome you must install software such as Coldfusion (www.allaire.com), Lasso (www.blueworld.com) or Netobject Fusion (www.esitestore.com) to pull information out of the database to create HTML pages on demand. This, in turn, means that you must not only run your Web Server and Database Server but also an Applications Server. Coldfusion, Lasso and Netobject Fusion are application server software that transforms the database data into dynamic Web pages.

A dynamic Web site can be an online store with an ever-changing product catalog so that when a customer requests information, a database can provide not only the product but also the current price, colors, sizes and the availability. Car dealerships, real estate, and ezine (online magazines) sites use dynamic data. There is one downside of utilizing dynamic page generation. Unless you carefully design and institute a good maintenance system, a large volume of traffic on your Web site can cause data traffic congestion and performance problems.

Database Publishing

A *data-driven Web site* (a dynamic Web site) collects data on the fly and then builds pages from that data. This is referred to as database publishing.

Database publishing offers the ability to distribute data updates on the fly. With the right interface, even a novice user can go into the database to update information that can be made available immediately. Maintenance is easy in the database-publishing world — for example, one can create an HTML template once and merge that template with new content to provide a reliable way to put information on your Web site in a consistent layout. Security is also easier since databases allow you to keep the wrong content off a Web site through the enforcement of security checks, such as "hide" flags, checking the date against the date a document is set to be posted, the date a product is set for delivery, etc.

Though database publishing can help you manage your Web site, it may take some time for you to learn all the ins and outs of the related software tools. Database publishing for your Web site requires Web server software, a database and the software (application server) that can bridge the two. All three of these must support the same standards, such as, CGI, ODBC or ASP scripts. If you do use one of the many tools available for dynamically generating content on your Web site, be sure to test. Check for things like slow pages, heavy pages, small pages, missing graphics, etc.

Interfaces

The Common Gateway Interface (CGI) is a standard interface between Web servers and other applications. It lets you create Web pages that can return information based upon a customer's input by calling a compiled C program or Perl script to access a database or another data source. CGI is inefficient, since it causes the server to launch a new process to run executable programs every time a new user makes a request. If you have a lot of traffic, your Web site's performance will suffer. However, CGI is a tried and true interface and is still the most common way to connect with Web servers.

On the database end, Open Database Connectivity (ODBC), which is a Microsoft standard database access method, is the common interface. For an ODBC interface to work, both the application and the RDBMS must be ODBC-compliant. ODBC, in simple terms, inserts a middle layer (a database driver) between an application and the RDBMS to translate the application's data queries into commands that the RDBMS understands.

Although, Java and Java Database Connectivity (JDBC) from Sun Microsystems will, in the future, be a viable way to publish a database on the Web, it's not there now.

JDBC is a Java Application Program Interface (API) that enables Java programs to execute SQL statements, which, in turn, lets Java programs interact with SQL-compliant databases (nearly all RDBMSs support SQL). Java runs on most platforms, therefore JDBC makes it possible for a Web operator to write a single database application that can run on different platforms and interact with different RDBMSs. At this time, the tools and drivers needed for Java database development are in their infancy. However, you do need to know now that JDBC is a lot like ODBC but is new enough that some databases don't offer a direct interface. If you plan to use Java now, one solution is to use a JDBC-ODBC bridge that allows a Java application using JDBC to connect to an ODBC database.

The Search Engine Dilemma

A search engine has three parts. The first is a spider (also called a "bot") that goes to every page on every Web site that wants to be searchable and reads it. Every search engine has its own criteria that its spiders use when crawling a Web site. The second component is a program that creates a huge database of the key words in the pages that have been read by the spider. Finally, there's an access program sitting on a portal that can take millions of search requests from users, compare them to the entries in the database, and return results.

Although dynamically generated Web pages are easier for the Web operator to manage, they are difficult for some search engines to index and incorporate into their database. The simplest answer to this problem is to use static pages as often as possible. Use the database to update the pages instead of generating them on the fly. Another little bit of advice: Search engines hate the "?" symbol, so don't use it in your URL.

CHAPTER 9
E-Commerce Software

Conspicious consumption of valuable goods is a means of reputability
to the gentleman of leisure.

Thorstein Veblen, *The Theory of the Leisure Class*

E-commerce software allows you to accept credit card payment for your product or service and provides your customer with the convenience of on-line shopping.

From just a few products to a catalog of thousands, whether you are a novice or an expert, starting a new Web-based business, or giving your brick-and-mortar business a Web presence, there is an e-commerce solution that is right for you. When making the decision for the right e-commerce solution for your Web-based business, take into account your "expertise" with computers and the marketing of products. Use your blueprint and consider what you can afford. Some e-commerce products are designed to grow with your business and other products work well only in a low traffic environment. Do you want to run your Web site from an e-commerce package, an "out of the box" solution, or do you need the flexibility that is more like a software toolkit that requires additional programming to provide a more complete solution. Here again, use your blueprint to lay out in a concise manner your site's exact needs and specifications. Then, with your blueprint in hand, start your investigation into the e-commerce software and services available to you.

E-COMMERCE ALTERNATIVES

Almost all e-commerce software packages provide a product catalog, a shopping cart, transaction security and bare-bones order processing. Note that it is of the utmost importance that you install your online e-commerce software on a Secure Sockets Layer (SSL) secure server to facilitate safe (and private) online transactions.

The author has made an attempt at categorize the various e-commerce solutions, however, please note that they often spill over into other categories. As you examine the various e-commerce solutions, consider:

- The ease of set up.

- Will the software integrate easily with your existing software?

- Is scalability limited to what is offered by the hosting service or can you integrate new software products?

- How are the orders processed?

- Is the software difficult to administer?

- Can it import product data from a database?

- How thorough and responsive is the documentation and support?

- Will your Web site operator have limited technical knowledge? If so, the software should make extensive use of wizards and templates.

- Or, if you have or you are an experienced Web site operator, the software can be more flexible and responsive to your needs such as software that can create CGI scripting and HTML pages.

The All-in-One Solution

Today you can find numerous all-in-one e-commerce solution providers. This type of Web-based service provides server space and the capability of setting up and running an online store through the simple process of inserting the proper information into Web-based forms and using a point-and-click interface. One reason you might consider one of these services is that they allow small businesses to take advantage of industry-leading e-commerce power without the necessity of purchasing or maintaining sophisticated e-commerce software. However, what makes this option easy for the novice to use also means that your design options are limited — all the stores have a same "look". If you envision your Web business "standing out of the crowd," this is not the solution for you.

The best known of these offerings is perhaps Yahoo! Store, followed by (in no specific order) freemerchant.com, bigstep.com and LycoShop. There are numerous other offerings that you can find on line by using a search engine and simply typing in "all-in-one" or "e-commerce software".

Generally only the smaller Web-based businesses use the all-in-one solution since these packages, out of necessity, limit the breadth and scope of a business's growth. But, that is not to say that a larger business can't use one of these services. For example, to have a good, viable store that could meet the expectations of its 1999 Christmas shoppers, FAO Schwarz (a very large toy store) placed its catalog in Yahoo! Stores. Be aware though, that many all-in-ones have very restricted space for catalog inventory.

While Yahoo!'s fees range from $100 to about $300 per month (based upon the number of items you are offering), freemerchant.com is an all-in-one that will provide basic store building tools free. However, there is a catch — you must allow freemerchant.com to place advertising on your site. Both sites offer nice, robust store building tools that are easy to use, even for the novice. Check them out, one may fit your needs.

Another very nice all-in-one solution is Bigstep.com. Not only does it offer a top-drawer e-commerce and catalog service, but it also provides numerous ways to expand your Web presence. Surveys, FAQs, Press Releases, Maps, Marketing benefits such as registering your site with search engines and sending e-mails to your customers (upon receiving the list from you), internal corporate pages — job listings, employee-centric offerings, etc. are just some of the benefits. Bigstep.com also has great software for product shipping plus some of the best customer service features of the all-in-one products. Most of Bigstep.com's services are free. To set up a merchant's account and offer real-time credit card processing, there is a fee. Check this service out, it might fit your needs.

If you decide to go with LycosShop your Web-based business will be integrated into all areas of the Lycos Network, including Wired.com, Tripod.com, Angelfire.com, HotBot.com, and Lycos.com. LycosShop offers features such as a universal shopping cart with a single check-out no matter how many stores are visited, one-click buying, an easy-to-browse product catalog, and product recommendation and comparison engines. The cost for this service starts at approximately $150 per month.

Another good e-commerce option — Nebulis International (www.nebulis.net) has a number of e-commerce options that allow businesses to establish an Web-based business, without the hassle and expense of traditional e-commerce solutions. Whether you choose their easy-to-set-up small business package or their affiliate ready enterprise system capable of storing thousands of products, Nebulis is worth considering.

Nebulis' e-commerce options range from do-it-yourself software packages such as EC-Builder from MultiActive Software to their Enterprise E-commerce Setup that offers full featured e-commerce options while allowing you to incorporate your own design into your Web site.

Here are just some of Nebulis' e-commerce features: HTML Shopping Cart with running totals, E-Store design affiliate program with comprehensive commission tracking, assignable order approval, instant credit card payment processing, Web-based admin control panel, customized e-mails to customers and affiliates, secure server ordering (SSL), sales tax, and shipping calculations.

There are many e-commerce solutions on the market. You can use one of the many standalone applications on your server (in-house or hosted), or use your server and link to an on line service such as Yahoo!, or take the whole package, which almost all the services mentioned in this chapter offer. Whatever solution you are considering be sure to get the answers to the following questions before making your final decision.

- What about my domain name? Can I use it?

- What type of credit card processing is offered and is there an additional charge for this service?

- Am I required to host ads and/or other types of branding?

- What is free and what do I have to pay for?

- How will they help you drive traffic to your site?

- Does the service offer special promotional features?

- You must read the fine print and get down to the specifics or you might find yourself with an unpleasant surprise at the end of the month.

Remember that each e-commerce solution offers something unique — you decide which solution fits you and your Web-based business. Do your research then perform the necessary due diligence to ensure that whatever company you choose is stable and has the financial wherewithal to provide you with the services it promises a year from now.

"Out-of-the-Box" E-Commerce Packages

E-commerce packages of this type enable you to get your Web site up and running quickly. "Ease of use" is a subjective term — what would be considered an easy-to-use product by one person could be viewed as difficult by another. But if you know HTML and have

CGI experience you may want to use a package that gives you some flexibility, such as designing your own HTML pages.

E-commerce packages should allow freedom of choice to incorporate software from a variety of offerings and should provide, at a minimum:

- good documentation and support
- the ability to import data from a database file
- order processing features such as the availability of a virtual shopping cart
- the ability to transfer data securely using SSL and not leave it in an unsecured area of a server where unauthorized parties might find it
- the ability to send customers' details to you using encrypted e-mail
- simplified day-to-day operation of your Web site such as allowing changes to be made offline and then uploaded to the server, which means that you can only use one specific computer for the updates
- the ability to add, delete and amend product data as well as run special promotions
- good, detailed reports of the analysis of server logs, such as the number of hits and referrer information which in turn can give, for example, a sales history analysis and information about the most common entry and exit points your customers are using in your Web site

The majority of the e-commerce packages will have in addition to the features set forth above:

- the ability to accept orders and payments in as many ways as possible — credit cards, debit cards, paper checks, electronic checks, digital cash, fax, telephone, or snail mail
- maintain pre-set tax tables so that the correct tax is collected on each order
- the ability to interface directly with carriers such as UPS and Fedex, along with automatically calculating shipping costs
- the ability to automatically send an e-mail order acknowledgement to the customer along with a unique number for order tracking
- the ability for your Web site to be updated online from any Internet-connected PC

There are also e-commerce solutions that offer services such as:

- domain name registration

- automatic search engine submissions

  And more advanced features such as:

- autoresponders (mail utilities that automatically send a reply to an e-mail message)

- chat rooms

- the ability to easily handle online processing (although you might process your orders offline, it is good to have this flexibility for future growth)

- discount clubs that let you give discounts to repeat or high-volume customers

- online order tracking that lets your customers check the status of their orders

- inventory management facilities, which can automatically remove a product when supply dips below a certain level

- additional marketing tools such as the maintenance of customer-buying history and preferences, targeted e-mailing capability, and affiliate program management

Many e-commerce solutions lack support for the fundamentals, such as back orders and most lack the modularity needed to mix and match applications from competing platforms. A sampling of the many products available can be found at: www.onlinemerchant.com, www.merchandizer.com, www.starvisor.com, www.holt.ie, and www.cobuildit.com (this one is a little different, but I like the concept).

Online Catalog

Although there are online catalogs on the Web (basically classified ads), they are not a true e-commerce solution. But an online catalog is a very good tool when it is used with a modest e-commerce site. A business with a brochureware site ready to move from 800-number ordering to e-mail orders, might use an online catalog option. An existing brick-and-mortar looking for an online presence with too many items for a Web store option but not yet ready for a full commerce-server solution might be happy with an online catalog option.

Online catalog software should be able to organize the products into groups as well as to offer a search utility that can aid in finding the right product. As a customer browses, the software should be ready and waiting for the customer to click on a button to place a selection into the shopping cart that in turn stores the selection in a database. The customer should be able to review his or her selections before finally "checking out." Lastly, the software should be able to interface with your accounting software to track total sales and inventory. One of the advantages of the online catalog is that it is scalable. But it does not always offer true e-commerce capabilities.

Look for:

- meta tags

- shipping options

- order forms

- e-mail order fulfillment

- secure ordering

- built-in FTP

Some sites you might want to visit in your quest for the right online catalog solution for your Web site are: www.gttpp.com/gttpp/catalogs, www.budgethosting.net/alacart, www.friendlywebpages.com/catalogintro, and www.cyberstore-builder.com/forms/evaluationform.

Link-based Web-Stores

If you want e-commerce capabilities, the easiest way to achieve this is to link your existing Web site with a Web store and use their e-commerce options. Some of the new Web store offerings host the back-end e-commerce services on their servers but either require or give the option of allowing retail merchants to place their Web sites on a local ISP. Using such a Web-store package requires no additional software on your server; just a bit of coding that can make the Web pages commerce-enabled. There's an additional advantage in that the Web-store provider can offer plenty of services in a secure environment.

The main issue to consider when choosing a Web store site is what type of payment processing is offered, and what are its limitations. You could find an e-commerce solution near you by going to your favorite search engine and typing the phrase "e-commerce packages" or you might want to check out these sites: www.web-impressions.com/ecommerce, www.shastamarketing.com/business/ecommerce, www.storemaster.com/ecomm, www.aksi.net, www.santel.net/pkgecommerce, www.norlink.net/business/ecompackage, www.mm2k.net/ecommerce/packages, and www.wdgonline.com/e-com/ecommerce_solutions.

Online Malls

Online malls are similar to traditional shopping malls, offering entrances and integrated shopping experiences across a variety of product lines and vendors with everything under the same URL. Most of the businesses also run on the same server(s), taking advantage of a unified shopping infrastructure including credit card checking, digital cash acceptance, personalization tools, etc. The main advantage of placing a Web-based business on an online mall is that your Web site resides on a server that has been specifically created for online selling. The mall operator may also offer other services such as promotions, marketing advice, and design assistance. However, you do give up some control of how your site looks and even how you operate your site. Be sure to verify that you can use your own domain name rather than www.megamall/yourname.com.

This is a great option for small or home-based businesses with a unique product or idea, limited production, and not much experience with computers who want to take their product to the Web as inexpensively and with as little hassle as possible. There is no question that aligning your new Web-based business with the mall areas of specialized online services like America Online and CompuServe will give you a leg up in the initial start-up phase. However, please note that the mall operator charges businesses a rental fee for space, takes a percentage of every transaction or requires each business to allow ads and/or other promotional devices to be placed within each individual Web site. As with all partnerships, verify that the mall operator has a successful operating history and is financially secure.

There are many online malls ready and willing to accept your site. The author has set out only a few online malls to get your started: www.cybershoppes.com, www.bargainstrike, www.women.com, www.oxygen.com, www.doughnet.com, and www.shopnow.com.

Commerce Servers

Here is the best solution for any large enterprise taking their business to the Web. Commerce servers are Web servers enhanced with support for certain commerce activities. Commerce server platforms are anything but plug-and-play and the implementation of an e-commerce Web site can give rise to many performance, scalability and integration problems that only patience and time can solve. Choose carefully, e-commerce software must integrate seamlessly into your legacy software. Commerce server platforms offer a diversity of services including:

- transaction, payment and personalization engines

- tax and currency calculation capabilities

- workflow automation

- content management software

- database and ERP (enterprise resource planning) integration modules

- proprietary and open application servers

- customer-service offerings with "800" number phone support integration

- smart catalogs

Although commerce server software has come a long way in the last couple of years, many still lack support for necessities such as back orders or contracts that require purchases at a specific interval. Proprietary architectures often make it difficult to customize some commerce offerings and back-end integration issues may require writing your own custom code for each legacy system that needs integration.

Most of the software offered now doesn't have the modularity necessary to meet the performance, scalability and integration needs of today's Web-based businesses. However, that being said, unless you have the resources to write your own software, you will be forced to buy into a commerce server solution, whether or not the technology is "up to snuff."

That is the bad news, now for some good news — there are BroadVision's commerce server called One-to-One Business Commerce (www.broadvision.com), Art Technology Group's (ATG) all-Java server called Dynamo (www.atg.com) and IBM Corp.'s Websphere Commerce Suite (www.ibm.com) based on an open Java application technology, which the large enterprise will find very useful. For the small to mid-size enterprise, Microsoft's commerce server is a viable option.

When looking for commerce server software, look at the companies offering:

- a modular system (to enable you to choose the best fitting elements for your enterprise)

- rules-based workflow automation, especially for content management

- support for monthly supply replenishment or back-order provisioning

- EJB/XML support

- scalability when the shift from back-end systems to multi-company workflow integration (i.e., product descriptions that will be provided directly by the supplier) becomes the norm

There is, in all probability, a commerce server platform out there suitable for any particular Web-based business. You must consider your budget, existing architecture, and software development capabilities when making the decision to purchase a commerce server platform.

CHAPTER 10
Quality Assurance

The first rule of intelligent tinkering is to save all the parts.

Paul Ehrlich

A good Quality Assurance Plan (QA Plan) will formally determine how and in what order each aspect of your Web site should be tested. A QA Plan's first priority is to avoid a situation that will force you to hurriedly accelerate or change the plan because of some sudden major problem. For many Web sites, by the time a problem becomes too obvious to ignore, considerable financial damage may have already occurred. If you do not test often and thoroughly defects will accumulate or be missed. A good QA Plan will orient the project toward detecting defects early, close to the point of insertion, and not allow defects to infect work later on.

This can't be said enough — quality assurance testing is essential to developing a successful Web site. The ever-growing list of operating systems, software choices, browsers and user preferences combined with the multitude of static Web pages and dynamic database-driven Web sites results in everything from customers having a problem-free experience while visiting your Web site to customers being driven crazy because their browser crashed. Most of the problems could easily be solved with a slight change in the HTML or other coding on the site.

THE QA PLAN

To assure that visitors to your Web site have a pleasant and problem-free experience you need to develop and implement testing protocols to improve production specifications, visual and HTML style guidelines, and process flow — your Quality Assurance Plan.

A properly implemented QA Plan can:

- solve browser incompatibility problems

- help you to stay current with HTML standards

- help you with the use of browser-specific HTML

- aid in the review of your site for bugs

- set up usability testing to insure that Web site user interfaces meet user needs

Test every aspect, from Lynx to Netscape to WebTV and other Web appliances, for validation that your Web site provides a problem-free experience for your customers, no matter how they surf the Web.

After following the design guidelines set out in Chapter 2, and before your new Web site is ready for launch, you must "freeze" your prototype and intensively test it prior to giving the public access. Lay out the tests in a structured manner per your QA Plan and be prepared for tinkering and testing to go on for probably a month. Remember to stop all development and changes of the site during this testing period.

Consider investing in specific software tools that can test content accessibility, basic functionality, and behavior under controlled access loads. As your last test, perform stress testing to see how the entire system reacts under really heavy or "bursty" traffic.

You will find numerous Web site testing tools that can help illuminate what happens as traffic and load increases. However, some of the software that can help you implement your QA Plan can be hard to use and/or require a bit of effort. But persevere, setup your test plans and check out software testing tools such as:

Watchfire's Website Quality of Experience Management Solutions (www.tetranetsoftware.com/products), which can help put you in control of your Web site by supplying intelligence on simulated visitor interaction with site content and Web site transactions. Reporting, analysis and measurement solutions provide you with a real-time view of your Web site.

Webtrend's Enterprise Suite (www.webtrends.com) can assist you in improving the quality, performance, and integrity of your Web site. It can illustrate broken links, chart biggest and slowest pages, document the loading time of connections, check the syntax of various HTML components, find the availability of external servers linked to your Web server, and more, such as crawling your Web site as a user would.

Segue's SilkPerformer Suite (www.segue.com) lets you rigorously test the performance of your Web site test using as many simulated concurrent users as your site and network will support. Its ability to stress test Web applications under heavy loads and simulate bursts of activity make it ideal for use by virtually any Web-based business. In addition, its reporting features enable you to chart and correlate response time results with server statistics to quickly identify bottlenecks and problems.

Or perhaps you might want to look into OTIVO (www.otivo.com) a full-service QA consulting firm whose services include browser compatibility testing, functional testing, and usability testing.

Testing the Prototype

The majority of your QA Plan should cover testing your Web site not only during development but also during your prototype stage before "going live." The optimal situation would be for your Web site to be developed on a development server and launched to a staging server for QA. The author realizes that smaller Web-based businesses will not have the resources for these additional servers. Nonetheless, your QA Plan should set out a full testing plan to ensure you tested as much of the expected customer interaction and site functionality as possible.

Since your Web site's design should already meet the "browser neutral" criteria specified in Chapter 2, you should test your design to see how it looks when viewed with:

- different screen sizes
- different browser window settings
- different color resolutions
- high security settings
- minimal feature settings
- different browsers and version
- different client platforms

When testing go to the browser's options settings and change them so that the page has a white background and the links are presented in the default color, and turn on the "don't load images" menu item, since some of your customers will have their browsers set this way. Note the results to each of the following questions.

- How does your Web site look with these settings?

- Can you still navigate your site with ease?

- Does your Web site use a text font that isn't one of the defaults? If so, does your site look okay?

- If you opted to use Java on your Web site, test it with a browser that doesn't support Java and a Java-enabled browser with that feature turned off.

- If your Web site requires a special plug-in, a special helper application, or special file type, test it both with the special "whatever" installed and then without the special "whatever" installed.

If you can, test your site with WebTV and other Web appliances. Some of these products are relatively primitive, generally only having limited capabilities and lower resolutions. You'll also find that Web pages must be reformatted so they can be read on a TV screen.

Your QA Plan should take into account each static page and each of the unique templates so they can be tested at least once in each browser configuration to ensure cross-browser layout and functionality. All other non-browser-specific functionality should be tested in at least one to three browser configurations.

Next, your QA Plan should have a "go live" criteria defined to be "No Open Bugs." In other words, before your Web site is completely available to the public-at-large, all problems and errors found on your site should be fixed. The best way to accomplish this task is to create and maintain a "bugbase" file set out as follows:

BUGBASE FILE

Bug Description	Date Fixed	Pending (y/n)	Date Closed	Deferred W/Explanation

Place all reported bugs in the bugbase as they are found. As each bug is fixed on the development server, launch the fixed elements and pages to the staging server as a new version of your site, as you do so change the bugs' status in the bugbase file to "pending." Then verify the "fixed" bugs and either re-opened them (if they weren't fixed) or close them (if the fix was verified). The final step is to document your testing procedure detailing the testing activity, remaining bugs and their statuses (deferred for later fix, feature requests, etc.).

Server Error Log

One of your *main aids* in tracking down bugs is your server's error logs — look for such items as missing images, bad links, and errors from CGI scripts, just to name a few. Use this excellent tool on a regular basis and after every update to your site. Web site errors mean lost traffic. It is normal to have a few errors in your log files, but if the error rate starts to rise precipitously, then look for what's causing the problems and fix them.

Spell Check

Don't forget to run your spell check and manually copyedit your Web site's text. I am always amazed at the Web sites that have misspellings.

Hang Time

Don't forget to measure the various browsers' "hang time." This is how long the browser hangs with a blank screen before loading your Web page.

Printing

Test how your Web site prints using different browsers. This is particularly important if your Web site is brochureware, subscription based or is a supplement to your technical help desk.

Some browsers can not start a new page if a table won't fit on the current page; however, tables can force page breaks when the document prints out. By using tables you can add some control as to how the pages will print.

Avoid browser-specific code since your Web site may not print out properly if the customer has a different browser.

Other printing problems can occur if you use an image for the background or a black or colored background. Frames seem to constantly cause printing problems. If you think that your Web site's visitors will be regularly printing your pages, you might want to provide a non-frame version such as www.ecominfocenter.com does. Note: This is a good information site for Web-based businesses, so bookmark and refer to it often.

One common mistake is that contact information, support, and the Frequently Asked Questions (FAQ) pages are not easy to find. Always keep those links clearly visible on every page.

Test and Re-test

Okay, you've tested the design/front-end of your site and now you are ready to put the site on your staging server. Test it again. Make a hard and fast rule to always test every time you make any change to your site just to be sure you haven't accidentally introduced an error when instituting a change.

Other steps you should take during the testing stage include having other people test your Web site and proofread the text. You and your staff are just too close to the project to notice what would otherwise be embarrassing errors.

If you developed a site that exists simultaneously in different formatted versions — flash/HTML, frame/non-frame — then, depending on the browser, you must test every version with every browser and with all of the possible option settings.

CONTINUAL QUALITY ASSURANCE

Once your site is "live" and you have customers, don't drop your QA Plan, it is just as important now. With frenetic deadlines and constantly changing requirements, it is very easy to ignore the basics of quality assurance. An active, dynamic site means your Web pages will be in a continual state of change. This means they will be revised by different people (in all probability) who bring their own individual coding quirks (although I am sure all will try to follow the HTML on the templates), which can and will introduce HTML and other coding errors.

If you have a Web site that is operational and brought to the Web without a QA Plan, gather your entire staff together (including consultants) and discuss ad hoc processes and standards that you currently have in use. In these discussions you can find out what causes the most problems on the site. This will give you the basis for setting up a QA Plan to address those issues as well as HTML and other coding guidelines. It is generally not practical to go back and try to "update" your older content to adhere to the new QA Plan, but do initiate the QA Plan for all new content.

Listen to Your Customers

Listen when you are told that a customer has problems with your Web site. When someone takes the time to report a problem, pay attention. For every person who took the time to inform you about the problem, there are probably about a thousand others who didn't take the time and effort — remember competition is just a click away. Be diligent, pay attention and you will be one step ahead of most Web sites when it comes to neutralizing the little annoyances. Are you building your Web site to drive customer traffic to your competitors or to enhance your bottom line?

TEST AND RE-TEST

Map your customers' experience. How? Fire up your browser and pretend you're a customer. Walk through the customer's complete shopping experience — run numerous tests from the first moment your customer enters your site through the entry of payment information and shipping preferences.

- Test the Web site's ordering process, from the user's point of entry through to the shipping preference.

- Test the credit card verification system, as well as the billing system that comes afterward.

- Stress-test all of the servers with simulated loads.

- Check the Web site's impact on any back-end systems.

- Test not only the servers, but also the personnel and processes that support the systems.

- Test e-mail response times.

- Test customer usability through focus groups or random-sample surveys.

- Test the offline side. How is the payment information received, verified and processed, including the receipt of payment into your bank account.

- Test your servers using simulated loads to see how they stand up under the stress of heavy traffic.

In addition to the products listed earlier, look into:

- RSW e-Load (www.rswsoftware.com), a component of the e-Test Suite, is the easy way to test the scalability of a Web site running on Windows NT. RSW offers a 30 day free trial. You can use e-load early in your Web site's development process to validate the scalability of the overall architecture and avoid costly rework later. It can also be used to test and tune your completed Web site under load prior to deployment. e-Load utilizes Visual Scripts to emulate thousands of "Virtual Users. " You can change the number and type of users on-the-fly to try "what-if" scenarios as you vary the loading conditions or application settings. Also e-Load's integrated real-time graphics and reporting capabilities allow for easy interpretation of the testing results.

- Facilita Software Development's Forecast (www.facilita.co.uk) is a non-intrusive Web server load testing tool that simulates users on a system. It allows you to perform extensive and realistic load testing before a system goes live. It supports the UNIX family — Solaris, AIX, SCO, Digital UNIX and Linux along with Windows NT.

Software Research, Inc's Testworks/Web (www.testworks.com) allows you to ensure the quality and reliability of your Web pages prior to publication. Components included in TestWorks/Web, such as the XVirtual tool, can simulate thousands of hits against your Web site by fabricating hundreds of synthetic interacting users, thereby helping you to assure 100% load accuracy. You can run the product on most UNIX and Windows systems.

Now, test your Web site's integration with your offline business systems such as your in-house database, accounting, inventory management system, etc., by simulating numerous transactions. In doing this you're not only checking out the hardware and software but you're also testing your personnel and the entire process that supports your Web site.

Last, but not least, check your customer service processes by testing your e-mail response time, your Web-based call center, etc.

Never launch an e-commerce site or enhancement without solid quality assurance. A month of intensive, structured testing is the minimum for a large-scale e-commerce site.

FOCUS GROUPS AND SURVEYS

These are not in-house focus groups — don't use employees and friends — you need the find your intended audience for these tests. The only way to do this correctly is to employ market researchers with Internet testing experience or use the service OTIVO mentioned above. These services can be expensive, but they are necessary. Here is where you can discover, prior to opening your site to the general public, if you have any features that your Web site's typical customers will find problematic or annoying.

Focus group usability testing includes asking the potential users about their expectations and usage, such as: Do you know what's in this site? Is it informative and useful?

Give the testing company your customer experience map so the focus group can do various scenarios typifying an average customer. The tester then should give you a report comparing the different approaches the individual members of the focus group used to navigate your Web site. In this way you can determine what will work best for your customers.

The company that you choose to conduct these tests should be prepared to provide you a complete report at the end of the testing period. This report should include:

- a short executive summary

- description of methodology

- key findings

- recommended actions

- summary of user comments

- the full results including any handwritten notes gathered during the testing should be made available upon request

There are two advantages of taking this approach:

1. Once you have the results from the focus group testing you can intelligently change content organization and navigation structure as needed.

2. The results will help you understand your Web site from a customer's perspective, allowing you to refocus your site's future development on your customer's experience.

You could possibly cut the costs a bit by using a formal random-sample survey which means the marketing firm would not need to have access to a computer for each individual but would call individuals, ask them to use your site and fill out a questionnaire.

CONCLUSION

Remember, this is important — don't skip this step — Not only must you execute a quality assurance test prior to launch but at any time you make an enhancement to your site.

CHAPTER II

Web Site Maintenance and Management

If you want a place in the sun, you've got to expect a few blisters.

Everyone pines for those uncomplicated days of (literally) yesteryear, when maintaining a Web site was simply a matter of updating HTML files. Alas, that is no longer the case, today's Web-based businesses are more robust, complex and demanding than ever before. As a result, more and more Web-based businesses are adopting an effective Web site maintenance and management system in sync with their overall business scheme.

Incorporate in your blueprint a system to refine and update not only your Web pages to keep them fresh and new, but also your entire infrastructure to take advantage of new and evolving technology. Thus keeping your site in peak condition for outstanding performance. In doing so you are ensuring that your Web site will provide the two most important features of a Web-based business — a compelling customer experience and minimal administration costs.

ESTABLISHING A MAINTENANCE AND MANAGEMENT SYSTEM

How do you establish this type of system? Use the Internet and take advantage of its dynamic and interactive attributes. Your first step should be to put a customer feedback form in a prominent place on your Web site. Feedback forms are invaluable in getting your online customers involved in the process of analyzing your site. Most of your customers will be eager to participate. Take this information and use it to ensure that your site always achieves optimum performance from a user's point of view. Don't be afraid to experiment as long as you constantly monitor the results. In this way you can make your changes, measure the results against other experiments, and settle on the best-performing choice.

Another tried-and-true approach when it comes to maintaining and managing a Web site is to devise a range of marketing strategies. It is important to measure the results of your marketing campaigns to determine if any particular campaign is on-track. If you are a click-and-mortar, your Web site strategy must fit with your click-and-mortar's business strategy. Closely monitor whether your Web site is meeting your stated business objectives. If you find shortfalls, bring out the blueprint and re-evaluate your Web business plan. You must not only define the process but also institute a methodology that provides the means for a continuous evolution of your Web site's objectives. Remember, as the new century progresses, and technology races ahead, you will continuously redefine the role that your Web site plays in the brick-and-mortar's overall business goals.

The establishment, management and maintenance of a Web site requires a significant investment of time and resources on your part, but first start with the basics:

- design your site for ease of modification

- avoid sloppy formatting, image maps and links on every page

- know who will maintain and update your Web site and have more than one person that can easily step in and take control

The Small Web Site

There are tools that you can use to create and implement a set of uniform formats and styles for a small Web site so that you can instantly create a new Web page by copying and modifying an existing page. This will help in keeping all coding uniform, thus eliminating problems caused by errant code. Check out SiteRefresh at www.spaceweb.com, SiteSentry at www.site-sentry.com, EasyWeb at www.topfloorsoftware.com, and Website Director at www.cyberteams.com.

The Large or Enterprise Web Site

A larger Web-based business may require a seamless integration between the Web site and its back-office systems. This will, among other things, have an added benefit of decreasing your Web site's overall maintenance costs by eliminating manual intervention, thanks to automated updates. By implementing the right system design, your Web-based sales can be instantly recorded in your sales order processing system, and information about new inventory items can be made available for sale online. Updated inventory information, such as, price changes, item descriptions and images are automatically updated as well. Of course, all of this must occur in accordance with defined preset "business rules."

Business rules: A conceptual description of an organization's policies and practices. Business rules enable organizations to automate their policies and practices, to increase consistency and timeliness of their business processing, and they aid in decision-making.

The best way to implement your business rules is to have them defined by a manager or systems consultant in English along the lines of "IF-THEN" logic. The same way that a "knowledge engineer" and programmer may sit down with an expert in a specific system in order to come up with the underlying logic of that system. Business rules can be associated with events such as creation, deletion or update, or to meaningful business events (ex. 'overdue')

Software code is later produced, both for the back-office processing as well as for the Web site to support these business rules.

If you wish to create end-to-end solutions connecting customers' Web browsers to data servers, then you'll also certainly want to integrate back-office applications, both within your company and in business-to-business relationships, such as with your distributors' applications or with your own legacy systems. This collection of needs means that you'll probably implement business logic specifications at many different levels.

Business rules can be explicit (actual software code that is triggered if a certain condition is met) or implicit (if one field is filled out by a user on a Web page then a series of related fields must be filled out too).

Business rules can have exception conditions (ex. "except those customers who do not have an approved account") and they can also have "immediate" or "deferred" enforcement (i.e. the rule doesn't stop processing but logs the non compliance as an exception condition, to be dealt with after all of the information has been collected and analyzed).

Usoft (www.usoft.com) has an interesting suite of software development products that enables you to deliver products and services on the Internet using business logic as the basis for your whole system. USoft's architecture is based upon delivering dynamic transactional Web sites, whereby the front-office and back-office are integrated. By using business logic as a central starting point to define business products and services, USoft increases maintainability and delivers unlimited flexibility that can take into account future Internet and software developments.

USoft's "Rules Engines" are at the core of their architecture. These Rules Engines transparently perform rules-based behavior, such as calculations, data integrity, complex data interdependency and validation checks.

USoft's rules-based application development products and services for the Internet are preferable to business logic implemented by ERP applications or coded into EJB or Microsoft Transaction Server (MTS) components. They give you:

- Rich data integrity. Business rules are ideally suited to guard not only parent-to-child relationships but also complex forms of data integrity such as discount schemes.

- Highly flexible application components. A large rulebase is much more maintainable than large sets of middle-tier components. Business rule implementations essentially contain their own event programming: no longer do you need manual programming, method invocation, procedure calls, or application or database triggers for your business logic.

- Excellent back office integration facilities. These include USoft's Rules-Driven Method Invocation (RDMI) that offers additional integration between business rules and third-party back-office applications, as well as transaction control via MTS components. RDMI lets you link rules-based data operations to non-USoft component calls. In this way, any component can participate in the enforcement of a business rule. For example, you could use RDMI to have a mail server send an e-mail based on USoft business rule specifications.

- Independence from front-end solutions. Business rules are automatically re-used (shared) by current and future Internet, intranet/extranet and back office applications, as well as by batch applications.

Another choice might be Computer Associates's PLATINUM Aion www.cai.com/products/platinum, a rule-based tool for developing and deploying intelligent components across the enterprise, including Internet, intranet/extranet and back-office applications. Aion combines business rules and object-oriented programming to efficiently create and maintain complex, knowledge-intensive applications. Its code generation technology provides the flexibility to deploy the applications as distributed components across a range of enterprise architectures and platforms.

Aion is one solution you might consider for creating, automating, and maintaining complex and frequently changing business policy logic. It's rule-based processing is critical for complex, dynamic applications because it enables the representation, processing, and easy modification of business policies and procedures that embody judgment and experience.

Aion separates and encapsulates business logic into a set of declarative statements called 'rules'. Each individual rule defines a premise and one or more resulting actions. It can give you a lot of functionality that you don't get just programming in C. Instead of focusing on a programming language, developers can approach their job as a series of "if-then" events.

LINKS MANAGEMENT

Another major part of a comprehensive Web site maintenance and management system is to vigilantly identify and fix broken links. A broken link occurs when a page or location (whether on your Web site or some farflung Web page) pointed to by another page has been moved, deleted or renamed. Unfortunately there are no automatic repair mechanisms standing by to sort the problem out. Most often the source page is simply left with a broken, or dangling link.

Any way you look at it, Web-based businesses are *heavily penalized* for both broken out-bound links (which are arguably under their direct control), and broken inbound links (to which a number of unsatisfactory solutions apply). Some obvious consequences of a failure to deal with broken links on your site and broken links that once pointed to your site are:

- Loss of revenue as potential customers attempt, and fail, to follow a broken link to your site.

- Brand damage since a broken link on a Web site is as bad if not worse than a mis-spelled word in a brochure. It takes diligent oversight to guarantee that a Web page that revealed no flaws when placed on the Web, remains flaw free (no broken links includ-ed) as time goes on. A business with a Web site with broken links and broken links pointing to that business's Web site might lead a consumer to the conclusion that the error is caused in some way by poor standards or administration by your business.

- Loss of productivity for the people who maintain your site. Broken links are a time-con-suming headache and at large sites it is practically impossible to repair all broken links.

The author has noted that today the average Web site has 1 page in every 4 pages that contain a broken link. It has been written that over 10% of the total links on the Internet are broken. Just think, maybe 1 page in every 4 that points to your Web site could be send-ing your customers on a one-way trip to your competition!

Do you have links to other sites? If so, you must keep checking these links regularly and update or delete them when the links are inaccurate. Be diligent about keeping your links updated so you can quickly identify broken links and pinpoint the pages you need to fix to keep your site at peak performance all the time. You don't want your customers to see a "File not found" message when they are looking to buy. There are applications and ser-vices available that can help you with this, such as:

- LinkGuard (www.linkguard.com) has a growing set of services that detect, report, repair, bypass and prevent broken links on the Internet. Check out the free services - like LinkGuard Online and LinkGuard Watchdog.

- A spidering software that checks Web sites for broken links is Xenu's Link Sleuth (http://home.snafu.de/tilman/xenulink). Link verification is carried out not only on "normal" links, but also on images, frames, plug-ins, backgrounds, local image maps, style sheets, scripts and Java applets. It displays a continuously updated list of URLs which you can sort by different criteria.

- A free PERL utility that checks internal and external links via http, writing the results to an HTML file is Checkbot (http://degraaff.org/checkbot/). It can check a single document, or a set of documents on one or more servers. Checkbot creates a report that summarizes all links that caused some kind of warning or error.

- An expensive link-checking and site management application for Windows with three great site-mapping views is WebAnalyzer 2.0 (www.incontext.com/WAinfo). It checks your site for broken links, missing images, duplicated files and other Web site problems. It features sophisticated custom-built reports, automatic scheduling and updating and multiple domain analysis.

Two established software companies discussed in various chapters of this book also provide very good software with link management capabilities. You can check their offerings out at LinkBot (www.linkbot.com) and WebTrends (www.webtrends.com).

If you are diligent, and use one of the above-mentioned (or similar) software packages with intelligence, your customers, when trying to access your site through a link or browsing your site, should seldom see some of the common error codes listed below:

Error 401 - Access to this page is denied

Error 402 - A payment is required

Error 403 - The request you have asked for is forbidden

Error 404 - File not found

Error 408 - Server timed out waiting for request

Error 500 - Internal server error

Error 502 - Error response received from gateway

CONTENT MANAGEMENT

Managing the content of a busy Web site is crucial for the optimum maintenance of a Web site. For example, you may have the problem of size — it is not unusual for a site to routinely publish hundreds of pages per week. However, the people creating all of this content are usually writers and marketing types who rarely consider the need to or know how to clean out dead files let alone the problem of tracing a chain reaction of errors caused by some simple change in code. Then you have those businesses whose entire Web site consists of constantly changing content — newspaper, ezine (an online magazine), B2B vendors and catalog sites. These kinds of sites require a tighter control of style and format, and easy re-purposing.

Web-based businesses are encountering increasingly complex logistical problems coordinating the updates to their site. Large and enterprise sites have Web teams consisting of software and content developers, Webmasters, graphic designers, testers, and approvers. Frequent changes by such a diverse team make it increasingly difficult for a Web-based business to ensure high quality while changes are being made at Web speed.

One way to help you with content management is to investigate some of the software alternatives. Many can help with the management of content on Web servers, keeping track of individual HTML and graphic files, analyzing links, generating dynamic pages and creating staging areas. I have set out just a few that you might find helpful:

TownSource Interactive (www.webpublishintoos.com) is a turn-key suite of dynamic content management applications built exclusively for the Web. All its core content management elements allow authorized users to self-publish information in real time. Web-based businesses can self maintain their directory pages, news, jobs, e-promotions, events calendars, and catalogs. With TownSource's automated removal of time sensitive listings, the administrator's job primarily becomes one of managing content — reviewing, editing, and highlighting information.

Continuus/WebSynergy www.continuus.com/websyn is an enterprise software application designed to manage the creation, acquisition and deployment of all Web-based assets. It is specifically designed for the large and enterprise Web site that must tightly manage their dynamic Web projects. It supports the collaborative development of both content-rich and software enabled Web applications.

Idetix's Revize http://axil.cpg.com is a Web-based content management system that enables you to quickly and easily build secure content editing capabilities into new or existing sites. With Revize, authorized users can use any Java-enabled browser to edit Web site content, while site design and page layout remains intact and protected. This means that individuals can each edit/manage their own content.

HARDWARE AND INFRASTRUCTURE MAINTENANCE

Time-to-market pressures have forced many Web-based businesses to create Web infrastructures (everything that makes your pretty pages work) in a haphazard fashion. These Web sites sometimes experience substantial downtime as a result of poor planning and/or maintenance — a flaw immediately apparent to customers and business partners. Keeping your Web site up and available is the goal. Attaining 99.999% availability "five nines" is a exhausting and arduous neverending pursuit. Your Web site's failure points can include:

- human error
- faulty software in routers and switches
- increased bandwidth traffic that crashes servers
- configuration problems
- power failures
- major carrier outages
- any of the numerous applications that runs your Web site

The total "end-to-end" performance of the Web site's infrastructure must be understood and analyzed in order to ensure that it delivers the performance demanded by today's Web-based business' customers. However, this is not achievable by the simple addition of a Web site management component to the melange of existing systems, network, and application management solutions already peppered throughout the average enterprise-size Web-based business.

But the case is not hopeless. Although a majority of all Web sites are now hosted externally, it is still vital that a Web-based business understand the importance of real-time management and capacity planning. Many Web sites are sophisticated systems that incorporate transaction processing and any problematic component between the customer and the Web site can affect performance and reliability. Help is on the way.

A formal management and maintenance system for a Web-based business ran on in-house equipment is crucial. This scenario requires that a robust management system must be designed and implemented, i.e., the full "end-to-end" system — application, network, connectivity and systems — if the site is to remain reliable and maintain cutting edge technology.

To accomplish this, all of your servers including your Web server should be as self-documenting as possible. All programs and other source code should be published and you should have a Web policy document with goals, practice, management, etc. that is frequently updated and in a location that is easily accessible (but in a secure location).

Here is the help:

One all-in-one tool is NetMechanic www.netmechanic.com. This free online Web site maintenance service performs whole site link checking, HTML validation, load time analysis, and server reliability testing with its Server Check Pro.

Another company to check out is Stone Bridge Systems www.stonebridgesystems.com. It designs and implements Operations Management Systems, which manages the full "end-to-end" system that enable a Web site's support staff to monitor and manage users, applications, data, systems, and networks in an integrated, pro-active manner.

Or look at Platinum Technology www.unixsolutions.hp.com/products/hpux/pp/platinum_content. They provide software products and consulting services that improve the IT infrastructure — minimizing risk, improving service levels, and helping to leverage valuable business information for better decisions. This can help any Web-based business to overcome the most difficult IT infrastructure challenges in the areas of systems & database management, data warehousing, and application life cycle management.

With the *proper* management and maintenance system in place, the Web-based business can monitor and manage applications, data, systems, and networks in an integrated, pro-active manner using sophisticated software tools. In addition, the data gathered and reported can be used for other functions, such as: security, capacity planning, etc. However, when it comes to high-availability (five nines) there's no single answer, just as there is no single point of failure. While a Web site should implement best practices to improve its chances, there are just too many factors that can bring down your Web site. The only sure thing is planning and preparation.

In this chapter, I've set out various software and online solutions to aid in your quest for the perfect, problem-free Web site. However, there are many such tools available and you may find yourself relying on a blend of technologies. But Web site management and maintenance tools often overlap so sometimes it is possible to purchase a single suite of tools that can handle most, if not all, of the tasks necessary for a properly managed site.

CHAPTER 12

What Are the Costs?

Forewarned, forearmed; to be prepared is half the victory.

Spanish Proverb

The cost of building an effective e-commerce site will vary greatly. This chapter discusses in general terms the range of costs for building different types of Web sites so that the Web-site builder will have a starting point in constructing an appropriate budget for the project.

Hopefully the readers won't faint when they read the following few paragraphs! These are the cold hard facts, but don't give up, continue reading, as there are limited alternatives for those of you on a budget.

Sticker Shock: Developing and launching an e-commerce site costs an average of $1 million, according to a survey by the Gartner Group, reported by InfoWorld Electric. The survey participants spent from less than $350,000 to more than $2 million to develop their sites.

Brass Tacks: A small to medium size e-commerce Web site's average start-up cost is between $250,000 to $1 million. This will get you a Web site that is adequate but functionally behind most industry participants.

The Facts: If you can spend from $1 million to about $5 million, you can build a fully functional e-commerce Web site that is equivalent to most industry participants.

The Gold Ring: A Web-based business that has a budget of somewhere between $5 million to $20 million can create a site that raises the industry competitive bar and changes the nature of online competition.

ESTABLISHING A BUDGET

It is *essential* that you set out a comprehensive budget for your Web site or you will find your costs growing out of control. This budget must be as detailed as any financial record. The costs of building your new Web site (including design and infrastructure costs, the cost of maintaining your Web site once it is built, and the cost for the continuous marketing and promotion of your Web site) should be broken down into fixed and variable expenses.

This sample budget offers a good starting place. However, it only covers the expenses incurred for the site, not the business' total operating expenses, i.e., physical plant.

	ESTIMATED COSTS		
Expenses	Start-Up	Monthly	Annual
Fixed:			
Registration			
Of Domain Name			
Merchant Account/			
Banking			
ISP			
Web Hosting Contract			
(if not hosted In-house)			
Local Telco			
Insurance			
Accounting			
Legal			
Miscellaneous			
Variable:			
Payroll			
Consultants			
Web design, database			
Etc.			
Software			
If hosting service used:			
E-mail, contact, accounting,			
Etc.			
Web-centric Software			
Log Analysis, e-mail lists,			
Autoresponder, QA, Web site			
Maintenance, etc.			
Hardware			
Graphics and images			
Acquisition			
(or digital equipment and			
graphics program)			
Marketing			
Includes banner ads and			
Search engine registration			
Public Relations			
Customer Relationship			
Management			
Includes Call center costs			
Personalization Software			
Includes Data mining			
Miscellaneous			

With a few additions, this budget can also be used by the brick-and-mortar making its move to the Web. For example, there would be increased payroll expense incurred for handling e-mail, credit card processing, inventory control, Web design and maintenance, etc. A brick-and-mortar will see its credit card and banking fees increase along with its monthly telco expenses. Also don't forget the added expense involved in updating all of your current stationery, brochures and promotional material.

RETURN ON INVESTMENT

After you have finalized the budget for your new Web site, you must establish a goal for a return on investment (ROI). How are you going to do this? The factors you must consider are:

- What return is realistic?

- How will you measure the return?

- Are you only interested in tracking a financial ROI, or is a value to be placed on: improved customer service; the marketing value of the Web site; or the savings instituted in specific areas of your brick-and-mortar business due to the Web site?

If you are an established brick-and-mortar, what is important is that the ROI measures the value of your Web site against your overall business. If you are an entrepreneur then it's a different story, you do, in fact, need to establish the criteria to measure a realistic return on investment. Either way, it is *essential* that you institute a system to keep track of the ROI so you can measure your new Web site's progress. By doing this you will never have any doubt about where your site stands at any point in the future.

HOME-BASED BUSINESS

There are more than 5 million small (I call them "home-based") businesses in the United States with $100,000 or less in annual revenue. There is an enormous opportunity for a number of these businesses to succeed on the Web. This type of business can get a very basic e-commerce Web site up and running for a small up front investment.

Although it is not the author's advice that you do so, you can go with one of the "free Web hosting" services offered by various Web hosting services and ISPs. This option gives you a very small amount of virtual hosting space plus Web authoring tools giving you the ability to put your content on your site. Don't forget to check if you are allowed to use your own URL. Also remember that some of these "free" services require that you learn the technology — HTML, basic CGI scripting, PERL, etc. — and use your own Web design or Web authoring tools. These tools, including those listed below range in cost from $30 - $500.

Allaire Homesite (www.allaire.com) is an HTML Design tool that includes some site maintenance features.

HotDogPro (www.sausage.com) is an HTML authoring tools with a lot of customizable features.

Microsoft Frontpage 2000 (www.microsoft.com/frontpage) gives you what you need to create and manage a Web site.

Web Weaver (www.macwebsoftware.com) is an HTML editor that has all the tools to help the novice Web designer produce tables, frames, and forms.

Another option (which the author leans more towards) is to put your products on one of the many e-commerce shopping malls for very little up front costs and a small per transaction fee.

The caveat: Be careful going some of these routes. Investigate thoroughly and look for:

- whether there is severe limitation in the size of your site
- a banner requirement, i.e., are you required to place banners on your pages that are provided by the hosting service
- whether there is a limitation on the number of items you can list
- the search capabilities, i.e., will customers be able to search for a specific item
- whether you can use your own domain name to promote and brand

Although the above options do give your business a Web presence, it will be small, somewhat problematic and it will not be scalable. As soon as your budget will allow, you should look into the following options.

SMALL ENTREPRENEUR OR LOCAL BRICK-AND-MORTAR

Let's talk about the costs, both the direct and hidden costs. Even if you are on a budget and watch your costs very closely, your e-commerce site can still cost anywhere between $15,000 to $80,000. Of course, if you do everything yourself, you might cut some costs in exchange for your sweat and toil.

After the Web site launches, the next expense you will incur is the hosting fee. This is usually around $1,000 per year at the low end and can easily be much more expensive, especially if you use one of the virtual hosting options. It is not unusual for an annual hosting fee to run around $50,000 per year if you go for dedicated servers rather than virtual servers.

MAINTENANCE

You also must consider how to systematically maintain your new Web site. In a traditional business, if you don't keep your place clean, neat and filled with current product, your revenue will suffer. The same holds true for your Web site: The content must be kept current, fresh and exciting and the site must be maintained so your customers need not suffer through page errors and downtime.

Please, take a minute to consider where your core expertise lies; if it's not Web mastering, you should seriously consider hiring a consultant to perform your Web site's maintenance duties, including content update. Depending on where you live and the size of your site, the costs should run from $1,000 to 12,000 per year.

If you decide to perform your own Web site maintenance and upkeep, you need to answer this question: Do you have the time, aptitude, and desire to design, build and maintain your own site? If you answered yes, then you must budget a monthly time and energy expenditure of at least 10% of the man hours it took to build your site for updates and maintenance. In other words, if you spent 150 hours designing and building your new Web site, you should budget at least 15 hours per month for the daily upkeep of that site. (You can also use this formula to calculate how much it would cost to outsource the project.)

BUSINESSES THAT HAVE VISIONS OF GRANDEUR

Find yourself a good, qualified consultant and together draw up your blueprint and storyboard for the entire site and let the consultant take care of all the daily necessities. Of course, the consultant should keep you apprised of every step taken. Even with a consultant it will take you at least 6 weeks, and perhaps up to 4 or 5 months (if the site is complex), to have your site up and running. You want your new Web site to be a revenue producer sooner than later, do it right from the beginning. The costs for designing and building this type of site can be as little as $150,000 and go up to as much as $1 million. The variation in price depends mostly on how you decide to deal with the software and hardware:

- build and host in-house

- use your own software but let a Web hosting service handle all the hardware needs

- use a hybrid hosting service and you license the software and lease the hardware from that service

- outsource all of your Web site's infrastructure either on virtual servers or dedicated servers, keeping only a staging server in-house

Now you must address the maintenance fees and the daily upkeep of your site. This type of Web site needs not only frequent additions of fresh and exciting content, but also daily upkeep and routine maintenance. This type of site is really too much for an individual to handle unless that person is well versed in all the relevant technologies. You can outsource these services for an annual fee ranging from $15,000 to more than $300,000.

If you are "reaching for the stars" but your budget is limited, you can save money by taking a more active role in the design and building of your Web site. Find yourself a good, qualified consultant to be on hand for the planning stage and on-call for limited consultation during the building stage. This method requires a close working relationship between you, your in-house staff and the consultant. With a good relationship, your Web site can be successfully launched within 6 weeks to 5 months after you have signed the consulting contract. Your costs will run probably around $100,000 at the minimum and up to $700,000.

The entrepreneur or business that has visions of grandeur — but just absolutely refuses to hire a consultant — can play in this field too, but only if they have the technical expertise necessary to design, build and do the necessary programming to get the correct software up and running. It will take longer to launch a competitive Web site in this way, but it can be done. Remember you are taking on a project that is probably not within your core competency. Not only do you need patience, but an income to support you over the time period it will take for a proper launch. Perhaps you could launch a small Web site in 5 months' time, but in all probability you should plan on spending a year working on a site before it's up and running and generating revenue. This kind of site will still cost you. It's just that you'll be exchanging the up front costs of a consultant for the costs of your own time and energy.

Design

You should set a generous budget for design work. Why? A professional graphic/Web design service can give your new Web-based business a real-world image. (Or an unreal one, if that is what you desire!). Basic graphics and design will run anywhere from $3,500 to $25,000, if you want more than the basics, i.e., sound, streaming video, flash, the cost will increase substantially. As with any consultant, make sure you choose your design service only after you have made a rigorous check of references and reviewed their previous work. Your initial meeting with them should be sufficient to ensure that you are "on the same page" when it comes to realizing your vision for your new Web site.

Hardware

You will need at least 3 servers, one for your Web server, one for your database and one for your e-commerce software. See Chapter 4 for information on some the actual configurations you might want to consider.

Operating System

You operating system can cost virtually nothing for a Linux version downloaded from the Web to more than $15,000 for one of the Unix family of products or Windows NT/2000.

Web Server Software

Again, the cost can be next to nothing for obtaining a copy of the many available free Web servers but you will still need to configure and optimize even "freeware" for your Web site's specific needs and these costs need to be budgeted. Or you may opt for something like the Lotus Domino server whose licensing fees start around $2,000, but in some instances it is well worth the cost.

E-Commerce Software

Depending on the e-commerce model you decide to build, your software can cost from next to nothing to more than $500,000. For example, at the low end, a simple e-commerce software package, such as iCat's (www.icat.com) basic online shop, is free. At the high end, which allows you to be in league with your largest competitor (such as e-toys if you are a toy store, or CDNOW if you are a music store), the cost starts at $500,000 or so. In other words, if you plan to build a Web site anticipating millions of hits a day and selling millions of items every day, then plan on spending a huge amount of money.

Database

If you have a large inventory, such as that found in a department store, you will in all likelihood have a database that must be put online. If you are an established brick-and-mortar business moving some of its operations to the Web, or even establishing a Web-based division, then this integration can be done in several ways: (1) software which can rummage through your stock system and produce something your online software can recognize and put on your Web site, or (2) you can have a real-time live link between your in-house database and your Web site.

The first solution can cost just a few thousand dollars for database design and updated software, along with a set cost per update. The second option requires a dedicated computer, which will run at least $4,000, along with a couple of modems and routers, which will cost at least $3,000. Then there's the link itself, which can range from about $12,000 to $100,000 a year, and a server-class software installation with the attendant firewall, backups, fault tolerance and redundancy, which is priced at around $35,000.

As you can see, the costs of establishing a world-class e-business can approach what a real-world business would cost, and waiting for your first profitable year can take equally as long, so I advise that you base your budget on a three-year plan.

ENTERPRISE BUSINESS

Don't stop the heavy breathing yet — the average cost for an enterprise size e-commerce Web site is more than a $1 million and that dollar amount can increase by 25% yearly during the first couple of years of operation. More than 75% of these costs are directly related to labor and professional service firms that you will need to employ. I know of Web sites where the total cost ran as little as $300,000, as well as sites that cost as much as $2 million. All of these sites, though, had one thing in common: An established, proper budget that they adhered to for the entire project.

It is interesting to note that the average time to build out a complete e-commerce site is just five months. However, it might be more than a year before some sites actually launch. It can vary.

As stated previously, more than 75% of the cost incurred when building an e-commerce site is for labor and consultants, the other 25% is usually divided just about evenly between hardware costs and software costs.

One factor that causes a big rise in the cost of a large e-commerce site is the many different types of consultants and vendors you need to take your business to the Web. You need a designer, an e-commerce application vendor, a media consulting firm, and systems integrators, to name just a few. In other words, a great deal of effort is needed when you start to build the front-end and back-end of an e-commerce site.

You really don't have a choice — an e-commerce site is a requirement for any midsize to large business that wants to remain competitive in today's business environment. It is also an unfortunate fact that a state-of-the-art e-commerce site launched today will be an outdated e-commerce site in just a few months if you are not careful when you build your infrastructure — it must be built so it can *keep pace with new technologies* as well as your business goals as they evolve.

CHAPTER 13
Consultants and Vendors

*A consultant is someone who takes your watch away
to tell you what time it is.*

Every Web-based business risks getting mired in an outsourcing dilemma as they seek to obtain valuable expertise that is either not present internally or in short supply. There are literally hundreds of capable consultants, vendors, and matchmaker companies out there clamoring for your dollars. For the typical Web-based business to choose among the myriad of options available to it, requires that it be able to identify which consultants and vendors have the capability and commitment to be able to help the Web-based business to reach its goals.

This chapter contains information about consultant contracts, costs, types of consulting services available, when to outsource and when to do the work in-house, etc. Surprisingly, nearly all entrepreneurs and most of the brick-and-mortar businesses do not have a formal process for selecting consultants or vendors and most selections seem as random as using the flip of a coin to make the ultimate decision. But with an effective selection process in place your new Web site will meet the needs of everyone, including your customers.

SELECTING A CONSULTANT

At some point, every Web-based business will need to retain a consultant. Consultants are the 'hired guns' of the Web industry that eliminate an endless number of problems in a timely and cost effective manner due to the wealth of related experience that they can bring to the table.

Your specific talent needs may be for a Web site architect, a Web designer, a Web developer, a marketing expert, a planning consultant or some other form of technical assistance. Formalizing an effective selection process is key to obtaining the best services for your needs.

As part of the process of sorting out your expectations and selecting your consultant, write a summary of your project and objectives. Include a concise description of your Web site (either as it exists, or as you anticipate it will be). This summary can be a handy reference tool when making initial contact with perspective consultants.

To begin, assess the project's specific requirements, review your objectives to ensure they are well-defined, then determine what your staff can handle and what you need to outsource by asking yourself and your staff:

- How much of the work can be done in-house?

- How much of the work is beyond your staff's capacity and must be outsourced?

- What is the budget?

- Are there desired cost savings? If so, what is the expected payback period (i.e., ROI of hiring a consultant vs. trying to do it in-house)?

- What is your business' commitment to the project? (In other words, after you spend all the time in the selection process, which in and of itself is very expensive, will the project move forward to completion?)

- What is the timetable for completing the project?

The Consultant's Role

After the project's objectives have been determined and prioritized you then need to compare those objectives to the types of services consultants offer. Including:

- a specialized expertise

- ability to objectively assess a specific situation

- a temporary supplement to your staff and knowledge base

- technical and economic analysis of alternatives

- development of recommendations

- design and programming support

- assistance with hardware/software selection

- assistance with implementing operational changes

- completion of one-time projects

Consultants can help improve your Web site's operations and productivity, but don't forget that you and your staff are the experts in the operation of your Web-based business, a consultant should enhance that expertise, not be a substitute for it. Do not depend on a consultant for decision-making — including purchasing decisions. Not uncommonly, consultants sometimes receive a commission when you (as their client) buy one of their recommended products or hire someone the consultant recommends.

The Consultant's Qualifications

After deciding to take advantage of a consultant's service, begin the process of identifying the type of consultant that will best meet the needs of your project. To find the right consultant:

- Re-visit consultants you have used in the past, assess that consultant's capabilities and limitations before deciding if you need to find another consultant.

- Obtain referrals from other similar Web-based businesses, trade associations, or consultant referral services.

- Contact prospective consultants to identify their expertise, qualifications and interest in your project. Request their marketing materials, including relevant educational background, experience and professional certifications.

- Obtain references and a list of previous clients. Checking past work performance is one of the best ways to evaluate a consultant.

When checking a consultant's references and previous clients, find out whether the consultant:

- has worked on projects similar in size and nature to the proposed project

- met the stated work and project deadlines

- was responsive, available and trustworthy

On a more personal level ask:

- If there were any problems and, if so, were they satisfactorily resolved?

- If it was easy to work with the consultant?

- Whether the consultant was knowledgeable and what was the overall impression of the consultant?

- If the final outcome was more expensive than originally thought — i.e., did the consultant bill for additional expenses? Find out if the final cost seemed in line with the original estimate?

The Request for Proposal (RFP)

Once you have narrowed your selection down to 3-5 perspective consultants, and before inviting them to the next meeting, prepare a Request for Proposal (RFP). A RFP is a formal request to the consultant describing everything you want the consultant to accomplish and requesting the consultant to write a proposal outlining how they would go about meeting your demands and the costs thereof. The RFP can be as informal as an e-mail or a telephone call, but it is best presented as a formal written document. The more information it conveys, and the more specific your requests, can enhance the consultant's ability to draft a relevant proposal.

There are basically two types of RFPs. A defined, rigid proposal wherein is laid out, step-by-step, your goals and requirements; and a creative proposal, which is a 3-4 page document setting out what the job will entail. The defined, rigid style of RFP allows for an easy comparison of costs, approaches and other criteria submitted by the consultants during the selection process. A creative proposal gives the consultant less structure thereby allowing for a greater diversity in response, which makes the proposals more difficult to consider. But the creative proposal does allow you to observe how the experience and knowledge of the consultant can be creatively applied to provide an exciting and unique approach to the project.

The Interview

Once you have compiled a list of consultants whose skills fulfill your requirements, invite them in for an interview. Be sure to:

- Explain your objectives and how you view the division of labor and responsibilities between the consultant and your staff. Be specific.

- Solicit the consultant's opinions — an outside perspective can be valuable.

- Set out your timeline.

- Ask the consultant to specify who would be working on the project.

If the meeting appears to be successful, immediately take the next step. Provide a Request for Proposal (RFP) as discussed above and obtain the information necessary for you to do your due diligence. Such as:

- Obtain a clients' list, including names and phone numbers.

- Find out how long the consultant has been in business.

- Ask what kind of projects the consultant has handled.

- Obtain some samples of the consultant's work, if possible.

- Ascertain what resources the consultant has to complete the project (i.e., staff, sub-contracting, etc.).

- Ask the consultant if there are any foreseeable problems in meeting your time schedule.

- Find out how the consultant charges — is it per hour, per day, or per project and if a deposit is required.

In any communications thereafter, endeavor to provide a written answer to any additional information requested by the consultant — clear communication is important, and it ensures that you get the results you want.

Review the Proposals

You should review the proposals received from the each of consultants and compare them to your established selection criteria to determine whether:

- the consultant responded to the principle needs based on the RFP's outlined objectives

- the services set out are specific to your RFP and are clearly defined

- the timetable covers both the consultants time and your staff's time and that it is reasonable

- all fees and costs are clearly defined, the billing procedures are specific and the consultant's fees seem reasonable

- the consultant has clearly defined the division of responsibility between your staff and the consultant's staff

- the consultant sets forth the consulting personnel assigned to the project, including resumes, experience and billing rates

The Contract

You need to protect your investment so get a written contract. Some of the specific issues that should be addressed in the consulting contract or letter of agreement are:

- Does the consultant use subcontractors? If so, does the consultant receive a commission for their services?

- Who provides the necessary insurance coverage? What type of coverage does the consultant have?

- How will unforeseen costs be handled? Is your approval required before such costs are incurred?

- Where will the majority of the work be performed? If at your place of business, is there adequate space?

- If information accessible to the consultant is confidential, a nondisclosure clause must be included.

- Include specific dates for the project's milestones, reports that may need to be submitted and the project completion.

- What is the procedure for handling problems that might occur?

- How will revised work and costs be determined?

Work Plan

Most consultants bill on a time and material basis; therefore, to protect the interest of both you and the consultant, it is necessary that you set out a reasonable work plan with a not-to-exceed (NTE) cost. A work plan is like your blue print, you need to map out exactly what the consultant has contracted to perform, with timelines and estimated costs at distinctive stages. Use the proposal received from the consultant as a guide when drawing up your work plan. In some instances the work plan may need to vary due to the nature of the project, so a series of possible scenarios and costs should be built around best case, worst case and most likely scenarios.

SELECTING A WEB SITE DEVELOPER

Many new Web sites are contracted out for development to Web Site Developers, an independent contractor performing a "work for hire" service. In this case you will look for a person or entity with both the technical and conceptual ability to be responsive to your requirements. A Web site developer will also need to be someone that can produce a Web design that will be compatible with your business' image. Follow the procedure set forth in the "Selecting a Consultant" section.

You will also need to produce and sign a development agreement that addresses issues that cover the development of your Web site including payment and acceptance procedures. The bare bones of a development agreement should contain:

- Firm dates for specific design milestones and Web site completion.

- A budget covering everything from the start through completion of the Web site including specific payment milestones.

- The developer's use of subcontractors and any commission the developer might receive from them for contracting with them for their services.

- The procedure for handling any problems that might occur.

- A mechanism allowing for revised work orders, change orders and determination of the ensuing costs.

- The maximum acceptable download time for any Web page.

- The inclusion of a user option, if necessary, of a low graphics version of the Web site in order to minimize downloading time.

- A guaranty that the Web site is downwardly compatible with a specific version of Internet browser software such as Microsoft's Internet Explorer, Netscape, and WebTV browsers.

- A guarantee that a specific number of users are able to simultaneously access the site, as well as setting forth a minimum response time.

- Assurance that the site will be properly integrated with your business' network, intranet or other data server infrastructure.

- Assurance that additions, corrections or modifications to the Web site can be made by you and your staff without interference with Web site operations.

- Specifications of the security safeguards, procedures and firewalls that the site must contain.

- Guaranties of the functionality of online credit verification and acceptance procedures.

- Assurance of the scope and procedure for you to easily access, record and compile information about the site's visitors and customers.

- A provision for timely documentation and source codes for all software associated with development of the Web site.

- Training of your staff to use and maintain the Web site's software including upgrades.

- Delineate the responsibility for transferring and installing the completed Web site to the Web servers that will run the new Web site. This should include all software — either purchased or licensed by your business.

- Set out a provision for alternative interface designs that the Web site developer must provide for your review.

- A commitment by the developer to a set period for joint beta testing of the completed Web site and a subsequent specific number of days to be used for evaluation of the new Web site by you and your staff to ensure your new Web site performs in accordance with the agreement.

- The developer will promptly correct any bugs and failed links, including setting forth the maximum time for correction.

- The developer will promptly perform any revisions of the Web site that are necessary to comply with the functionality specifications.

- A right of rejection of the Web site if it does not meet the written specifications, setting forth certain options you may exercise regarding corrections at the time of a rejection.

- Any particular warranties or disclaimers by the developer.

- Assurances that any software for the site is free of any viruses or disabling devices.

- Conditions under which you have the right to terminate the developer's agreement and the liability of the developer upon such termination.

- A nondisclosure clause must be included, if information accessible to the developer is confidential.

- A copyright notice to be displayed on each page of the Web site.

The Contract
Once you have successfully negotiated the Development Agreement, to legally bind and protect

all, a contract with the Web site developer should come next. It must address several issues:

- Incorporate into it all of the provisions of the Development Agreement by reference.

- Ownership of intellectual property relating to the content, screens, software and information developed including who owns the rights to use any materials or software the developer creates for the Web site.

- In development of your Web site, the developer must covenant that it will not infringe or violate the copyright and other intellectual property rights of any third party.

- You will receive a perpetual, irrevocable, worldwide royalty-free transferable license to any intellectual property that the developer owns, uses and retains ownership of the same.

- Set out who is responsible for securing necessary rights, licenses, clearances and other permissions related to any graphics or other copyrighted materials used or otherwise incorporated in the Web site.

- The developer covenants that it will not ever use any trademarks, service marks or logos owned by you and/or your company, except with your express written approval.

- The developer will comply with all applicable laws.

- The developer will maintain satisfactory insurance and will provide proof of its policies.

Other issues you may want to incorporate into the developer's agreement or set forth in a separate agreement:

- The developer will submit the appropriate information about your Web site to a specified list of search engines and directories.

- The developer will not use its service affiliation with you for its own promotional purposes without prior written consent.

A Web Site Developer will be one of the first consultants you will need for your new Web Site. Go slowly, follow the steps outlined herein, choose carefully, and you will be on the road to a great Web site.

VENDOR SELECTION

A vendor has a product for sale that will require customization for you to be able to utilize it. Vendors sell you the product and their professional technical services, as a package. It is imperative that the vendor selection process not be handicapped by internal political agendas, "gut feelings," or the toss of a coin decision. Once it is known that you are "in the market" you will be deluged with specific vendor related solicitations. If not managed correctly, the vendor selection process can eat up time and resources and it can be quite costly, accounting for as much as 25-30% of the total vendor costs.

Some of the worst case scenarios can be:

- choosing a vendor without proper due diligence — i.e., the vendor might be experiencing financial problems — resulting in you being forced to make an ill-timed decision — i.e., in the middle of an integration project — to bring in another vendor to complete the project

- service and support problems

- differences in your visions that were not made clear

Vendor Evaluation

Establish a vendor evaluation methodology. A vendor's ability to execute a specific plan and its long-term vision is well worth the investment. In spite of the critical service and support that vendor's supply, most businesses don't take the time to create a vendor RFP — let your business be the exception.

Elements of a vendor RFP:

Functionality: This is usually the primary focus of any vendor evaluation, but in actuality it should represent no more than 40% of the total decision-making process.

Storyboard: To ensure that you cover all of the capabilities you want from a specific vendor product, use a storyboard. Draw the storyboard using the same criteria as set out in Chapter 2. In other words, don't forget:

- the design aspects

- ease of use features

- ability to integrate with other tools, both hardware and software

Example of Other Criteria: Does the product provide:

- tools that enable you to present content electronically

- configurators to easily target various vertical, and geographic markets

- the scalability to incorporate new media formats

- ability to easily interface with other e-commerce applications

- ability to enhance rather than decrease the security risks

Costs: Don't put too much emphasis on the initial cost of the product in your decision-making process. Remember that the majority of the cost is hidden — such as product training, customization and integration. Therefore, cost calculations should always include not only initial license costs for the product and any knowledge tools utilized, but also costs of installation and maintenance, help-desk gateway, ongoing education and training, and professional services such as customization and integration.

The Vision: What is the vendor's own stated and realized development plans for its product? For example, ask how the vendor plans to incorporate and utilize new technologies into its product's architecture and how it plans to evolve its current product by adding to or enhancing the current functionality. Let's not forget about service and support — how does the vendor plan to grow and change its general and professional services support. Remember to investigate (due diligence once again raises its ugly head) how the vendor treats its customer once the vendor has been paid.

As set out above, a vendor's vision is just as important as the vendor's ability to produce a viable product and execute its successful implementation. For most businesses, this can be used as the key differentiator when making the final vendor selection.

Service and Support: A product's functionality and cost provides, in many instances, the inducement for making a specific vendor selection. It is very important that you also consider the availability of quality service and support, for without them, the success of any product implementation is ultimately doomed.

Service and support needs to be broken down into two areas. The first is general support including installation of the product and continuing support — regardless of location, and the quality of the help desk services. The second area is professional services. This can be the weakest link in many vendor organizations and therefore due diligence must be stringent — i.e, evaluate the vendor's strengths in project management, systems integration, and business consulting skills.

Due Diligence

The author knows she has harped on performing proper due diligence throughout this section, but it has proven to be the weakest area in most vendor selection processes. Given the immaturity of the e-commerce arena and the fierce competition that exists, the author predicts that, in a few years, at least half of the current vendors will no longer exist. Have you taken this fact into consideration when making your vendor selection? If not, do so. What is the vendor's financial viability? You can answer this question through analyzing a vendor's revenues, growth, margins, sales and marketing investment, quick ratio, etc. The next step is to measure the quality of personnel within the vendor's sales and development departments. Ask questions, such as, if these individual departments

- Are able to meet industry milestones?
- Are historically able to meet time deadlines?
- Have historically delivered what they promised?
- Have R&D capabilities comparable with other vendors?
- Are suffering a high turnover among their talented people?

Finalizing the Selection Process

Once you have put in place the above stated selection criteria and structure, you must *use your storyboard* to guide you through each step in the selection process. The first step is to find out what your needs are, then research to pinpoint the exact requirements and then write the RFP and send it out. That's straight forward, right? The second step is to whittle down your vendor selection list, which can be complicated — use RFP validation, comparisons, scripts (the storyboard) and vendor presentations. In the end, hold a no-holds barred in-house meeting and review everything, you should wind up with a short list of no more than three vendors that fits all the criteria. You can now take the final step — negotiation and selection. Here you develop and sharpen your negotiating strategy. How? Decide what's critical to the project and put it all down in a contract (use your legal team for this part). Call in the short list vendors and the race is on. Once you have selected a vendor willing to work within the negotiated terms and conditions, you can begin the final documentation, presentation to management and getting those signatures on the dotted line.

Following the above procedures enables you to utilize the best evaluation criteria, gather the necessary and objective data and guarantee that your overall evaluation process proceeds in a structured format. You'll also end up with a great paper trail, which can be useful if you need to explain how you arrived at your selection. Following the advice in this section should usher your Web-based business into many successful vendor partnerships.

CHAPTER 14

Web Hosting Services

Technology...is a queer thing; it brings great gifts with one hand,
and it stabs you in the back with the other.

C.P.Snow

There are a multitude of Web hosting services (a third party that sells you space on its Web servers) available. Most small Web-based businesses, in all probability, will not create and maintain their Web pages on their own in-house Web server. Instead, they will contract with a Web hosting service.

Your Web hosting decision is in all likelihood the single most important decision you'll make for your Web-based business. Why is that? A good Web hosting service will provide a place where your site will reside and operate quietly and efficiently in the background. However, if you choose a poor Web hosting service, you can expect a great deal of pain and frustration. The trick is to shop for the right match between the Web host and your Web site.

In your quest for the right hosting service for your Web site, start with the basics — how good, how reliable, and how industrial-strength is your potential host's connection to the Internet. Then check out what other services are offered to enable your Web-based business to have more functionality.

Although, at one level, all hosting services basically provide some hard disk space on powerful computers (the servers) that have 24-hour connections to the Internet, there are many differentiations, which I will discuss in detail in this chapter.

WEB HOSTING SERVICE MODELS

I want to dispel a common myth about Web hosting services: They are NOT all essentially the same. There are a multitude of options available to a Web-based business — from dedicated Web hosting to free Web hosting. Because there are so many hosting choices, decide what your own Web hosting requirements are before venturing forth. This allows you to narrow your shopping down to just a few hundred rather than thousands of choices.

Internet Service Providers (ISPs)

Throughout the world, are thousands of local ISPs that provide dial-up access, some of which also provide some type of ad hoc Web site hosting service. Many ISPs don't really understand the needs of a small Web-based business. Nor are they quick to offer improved service because their bread-and-butter is dial-up access and that's where their focus and investment goes. Although there are a few large ISPs that have a separate division that specializes in Web site hosting, many ISPs just don't have an adequate infrastructure for Web hosting.

Dedicated Web Hosting Services

All large or enterprise Web sites should make this service their only consideration. Sites that include streaming media or specialized server requirements must also seek out this type of service.

Dedicated Web hosting service by definition means a service that provides you with server space (virtual, dedicated or co-location) for your Web site — but usually without producing the basic ISP Internet access. One advantage of this type of service is that your customers won't be sharing valuable bandwidth (a big concern when choosing any type of hosting service) with the casual Web surfer checking their e-mail, downloading MP3 files, etc. What this means is that your customers will experience speedy access times, fast loading pages, and no shopping cart lag.

A dedicated Web hosting service's primarily business is offering server and rack space for businesses that do not want to manage their Web-based servers in-house. Okay, Web hosting services just might also offer dial-up service (ye ole ISP) as a convenience to its customers; but it's probably not going after the "casual surfer's" business.

You can find good Web hosting services whose options run the gamut from the basics to the "whole shebang." The market is over-supplied and to stand out in the crowd some Web hosting services offer some very nice (but expensive) high-end features. You will find that a good full-featured Web hosting service has a more "services" oriented approach — offering expertise in networking, or offering and managing complex software — as opposed to just selling space on it's servers hard drives.

Local Web Hosting Services

Check out the Web hosting services in your local community. These services can offer personalized attention and customized service, such as visiting your business in order to evaluate your hardware, examine your network, etc., and then making specific recommendations. For a small Web-based business, a local Web hosting service will, in many instances, have the facilities to help you market your business, for example, by providing a link to your Web site on its local business directory. Therefore, a small local brick-and-mortar making its move to the Web may be willing to trade off certain features offered by a larger hosting service for the extendibility of such a local Web hosting service. Note though that local Web hosting services are less likely to provide 24x7 technical support.

If you choose one of the small local hosting services, and your site becomes very active, don't be surprised if the host asks you to move your Web site to another service. Why? Because a good hosting service, even if small, will look out for the welfare of their overall constituency and might be afraid that traffic to a particularly popular Web site on their service will hurt the performance of other Web sites that they are hosting.

Web Developer Hosting

This type of Web hosting service is just now coming into its own. What is it? Basically a Web developer that has installed the capability of hosting Web sites for its own clients. If you are a small Web-based business, this isn't a bad option.

A Web developer usually provides hosting services via a server that sits in a corner somewhere with a small pipeline to the Internet (either a ISDN or some type of partial T-1 service). Many times a Web-based business, especially one with a small niche market, will find that the great service provided by such a hosting arrangement is more important than a large pipe to the Internet.

A Web developer's business is particularly customer-centric and will usually have the staff to help you with problems that might arise. However, there is a price to be paid: a slightly higher contract price, total dependence upon one service, and lack of 24x7 technical support. One piece of advice: If you decide to go this route, be careful to ensure that your hosting contract does not lock you into using only the Web developer's services (hosting or otherwise) for an extended period of time.

Another problem that might arise when you use your Web developer's hosting service is that the developer's name might be listed as the "Administrative Contact" with InterNIC. This identity confusion can cause problems and delays if you (at any time in the future) want to transfer your Web site and domain to another hosting service. So just make sure that your Web site developer isn't listed as the Administrative Contact. You can find out who is currently listed as Administrative Contact for your domain name at http://rs.internic.net/cgi-bin/whois.

Sub-domain or Non-virtual Account

What 99% of you don't need or want is the 4 or 5 MB of Web space that you can get from an ISP for a small monthly fee or maybe even free when you sign up for a regular Internet dial-up account. This type of service is referred to sometimes as a "sub-domain" or "non-virtual account." It allows you to build a very small, simple Web site that can be accessed by a URL that looks something like www.mystupidsite.ISP.com or www.ISP.com/~mystupid-site/homepage.html which means you have a directory on your ISP's Web site in which you can build your site. The profound drawback to the option is not only do you have a hard-to-remember URL for your Web site but if you ever move the site, you'll have to change the site's address. It's just not something to use for a serious commercial Web site.

Free Web Hosting Services

You don't want to place your Web-based business in the hands of a free Web hosting service because:

- You will be severely restricted in the things that you can do with your Web site.

- You won't be able to use your own domain name. You'll have to settle for something like www.freewebhosting.com/yourcompany.

- Although these Web hosting services normally give you between 2 and 10 megabytes of server space, many require you to display their advertising banners (or put up with annoying pop-up windows carrying their ads) and many won't allow you to display advertising from any other company.

- Most won't give you the easy-to-use FTP services to upload your Web pages. This means you will have to find another way to put your changes on the Web server.

- Very few will give you CGI-bins.

- Few, if any, provide secure servers for credit card purchases.

- Search engines normally take three to four times longer to list the submitted pages and give more "weightage" to sites that have their own domain names.

- You won't get unlimited autoresponders, nor the POP e-mail accounts you need.

- Most free Web hosting services will not give you access to your own server log files.

- You and your customers will experience frequent downtimes because of the heavy loads on the hosting company's servers.

- You will find that technical support is almost non existent.

Get the message — Don't use a free Web hosting service for your Web-based business — EVER.

DIFFERENT HOSTING NEEDS

There is a big difference between the Web requirements of a small to medium size Web-based business' hosting needs (even if it is a full-scale e-commerce site) and an established large or enterprise size business moving to the Web with a huge catalog of products and heavy traffic.

Whichever category you fall into, my one caveat is to shop around for your Web hosting service provider and thoroughly check references.

The Small to Medium Web Site

It is important that strict attention be paid to how your hosting service and your Web-based business will work together, including how your chosen hosting service can compliment your Web-based business.

Shopping for the right Web hosting service for your Web-based business is a difficult task at best. Look for a Web hosting service that offers a basic hosting package that includes:

- unlimited data transfer

- at least 15 MB of space (if e-mail, log files and system programs are included in the amount of MB offered)

- the option of FrontPage extensions, since so many Web sites are designed with FrontPage

There are numerous hosting services offering small business-specific hosting services. Learn to differentiate between a pitch and a promise. Here's how to start. Ask yourself what do you want from a hosting service and what do you want your Web site to do? To help you find the answers to these questions, make a list with a minimum of three columns:

WEB SITE'S HOSTING NEEDS

Projected Needs at End Of:

Needs	Current	1st Year	2nd Year
Reliability	90%	100%	100%
Services you want			
- server space	5MB	20MB	25 MB
(average small site needs 5MB)			
- # of e-mail boxes	5	15	20
- e-mail forwarding	no	maybe	maybe
- traffic allowance	75 MB	100MB	200MB
- ready-to-use CGI scripts	yes	maybe	maybe
Tracking tools	yes	no	no
Tools to register with search sites	yes	yes	yes
Scheduled backups	yes	yes	yes
Cost you can bear	$3600	$5000	$7500

Use this list to start your comparisons. The reason there are three columns is that what you want and need now won't be what you need a year from now. Don't switch hosting services without serious consideration. You can often avoid doing so by selecting a hosting service that provides a full range of hosting packages.

Many Web hosting services' offer Web design packages and most of them leave a lot to be desired. But, if you do consider this route, subject their in-house design team to the same scrutiny as you would a Web design firm or consultant. If you opt to do your own Web site design work, scrutinize any prepackaged Web design tools offered by the hosting service. Most of the time they are inadequate. Your best bet is to buy and use your own design software.

In response to the small businesses that are racing to the Web, many large ISPs have put into place numerous programs that target small Web sites. So for the small Web-based business, these services — Web site hosting, Web design, e-commerce — have been consolidated. While not optimal, they are a viable option to the strictly Web hosting service. AT&T WorldNet has redesigned its Small Business Center, and Prodigy, through its acquisition of BizOnThe.Net, offers small Web sites their own business-specific hosting needs. MindSpring offers four virtual hosting plans: The low-end package offers 30MB of server space and 2GB of downloads for $30 a month, and the high-end package offers 75MB of server space and 6GB of downloads for $100 a month. Then others, such as, EarthLink takes a pay-as-you-grow approach, charging small Web sites a base fee then additional fees for incremental additions to server space and traffic needs.

You will find in almost every hosting package a set number of e-mail mailboxes, a pre-defined amount of server space for your files, and a traffic allowance, which is the number of megabytes downloaded when customers request one of your Web pages. As with everything else, the more e-mail boxes, file space, etc. you want, the more you pay. Unless your Web site is very well established and image-driven with, for example, a large product catalog, you can start with the one of the less expensive plans offered by your chosen Web hosting services.

For most Web-based businesses, a Web hosting service makes the best sense. Paying a relatively small monthly fee to a service to host your Web site on its servers, which are maintained by its technical people, and connected to the Internet via its pipe, allows you to ameliorate hardware costs and avoid hiring expensive technical staff.

The Large to Enterprise Web Site

If you plan to establish a very high traffic site that provides chat room features and/or serves up large media content, such as graphic files in your product catalog, streaming media, etc., consider only the large national Web hosting services. These organizations provide, at a minimum:

- OC-3 or better connection to the Internet

- mirror sites

- 24-hour staffing

- redundancy (including its connection to the Internet backbone)

- security

   Be sure to verify:

- how many hours a day the technical support staff is available (it should be 24 x 7).

- how fast they respond and if there is a response time guarantee

- how much help the technical staff actually provides under various contract terms

Expect to pay a substantial sum for 24-hour full service technical support since people cost more than computers. However, for most large Web sites, all high-traffic Web sites and all enterprise sites, this type of service is mandatory.

A hosting service that will fit an enterprise Web site's needs must have a big fat pipeline; high-performance; mission-critical services; and a secure, high-speed, dedicated connection from your location to your hosted Web servers.

The expensive enterprise class hosting service contract should provide a project leader and an enterprise management team to run your Web site's entire server infrastructure, including the firewall, on a 24x7 basis. This team should manage, support, and upgrade Web applications, whether standard or proprietary, and add networking options, including a Virtual Private Network (VPN), Internet, frame relay, and dial services. An enterprise class hosting service contract is based on the scope of the project but should include at the minimum:

- dedicated, point-to-point, unshared T1 or T3 access to the Internet

- 24 x 7 service and support

- complete DNS services

- end-to-end implementation management

- online network utilization statistics

- choice of CPE solutions

- a fully managed service

- redundancy - T3 connections to diverse backbones, UPS and generator power backup

- a redundant network operations center

- High Availability Cluster Multiprocessing consisting of a primary machine and a live standby. Data contained on the primary server is seamlessly mirrored on the standby machine. If the primary should fail, the standby server will immediately assume the role of the primary machine.

- dedicated e-commerce that offers customized systems for purchases, services, and delivering order status and Web application hosting

- Web applications such as e-mail, human resources, finance, and other operations to secure off-site servers with high-speed access and a single point of contact

- VPN and Virtual Private Dial-up Networking, enabling businesses to connect their LANs, Web sites, business partners, branch offices, telecommuters, and mobile employees in an integrated, secure, and simple manner

- managed software services enabling the enterprise IT organization to provide for asset management, software distribution and management, network management, network performance tuning, and desktop management

- streaming media delivery through scalable, on-demand capability that distributes images to single and multiple locations to support videoconferencing, PC-to-PC conferencing, and video distribution services

A service contract like this does cost a pretty penny but it is worth it. Just ask yourself, what will it cost if your site is down for any length of time? Believe me when I say that, over a year's time your site will go down for some reason or other. Do you know how you'll handle this situation? Can you afford it when it does go down?

High-end Web hosting services is a very competitive market. AppliedTheory, Digex, Exodus, Frontier/Global Center, MCI WorldCom (UUNET), PSInet, and Qwest are all high-end Web hosting services offering sophisticated, large-scale, end-to-end solutions tailored not only to the enterprise customer's immediate needs, but engineered to respond to future demand, with an emphasis on customer support and service.

The right enterprise class hosting service will have trained system administrators, along with other qualified personnel, on site 24 x 7, monitoring your Web servers along with the other Web servers they host. The hosting service's technical personnel monitoring your site provide instant attention and follow pre-arranged instructions for any situation that arises. These instructions can be as varied as a call to a named technical person in your business, to handling the problem themselves, or anything in between.

All good hosting services are positioned to provide first class security through, for example, multi-staged access control and trained security personnel monitoring the equipment and the system, 24 x 7. Also, they will provide a configured router and will offer front-line firewall solutions which you are advised to take advantage of since neither are easy nor cheap to set up. It is well known in the industry that security is an entity that has a life of its own; therefore, leaving the matter to the security experts at a good hosting service is a wise choice.

Also, any good hosting service will provide redundant power supplies, the right air conditioning, and correct physical locations along with the necessary network links. A service should also provide automatic backups of your data along with off-site storage.

THE SHOPPING LIST

Shopping for the right Web hosting service for your Web-based business can be complicated. Start by creating a list of your Web site's specific requirements. Be sure to consider each of the following topics.

Size of Pipeline

First the pipeline or bandwidth (which connects your server to the Internet) — the more bandwidth you have, the more it costs. It is the mind-boggling expense of installing an adequate pipeline to the Internet that prohibits most Web-based businesses from setting up their Web servers in-house. High speed access is obviously key to having a responsive Web site. The provider should offer a minimum of T3 (45 Mbps) connectivity with sufficient bandwidth available for each client. This bandwidth should preferably be connected to a high speed Internet backbone (the worldwide structure of cables, routers and gateways that form the Internet). The more direct access your Web server has to the backbone the less likely your Web site will suffer from a "data traffic jam."

Mainly Web hosting services will charge you a monthly fee based on the amount of traffic your site receives. Some will connect you as directly to the backbone as possible and provide you with all the bandwidth you can use for one set fee.

Typically, a Web hosting service's computers are connected to the Internet backbone by T1 (at a minimum), T3 (the majority of local services), or some type of OC line (large professional services). (See Chapter 6 for a complete discussion on connectivity.) Albeit, you will find some small local Web hosting services and Web developer hosts that might have just an ISDN or "fractional T-1" connection to the Internet. Generally, your best is to look for a hosting service that offers at least a T-3 connection (unless, for example, your Web site serves a small niche market).

One common problem is data traffic jams. Ask a potential Web hosting service what options are available to you if you find your Web-site's bandwidth (speed of connection to the Internet) is compromised by another site hosting chat rooms, or a large multimedia site offering streaming audio and video.

Know Your Traffic Limits

Find out how many page hits (the number of times someone transfers one of your Web pages to his/her browser) are included in the basic price of a Web host's service. This will probably be stated in terms of megabytes of file transfer (amount of data transferred out of your site); if so, ask the host to translate it into an average hit rate. Although some Web hosting services have no limits, others will apply a surcharge if you go beyond a pre-determined limit. Then the way hosting companies charge you varies. Some charge for the number of hits (the number of times someone transfers one of your pages to his browser). Others charge according to the amount of data transferred out of your Web site. Either way, the busier your site, the more you'll be charged under these kind of pricing schedules.

Unlimited use may not be the nirvana you think it is. It could mean that there are sites on the service that are very busy resulting in the dreaded "data traffic jams." Nonetheless, most Web hosting services provide a certain minimum data transfer for free, which is generally more than adequate for most Web sites. A small site will probably need less than 100 MBs per month.

Compare traffic allowances. The hosting services that limit the amount of material that can be downloaded from your site each month may hit you with a large surcharge when that limit is exceeded. If your site offers products/services that require download (software, music, white papers, tech support information), you need to find a service that doesn't set limits. Some offer huge traffic allowances (several thousand MBs per month) for the same price as others that limit you to a few hundred MBs per month. Remember to plan ahead and allow for future growth of your site and its traffic.

Space

Web hosting services usually assign a Web site a defined amount of disk space for "virtual" service. In other words, when you're using a Web hosting service, most of you are buying space on their server's hard drives. You don't want to handicap your site with too little disk space, but at the same time you don't want to pay for unused disk space.

5 MBs is plenty of space for the Web pages and graphics for most small Web-based businesses as long as e-mail, log files, and system programs are not counted in the 5 MBs. Otherwise, more disk space is needed — these items take up considerable space — about 10 MBs. As a rule of thumb, 10 MBs of disk space equals about 100 Web pages, which is more than enough for the average Web site. Of course, if your Web site offers lots of images, sounds, animation, or applets, you'll need more space. Planning ahead can save

you money later on. If you expect to grow, look for a place that offers sites of 100 MBs or more. Ironically, you can find some Web hosting services that offer 300 MBs sites for less money than others offering only 30 MBs.

Ask the hosting service how many Web sites are hosted on each of its computers. Although most hosting services are not too forthcoming about this information, you should be able to at least learn if the host has any policy limits.

Uptime
Check the hosting service's reliability or "uptime" — the percentage of time the Web hosting service is up and running. Most claim 99.9 percent uptime, but ask around. UUNET, Concentric (who claims it has never been down) and Digex all have the best uptime ratings.

Multimedia
If your Web site utilizes multimedia, look for a Web hosting service that supports the most popular multimedia technology.

CGI Scripts
Specific CGI (Common Gateway Interface) scripts (small but highly potent bits of computer code) are important for an e-mail response form, a site search engine, and e-commerce support. It's a way to provide interactivity to Web pages, such as the handling of the input from forms, like using CGI to take information from a form and send it to your e-mail account. CGI scripts enable your Web site to accept credit card orders, and track everything a visitor does once they get on your site.It can also automate otherwise tedious processes such as signing customers up if you have a "registered users only" section on your Web site.

You will find Web hosting services have inconstant policies regarding CGI scripts. Some services:

- offer libraries of CGI scripts (CGI-bin directory) for your use

- offer libraries of CGI scripts (CGI-bin directory) for your use and let you install your own CGI scripts (your own CGI-bin directory)

- don't have a library but allow you to install your own CGI

- don't allow you to add any CGIs

I recommend that you find a service that at least allows you to add your own CGI scripts.

CGI-bin directory: You will need to reference programs in a CGI-bin directory. This directory will include such CGI programs as the e-mail message that is sent out by Web page forms. To do this you need a good forms-to-email program in your hosting service's main CGI-bin. If you must provide your own, you will need your own CGI-bin directory. It is absolutely essential that you have full control over your own CGI-bin.

Telnet Access

A shell account is a login account on a UNIX server and is based on a UNIX operating system. A telnet shell account allows you to interact with your site in a multitude of ways. Telnet is a common way to remotely control Web servers. You can think of it as if you were sitting behind the keyboard of the server. It lets you change, remove, and make new files, you can check your disk usage, clean out your server logs, read files, test scripts, and FTP files from other servers. With telnet you can change the permissions of a CGI file, change your password, create new directories, or just use programming tools such as C and PERL. That's the capability a telnet shell account gives you.

> Telnet is a powerful tool. It is a terminal emulation program (a program that makes your computer respond like a keyboard) for TCP/IP networks such as the Internet. The Telnet program runs on your computer and connects it to a remote computer (your Web server at your hosting service). You can then enter commands through the Telnet program and they will be executed as if you were entering them directly on the server console. This enables you to control the server and communicate with any other servers you might have at the hosting service.

The ability to modify files and directories is very useful for an active site. Windows95/98/NT comes equipped with a built in Telnet program. To start a Telnet session, you must log into a server by entering a valid username and password. Although Web hosting services are split down the middle as to whether they provide a shell account or not since limiting Telnet access admittedly does help in keeping hackers at bay and can eliminate downtime caused by human error. Without telnet you can end up incurring longer programming development time, which adds to your overall development costs. If you are denied Telnet access you can't compile programs written in C, C++, PERL, etc. Instead you must rely on the hosting service's technical support staff, which usually results in very irritating and expensive delays.

Web hosting services will usually allow FTP access to a CGI-bin directory but many, as stated previously, will not allow Telnet access. Telnet access is not a do or die requirement. Still, if you find a Web hosting service that offers it, and you are satisfied with their security set-up, it is an added bonus.

E-Commerce

When considering a Web hosting service's e-commerce offerings, please follow the advice set out in Chapter 9. As a "quickie update" remember that before putting your e-commerce in the hands of a hosting service, look closely at the critical components. The software should be intuitive with some kind of "wizard" to assist you with the set up, such as tools that provide category pages with links to individual items along with "Buy" links that can take the customer straight to the shopping cart. Next, look at the catalog builder. Can you create your product catalog offline and then post it to your Web site and link it to the database you use to track inventory?

Any Web hosting service offering an e-commerce package should also be able to help you with setting up a merchant account — the agreement between your Web-based business and your bank that allows you to take credit card orders. Also, you may need real-time credit card authorization (see Chapter 3) which will cost extra. And, last but not least, consider security. Are your credit card transactions protected, at a minimum, by the Secure Socket Layer (SSL)? If not, what security does your Web hosting service offer for order processing, especially credit card data? (See Chapter 7 for a detail discussion of security considerations.)

Technical Support

First rate technical support should be your primary consideration, especially if you're not a technical wizard. The Internet has no down time. Your server must be available 24 hours a day, 7 days a week. In the event of problems, immediate contact and assistance from your Web hosting service's technical staff is mandatory. Look for a hosting service that provides automatic monitoring of your Web site. This way, if there is a problem with the site they will be able to respond to it immediately. Ask if the Web hosting service's stated "24 x 7 service policy" means that server support, server monitoring and server availability are all covered.

The best and easiest way to check out a Web hosting service's technical support is to do the following:

- Write down a few questions to ask. Such as, what the hosting service's procedures are for handling problems with your server, how quickly do they respond, how much help do they provide and the type of technical support available. Make sure they give you a thorough answer.

- Place a few telephone calls — are they toll-free or local calls — day and night on different days of the week.

  Ask your questions.

  If you get the right answers stated in language you understand (i.e., not technospeak), and you didn't have to let the phone ring a 100 times or hold for 15 or more minutes, you've hit pay dirt.

- Send them a question by e-mail and see how long they take to respond.

- Check out the quality of their online documentation.

Web hosting services handle technical support in a variety of ways. Some hosting services have a policy of handling all their support through e-mail. The problem with this is that it's too easy for them to ignore e-mail or delay responses. You will find that 75% of the time you will need to talk to someone. Most low-cost Web-hosting companies will have telephone support, although they will not offer toll-free numbers; but at least you get to talk to a "live person." Other hosting services, some with toll free numbers, charge for telephone-based technical support. Just be sure you know where you stand before signing on that dotted line.

If you need 24-hour technical support — and larger companies and high-traffic Web sites do — then expect to pay substantially more. People are much more expensive than machines.

The best practice is to find others using the service and ask them about their experiences.

Value-added Services

You can expect a quality Web hosting service to have (in addition to a library of scripts that you can use to add forms, guestbooks, statistics, and so forth, to your site), e-commerce with shopping cart software, merchant account setup support, real-time processing availability, and more. They should also have support for Java, Shockwave, Cybercash, Real Audio, Real Video, VRML, secure transactions, and other utilities.

It is important that your chosen Web hosting service technical staff is familiar with the applications you plan to use. For example, if you're planning to use a particular application that requires special setup parameters, make sure your potential host is familiar with the application. If not, you just might end up spending an enormous amount of time trying to figure out how to configure it, or perhaps never figuring it out!

Site Administration

Quite a few quality Web hosting services offer Web-based site administration, although it is not an essential requirement when searching for the right Web hosting service (just a nice extra, especially for the non-technical Web site owners). With the proper Web-based administration tools, you can do things such as set up POP accounts and configure autoresponders through your Web browser since it is basically all point and click.

Even if the site administration tools are not Web-based, you will still need to update your pages, manage files, collect orders, retrieve data from forms, get statistics, and perform other housekeeping chores to your site. So find out how secure and user-friendly is the software you'll be using to do these things?

Ask the Web hosting service:

- Can you make changes anytime you want?

- Do these changes need to be audited?

- Can you place custom ASP scripts on the server?

Remember that your Web site is a direct reflection of you and your Web-based business. As such, you want to have sufficient control of your Web site so as to portray your business in the best "light" possible.

Flexibility

As with everything in life, flexibility is a nice perk. Ask if the Web hosting service will accept special requests or instructions.

Another concern is the ability to upgrade services. As your Web-based business grows so will your hosting needs. Ask if you can start out with an economy package and then upgrade as your needs and budget increase. Also check out how much it will cost for you to add more disk space, transfer more data, create more e-mail accounts, and so on.

Security

Security is of paramount importance. As such, find out what security features your Web hosting service offers or supports. Although many Web hosting services claim to be secure, when closely examined they fall far short of their claim. Find out if your Web hosting service can actually protect your data from the growing menace of outside threats and hackers. For example, the hosting service should have expert security staff on call to dispose of any potential threats.

Some key security and reliability issues you'll want to cover with a Web hosting service include:

- What kind of Internet firewall does the Web hosting service have in place to keep uninvited visitors out of its servers?

- How often does it conduct security audits and what other proactive steps does it take to address potential security holes?

- How are hackers kept out?

- Are back-ups performed daily to ensure data is never lost?

- Are all servers on an uninterruptible power supply (UPS) so data is always available even when there is a power outage? Also, what is their generator backup configuration?

- Since you will be taking orders on-line and maybe transferring sensitive information, you'll need a secure server (often referred to as an SSL server — a Secure Sockets Layer server). For instance, credit-card information typed into a form will be encrypted before being sent to your Web server. Some Web hosting services charge an additional fee to use the secure server, so ask. Look for hosting services that support transaction encryption standards like SSL and SET (See Chapter 7). You don't have to have a secure server to take orders online, but many people won't place orders unless you do.

- How does the Web hosting service go about getting sensitive information from your Web server to your back-office in a secure manner?

- Is 24-hour tech support available since you will want a hosting service that can handle technical issues at any time? Also ask if there is a separate tech support line for hosting customers, so you don't have to stay on hold for hours to get your questions answered.

- Does the hosting service use redundant connections so your customers can access your Web site even if a line goes down or is cut?

- Is the site physically secured so that only authorized personnel have physical access to servers?

Finding a Web hosting service that will maintain the integrity of your Web site is nearly as important as maintaining the availability of it. Having your server "hacked" is not something you want to experience so find out if the Web hosting service has taken the necessary steps to secure your Web site. In addition, ask about partitioning of users on shared servers, ability to encrypt user access and how the software security of the server is set up to prevent unauthorized access.

E-Mail

Almost all Web hosting services provide at least one e-mail account with your Web site, although sometimes you'll get several accounts. However, some hosting services charge extra for an e-mail account, so ask. Note that with a single e-mail account, you can retrieve e-mail that has been sent to various "alias" addresses such as webmaster@yourcompany.com, sales@yourcompany.com or info@yourcompany.com and so on.

Ask the Web hosting service how many e-mail addresses you are allowed since some services allow you to set up multiple "aliase" as mentioned above. Another feature Web-based businesses might find useful is the ability for different aliases to be forwarded to more than one e-mail address. For example, you might have stores in many different locales, with e-mail aliases for each of them.

Another mail forwarding feature offered by some Web hosting companies is the ability to automatically define certain types of incoming e-mail messages that are to be forwarded somewhere else. For instance, messages to marketing@yourcompany.com could be forwarded to marketing@acmemarketing.com. Remember to ask if there is a limit on how many accounts can be forwarded.

Another feature you might need is POP (Post Office Protocol) e-mail boxes on your Web hosting site, although for some smaller Web-based businesses, the POP e-mail box you have with your local access ISP probably covers your needs.

Larger Web-based businesses will need a minimum of 10 POP mailboxes. In addition to unlimited e-mail aliases along with the option of designating a catchall POP account so that any mail sent to anaddresseeunknown@yourcompany.com will be automatically forwarded to the catchall account since a customer may enter the e-mail address incorrectly. Add to this unlimited autoresponders since they undoubtedly will be an important part of your marketing strategy.

A mail responder, or autoresponder, is a program that automatically responds to incoming mail sent to certain addresses. Autoresponders let you specify e-mail addresses that allow for automatic and immediate posting of a pre-determined reply. For example, if someone sends e-mail to sales@yourcompany.com, a brochure-type e-mail message can be sent back. This is a good thing, so find a Web hosting service that provides this service.

Among the many useful attributes of a good autoresponder are that it allows you to:

- save the incoming message

- copy the e-mail address from the incoming message and put it in a text file, which that allows you to easily collect e-mail addresses

- quote the incoming message in the autoresponse

Online Promotion

A nice perk that numerous Web hosting services offer is online promotion. Some help with the registration of your Web site with the leading search engines and directories. Or maybe the offer a place where the Web hosting service will promote your site. And some Web hosts will even assist your Web site with online advertising.

Access/Traffic Reports

The reason you are putting up a Web site is to attract customers. Find out what access/traffic reporting services your Web hosting service provides. Access/traffic reports show you information about customers who visit your Web site. It is vital that any Web-based business knows:

- how often your site is accessed

- what Web pages are most popular

- where your customers are coming from (i.e., search engine referrals)

- how your customers get to your site (i.e. browser type)

With the right access/traffic reports you have the tools necessary for you to make sure that the site is doing everything it should be.

A good Web hosting service will have software that tracks all the traffic to and from your site with the necessary statistical data on that traffic (your customers). Some hosting services will automatically e-mail reports to you at pre-determined intervals. There are hosting services that even provided nice graphics showing the break down of a number of detailed categories with charts and numbers.

Ask your Web hosting service if:

- They provide access/traffic reports, if so, what kind, how detailed?

- Are the reports accessible online at anytime?

- Are the reports held in archive for later reference and for how long?

- How often are the reports compiled?

Multiple Domain Names

Ask your Web hosting service if they charge a fee for extra domains. Extra domains are very useful. Your primary domain is for your main Web-based business but you could use additional domain names to promote specific products. You can structure this in various ways. For instance, all the domains can point to the same directory; you can have separate directories for each domain; or a specific group of domains pointing to a single directory. Web hosting services have a variety of billing methods for this option, such as:

- an additional fee for each extra domain

- allowing a set number of domains and charging for any over the limit

- no charge at all for domains

You have to ask.

File Transfer Protocol (FTP)

You don't want to be restricted in any way when it comes to updating your Web pages. Look for a Web hosting service that will provide unlimited FTP access since that is how you upload your Web pages to your Web server. Most Web hosting companies provide this service.

Another type of FTP service you will need, if your Web site offers software downloads, is anonymous FTP (sometimes referred to as "public FTP"). This is different from FTP access to your Web site. Although it is possible to transfer files directly from your Web site, customers that don't have decent Web access will want to use the anonymous FTP option. Another feature of some anonymous FTPs is that an interrupted download can be resumed, i.e., if a file transfer stops somewhere in the middle due to an ISP or telephone line problem, the customer can continue the transfer where it stopped when he/she is able to get back online.

Server Performance

Another must is high performance Web servers. Find a Web hosting service that has server hardware that is high quality, reliable, fast CPUs, a lot of memory (the more the better), high speed disk drives, and redundant T-3 connections or better. Find out the brand names, the operating system loaded thereon and the Web server software provided. Also ask how often the Web hosting service updates and replaces their server hardware and software. Do not compromise on this issue.

One way to test your Web hosting service's servers is to use Net Mechanic's Server Start www.netmechanic.com. This is a nice free tool that measures the speed of access for all facets of access (network speed, DNS lookup, connect time, download time, and absence of timeouts). This product allows you to watch server performance for 8 hours and will send you an e-mail report. Run the check during both peak and non-peak times.

Password Protected Area

Password protected areas is one of the best ways to keep unwanted cretins out of your Web site. Unfortunately they can be problematic to set-up. Ask your Web hosting service if it has technical aid to assist you in this area. Note, it is quite simple to institute a password protected area using Microsoft FrontPage.

Backups (Server and Power)

Information on your servers will be in a constant state of change. Making daily backups is essential in case of a major server crash. Ask the Web hosting service if they provide off-site storage of the backup tapes. If you also have your database on the Web host's servers, talk to them about their procedure for backing up the database or if they can help you backup the database yourself.

Another important issue is a power backup system. Most Web hosting services do this as a matter of course, but it doesn't hurt to check that your Web host provides UPS and generator power backup.

Redundancy

The ability to be up and running no matter what the crisis is of critical importance. There are many elements to redundancy — see Chapter 5 for the full picture. However, a good Web hosting service must have redundant Internet connections, which are essential for providing uninterrupted service to your customers. With only one connection point, if the Internet line goes down, then your Web site is down.

Scalability

The best thing that can happen is that your Web-based business experiences a giant spurt of growth due to its popularity. However, can your Web hosting service handle such growth? If you feel that increased traffic on your Web site may become an issue, find a hosting service that can easily add bandwidth and processing power to meet any level of demand. A good quality Web hosting service will automatically monitor on a 24 x 7 basis both the servers and the Internet connections so that it can respond appropriately to any traffic or congestion problems, without any action on your part.

Mailing List Management

A mailing list is a discussion group based on the e-mail system. You can also use a mailing-list program to distribute a newsletter. A Web hosting service that offers the option of mailing list software such as Majordomo, is a bonus for all Web-based business and a must have for others. Ask your Web hosting service if a mailing list option is available and if so, the cost, how many mailing lists are permitted per site, and if there is a limit on the number of members per list.

Databases

Databases have their own issues. Be very careful to place your Web site on a Web hosting service that offers an operating system compatible with the system you use to maintain your database.

TYPES OF HOSTING ACCOUNTS

As you have noticed as you've read through this chapter, when it comes to Web hosting services, *one size does not fit all*. The same goes for the type of account you opt for with one of these services.

Virtual Hosting

Most small e-commerce Web sites should consider "virtual serving." This type of hosting service lets you run your Web site as if you had your own in-house Web server but with the advantage of the Web hosting service's pipeline to the Internet. Virtual serving just divides a server's capacity into several distinct "virtual" Web servers. With this set up a hosting service can host several sites on one computer. You have the ability to load software, set up your own CGI-bin directories, etc.

Most Web hosting services offer several varieties of "virtual serving." If you require a more powerful server or a server with a limited number of sites sharing it or a combination of both, you can get it (for an appropriate fee). You are only limited by what hardware configuration and bandwidth you can afford.

Your Own Dedicated Computer

Another option for a small e-commerce site that has heavy traffic and needs high availability or serves dynamically generated pages is to have a dedicated computer. Instead of sharing a server, you run your Web site on an individual computer, which lets you take the advantage of the Web hosting service's high-speed connection to the Internet, technical support and redundancy systems. There are many Web hosting services that offer leases for individual computers with the same management options as a virtual hosting contract.

Co-hosting or Co-locating

A large Web site might go with co-hosting (which is also referred to as co-locating) since it provides you with the most freedom — but it is expensive. With co-hosting you rent space in an Web hosting service's network server cabinet and pay to access the network that's connected to the Internet. In this situation you put your own computers in the server cabinet and service them yourself by obtaining access to the hosting facilities. This arrangement usually includes, for a fee, some kind of limited maintenance and back-up service.

Basic Server Farm

A basic server farm usually consists of several separate servers performing different functions — all residing in one server cabinet. A large Web site running various applications can contract with an enterprise-class hosting service that can separate the various server applications over different computers, some sharing tasks and others going it alone. It's good practice, for example, to put a processor-intensive application on a single server and also isolate any risky tasks. See Chapter 4 for discussion of hardware configurations.

In-house Hosting

Throughout this book the author has discussed the possibility of hosting a small Web site yourself. Don't try this with a large Web site. It would be a nightmare unless your company is already operating servers on a 24 x 7 basis with a 24 x 7 technical staff on the premises. The cost of the large bandwidth connection (pipeline) to the Internet is daunting. So, please find someplace to put your Web servers that has engineers on site 24 x 7 to monitor them and, in doing so, you will find yourself dealing with a much less costly and less problematic Web site.

It is difficult for many of you to forego the opportunity for hands-on experience with your servers, but once everything is correctly configured and running, there's very little to do. What you might need to do can be managed remotely whether you are running UNIX or NT systems.

SERVICE AGREEMENT

One last important thing is the service agreement. While you might attempt negotiation of a service agreement, you probably won't get far. Be realistic, an Web hosting service will not guarantee to provide 100% uptime, nor will it offer more than pro rata compensation for down time or reimbursement of paid service fees. That being said, most of the down time your site experiences will probably be a direct result of something that is done from your end and not from service outages attributable to the hosting service. Good Luck.

CHAPTER 15

Marketing a Web Site

The market is a place set apart where men may deceive each other.

Diogenes Laertius

Your new Web site is up and running — let customers know it's out there. Marketing a Web-based business is just as important as marketing a brick-and-mortar business. Even though a marketing plan is probably one of the most important elements of a successful business, it is usually the least thought out aspect of any new business. Formulate a strategic marketing plan. A properly instituted marketing plan gives your Web site an acceptance level that is normally far above the average Web site by providing a rational direction for your marketing activities.

MARKETING PLAN

A marketing plan is an important aspect of any new Web-based business. It is the best thing that you can do to help assure its growth. It should be a guide on which to base decisions and should ensure that everyone (you, your employees and consultants) is working toward the same goals. A properly drawn up and instituted marketing plan provides a guide for how to spend a Web site's promotional dollars. Your plan should include a sizable budget for market research. What you know about your target market and the information gleaned from market research will give you the basis for your marketing strategy.

Design your marketing plan to reach the 25-35% of your Web site's customers that are not brought to your site by search engines and directories. Whatever campaigns you decide upon, they must encourage customers to place an order or take some kind of action that will allow you to respond and thereby establish a relationship with that potential customer. Optimally a marketing plan and budget should cover promotion and advertising for 6 to 12 months. Your marketing costs are an *integral part of your business' budget.*

Develop market objectives that are realistic and specific. If possible, hire consultants to assist you in identifying the available market, who will be competing with you for that market share, and what a realistic projection for your share of that market might be. Most of this information can be gathered from:

- your internal records

- published market information from government statistics, chambers of commerce, newspapers, magazines, trade journals, banks, utility companies, city and county planning organizations, colleges and universities

- surveys, mail, telephone and personal interviews, opinion polls, market testing and feedback from customers

Analyze your site from a promotional point of view. So, with your marketing hat on, look at your site with a fresh eye and consider:

- What would a visitor consider as the main purpose of your Web site?

- What kind of person would be interested in your Web site?

- What does your Web site do or offer that stands out from other Web sites?

Now look at the competition:

- Are potential customers using the Web now?

- What are the strengths and weakness of the competition?

- What can be done to make the campaign's overall message superior to your competition's?

- What message would be most effective in drawing potential customers to your Web site?

- What would cinch that a potential customer is converted to an actual customer?

This research will give you a good idea as to how you should go about reaching your current and potential customers. In other words, where you should spend your advertising dollars: banner ads, targeted opt-in e-mail, newsletters (online or e-mail), traditional advertising methods (print, radio, television), incentives such as discounts and gift certificates, contests, and surveys.

The information you have gathered gives you a good starting point for your strategic marketing campaign.

As you formulate your marketing plan you want to consider:

Competitive Forces: Who are your major competitors now and who is likely to be your major competitors in the future? What response can you expect from those competitors to any change in your marketing strategy? How does the structure of the industry affect competitive forces in the industry?

Economic Forces: What is the general economic condition of the country or region where the majority of your customers reside (demographic research)? Are your consumers optimistic or pessimistic about the economy? What is your target market's buying power (demographic research)? What are the current spending patterns of your target market? Are your customers buying less or more from your Web site and why?

Socio-cultural Forces: How are society's demographics and values changing and how will these changes affect your Web-based business? What is the general attitude of society about the Internet, your business and products/services? What ethical issues should you address?

Legal and Regulatory Forces: What changes in various government regulations (domestic and foreign) are being proposed that would affect the way you operate? What affect will global agreements discussed such as NAFTA and GATT have on your Web-based business?

Technological Forces: What impact will changing technology have on your target market, if any? What technological changes will affect the way you operate your Web-site, sell your products/services, and conduct marketing activities?

Identify Target Market: What are the demographics (the study of the distribution, density and vital statistics of a population) of your target market, i.e., characteristics such as, sex, age, income, occupation, education, ethnic background, family life cycle, etc.? What are the geographic characteristics of this market, i.e., its location, accessibility, climate? What are the psychographics (the study of customers' human characteristics) of this market, i.e., attitudes, opinions, interests, motives, lifestyles? What are the product-usage characteristics of this market?

Needs Analysis: What are the current needs of your target market? How well is your Web site and its products/services meeting these needs? How are your competitors' meeting these needs? How are the needs of your target market expected to change in the near and distant futures?

Market Positioning

Your Web site and its products/services cannot be all things to all people. Look at margarine or aspirin, for example, and the extremes that have been taken to create brand awareness and product differentiation. Marketing requires continual vigilance. Your marketing position must be able to change to keep up with the current conditions of the market. Constantly monitor what is happening in your "space" so that you always have up-to-date knowledge of your marketplace. After you accumulate accurate information about your customers, the segments they fit into and the buying motives of those segments, you can select the marketing position that makes the most sense.

Performance Analysis

At this moment, how is your Web site performing in terms of sales volume, market share, and profitability? How does this compare to other Web sites in your "space"? What is the overall performance of your entire competitive marketplace? If your Web site's performance is improving, what actions can you take to ensure that it continues to improve? What are your Web-based business' Strengths, Weaknesses, Opportunities, Threats (SWOT - you will hear this term a lot in marketing circles)?

Marketing Objectives

Once you have the answers to the above questions, you are ready to set out your marketing objectives. What are your current marketing objectives? Are your objectives consistent with recent changes in the marketing environment and/or needs of your target market? What is the specific and measurable outcome and time frame for completing each objective? How does each objective take advantage of a strength or opportunity and/or convert a weakness or threat? How is each objective consistent with your Web-based business' goals and mission?

Marketing Strategy

Next comes your marketing strategy. Once you have completed the research on your target market with specifics such as demographic, geographic, psychographic, and product-usage characteristics, justification for the selection of this target market, and competitors in this market, look at your marketing mix (pricing, distribution and promotion strategies). How does this marketing mix give you a competitive advantage in your target market? Is this competitive advantage sustainable? Why or why not?

Implementation

Now it is time to implement your marketing plan. Identify a marketing team. This team can be formed from your business' internal personnel and consultants, along with persons that have intimate knowledge of the Web, Web marketing and (if you are a click-and-mortar) how the Web can be integrated with current marketing plans. In addition, you need to find graphic designers, copywriters and illustrators. Once the team is in place, it should plan and focus on strategic revenue goals. Don't let the team focus on the number of hits your site receives due to an overall advertising, marketing and PR campaign while ignoring whether the campaign achieved the expected revenue goals. Make it clear as to whom has the decision-making authority. Who is responsible for what and what is the timetable for completion?

Don't forget to coordinate your marketing activities. What does this mean? Here are a few example: If you plan to unveil a campaign during the Super Bowl you must ensure that your Web site and your Web hosting service have the facilities to handle the added traffic. If you are a brick-and-mortar, coordinate special promotions. If you plan to offer a specific item as, let's say, a two-for-one promotion, take steps to assure that there is adequate inventory. Additional call center help is usually necessary when launching any kind of campaign.

Finally, institute a procedure to monitor the success or failure of your marketing activities. Will a formal marketing audit be performed? If so, what will be the scope of the audit? Will specialized audits be performed? If so, which marketing functions will be analyzed?

When drawing up your marketing plan, think about where you want your business to be in three years and how you plan to get there — that's your marketing plan in a nutshell. At no time should you forget that marketing your Web-based business never ends. Once you have all of your information and your marketing plan in place, you will need to continuously revisit, revise, refine and revamp it to accommodate changes in your marketplace.

Other Elements for Consideration

Some other elements that fit within a good marketing plan are:

- distribution channels

- pricing and terms of sale

- promotion and advertising plan

- marketing budget

- inventory selection and management

- visual merchandising

- customer relations

With a marketing plan in place you have a considered strategy to out maneuver your competition by capitalizing on their weaknesses and emphasizing your Web-based business' strengths. By increasing market awareness of the offerings of your Web site, you bring new customers.

Marketing Venues

Your marketing plan should include marketing through several venues, such as print media, banner ads, affiliates, television ads, radio ads, newsletters, e-mail, etc. However, with the Web's extensive capabilities available for a reasonable cost, you should make it the cornerstone.

Consistency

Create a consistent marketing message for your Web site that reflects its mission and goals. This theme will provide consistency to your presentation and continuity over time. The theme can remain constant, although the look and content will certainly change. Always keep the look and content focused on your potential customers' wants and needs and take advantage of your competitions' shortcomings.

Analysis

Your marketing plan should become the basis for analysis of whether customer needs are being met through analyzing sales trends, customer's comments, amount of returns, requests for unavailable merchandise, repeat customers, surveys, etc. At some point you will want to consider offering new products — either related or unrelated to current ones — and go after new target markets or penetrate current markets more deeply.

Brick-and-Mortar Advantage

If you have a brick-and-mortar, make use of it. How? By making certain that your Web site's information is prominent in all of the advertisements for your traditional business and check that your Web site's address is prominent on all your marketing and advertising material, business cards, letterhead, envelopes, brochures, shopping bags, giveaways such as hats and pens, etc. Also make your employees aware of the importance of promoting the online business.

If you are the owner of a successful brick-and-mortar brand, then you already possess a key advantages in your online venture — name-recognition. Just this fact alone will help make your Web site more valuable and allow it to obtain profitability more quickly.

SEARCH ENGINES, DIRECTORIES, ETC.

You've designed a wonderful Web site, but you are disappointed with the traffic and sales your site is generating so you look for a solution. As you research the problem, you'll find the majority of all Web sites' traffic come from search engine referrals — maybe your Web site is not getting these referrals. The reason probably is that you have not designed your pages correctly for search engine placement or you have not submitted your Web site correctly with the various search engines (or a little of both).

We all know that it's sometimes difficult to find what you're looking for on the World Wide Web. Even using a search engine or directory service you still need a fairly specific search — if you don't want a million returns. Your potential customers are in the same predicament. Take the time and make the effort to guarantee that your Web site is listed well for the keywords that are important to you. (Confused? — read on.) Most search engines spider the Web looking for new pages to add to their database or index. You can wait for one of these spiders to locate your site, go to the search engine site and tell them about your new Web site, or use one of the many site submission services.

Spiders: There are two types of spiders — shallow and deep. A **shallow spider** either spiders the URL given and stops or only spiders the URLs it finds within a single level of directories. A **deep spider** takes the URL and spiders every page within the Web site, despite the levels of directories it must delve into.

Once your pages are added to the relevant indexes, your potential customers can search using various keywords to find pages that best match their search criteria. Appearing within the first 20 returns of any relevant search is critical to driving customers to your Web site. Search engines use their own special "magic" to determine the rank or position of importance of each individual Web site. The exact rules that the search engines and indexes use to rank pages for relevance are generally tough to ascertain and change often.

How Search Engines and Directory Services Work

Search engines have spiders that crawl the Web 24 hours a day, finding and indexing pages. These spiders then return with the information they have gathered and that is what is returned when you type in a string of keywords in a search engine's "search box".

Directories, for the most part, use real people to compile their information and then supplement that information with a search engine.

There are three important elements to search engines:

1. The database operates on the same principles as your Web site's database. The database consists of indexed descriptions of Web pages including a link list with a small description for each link. When a search request is received from a surfer, these databases utilize special search algorithms, using keywords, to find needed Web pages.

2. Search engines give each page they find a ranking as to the quality of the match to the surfer's search query. Relevant scores reflect the number of times a search term appears, if it appears in the title, if it appears at the beginning of the page or HTML tags, and if all the search terms are near each other. Some engines allow the user to control the relevance score by giving a different weight to each search word. A search term used too many times within a page can be considered Web spamming (for which search engines penalize) so don't overdo the use of a keyword or phrase on a page (don't exceed the 15-25 count range).

3. Each search engine has its own peculiar ranking method. For example, if there are no links to other sites or pages within a Web site (a single page Web site) some search engines will not list that Web site.

This section has been written with the hope that when you have completed reading it you will understand what search engines do with all of your Web pages and with that understanding will come the search engine exposure that your new Web site needs. To find out what you can do to stimulate traffic, read on.

Designing for Search Engines

If you ignore the criteria necessary for optimal placement by search engines, your Web site will miss out on traffic that you would otherwise receive if your Web site had been designed so that search engines could find and crawl your pages. If your Web pages are listed but are not within the first two or three pages of results, you lose. When someone queries a search engine for a keyword related to your site's products/services, does your Web pages appear in the top 20 matches, or does your competition? This section has suggestions and ideas that will get you started on breaking into the coveted "top 20" inner sanctum.

When designing your new Web site, take into consideration the inner workings of search engines. Seven of the most popular search engines use spiders to index pages. They are Alta Vista, Google, Excite/Webcrawler, Hotbot, Go, Lycos and Northern Light. These spiders are small programs that gives weight to the placement and frequency of words. This includes related words and word relevance along with other criteria, such as title, placement of keywords, and meta tags within your HTML code. Be sure to give a descriptive title (five word or so) to each page of your Web site. After you have submitted your URL to a search engine, it sends a spider to "investigate" your new Web site. Here is why designing for search engines is so important: *The information the spider returns will be exactly what appears in the "results page" of the search engine.*

Search engines vary on how they rank Web sites, but every Web page should include:

- page TITLE tag

- keyword meta tag which is more than one word

- description meta tag

- !— comments tags —

- first 25 words (or 255 characters) of text

- NO FRAMES tag

- hidden FORM tag

- HTML tags

- ALT tags

Title: The title you choose will be the most important decision you make affecting search engine ranking and listing. There is no specific science to it — just make it simple. Look at the Web page and the first five or so descriptive words that come to mind can be the title. Another way to look it — think of your title as a catchy headline for an ad.

Text: When it comes to the text of a submitted Web page the search engines vary their indexing procedure. While some will index the text of a submitted page others will only take into account the first 25 words (or 255 characters) of a submitted page (25/255 rule). So, write the text of a submitted page using the important keywords more than once in the first 25 words.

Something else you can do is to create at the top of a submitted Web page, a transparent GIF image that is one pixel in size and inside the ALT tag insert a description of the page using the 25/255 rule.

Meta Tags: They are an indispensable tool in your battle for search engine ranking. Put them, along with keywords relevant to each specific page, on each page of your Web site.

When we discuss meta tags in this chapter we are discussing only description and keyword tags. A description meta tag is exactly what it sounds like — it gives a description of a Web page for the search engine summary. A keyword meta tag is again exactly what it states — it gives keywords (which should never be fewer than two words) for the search engine to associate with a specific Web page. These meta tags, which go inside the header tags, are crucial to properly index your Web site with search engines. Your meta tags should reflect the content of the first couple of sentences of the main body. It is important that you make certain that the words you use in your keyword tags are words that someone would type in to find your Web site. If you don't insert meta tags on each page the search engine's spider will just copy the first 25 words or 255 characters it finds (25/255 rule).

Keyword hints:

- Keywords are target words that will drive people to your Web site.

- Always use the plural of the word. Searching for "car" with find sites with "cars" in their keywords but searching for "cars" will not find sites with only the singular "car" in their keywords.

- Almost any site on the Web could use "Web," "Internet," "net," or "services," as a descriptive keyword. Don't! Using these and other like words to target potential customers is fruitless and most of the spiders actively ignore common words such as these.

- Include incorrect spellings of keywords that are routinely misspelled. For example, the word "accommodations" is commonly spelled as "accomodations" so include both in your keywords.

An example:

HEAD

TITLEBest Online Widget Store in the Universe/TITLE

DEFANGED_META name=""description" content=""An online store with all the Widgets you would ever want."

DEFANGED_META name= "keywords" content= "widgets, widget accessories, widget howto, widget books, widget articles, widget technical papers, widget software, working with widgets, designing with widgets."

For guidelines on what you should do with meta tags, go to a search engine, say Hotbot, search for a term or word that you hope someone would use to find your Web site. Then go to the first 20 Web sites and use the "view source" feature of your browser to see what kind of meta tags each of these sites use. Study them and understand their relationship to the Web page, then use this information when you are composing your own meta tags.

Keywords: There are two ways to approach keywords: A *blanket strategy* and a *targeted strategy*. When you use a large list of keywords, your pages will be found by a variety of surfers using a extensive range of search strings, but your Web pages will not, in all probability, be among the top ranking pages — this is the *blanket strategy*. When you use a limited number of keywords, the density of these few keywords increase and therefore put them higher up the list — the *targeted strategy*.

If you have a Web site that offers either a limited number of products/services or products/services that can be adequately covered with a short keyword list then the target strategy is for you. In other words, you're confident that potential customers will search for those specific words above all others. However, if you have a wide variety of products/services on your Web site (such as drugstore.com or outpost.com), then you might use the blanket method. Or consider the doorway page, mentioned later in this section.

Keyword Mix: Pay attention to your keyword mix. Keyword density (the ratio of a keyword or keyphrase to the total words [depth] on a page) is the factor that search engines most consider when assigning relevancy ratings to Web pages. Achieving the right keyword or keyphrase mix has become almost a science. Some search engines look for various combinations of keyword density, i.e., the number of keywords versus total word count must be within a certain range, and to complicate matters, they assign different "weights" to components such as Title, Meta Tags, Links, Body Text, Headline, etc.

If your keyword density is too low, your page will not be rated high enough in relevancy and, conversely, if too high, then your site may be penalized for "keyword stuffing." I know this sounds very complicated but there is some help — keyword optimizing tools such as GRSoftware's Keyword Density Analyzer (www.grsoftware.net) and Webposition Gold at www.website-promoters.com. Or check out www.keyworddensity.com and www.webjectives.com/keyword, which provide free online analysis of any Web page.

Doorway Pages: Search engines do a poor job of indexing and scoring Web pages using dynamically generated pages, frames, or Java Script. This is where doorway pages, entry or bridge pages (they all mean the same thing), come in.

Another use for doorway pages is to create alternate entrances (doorway pages) to your Web site so as to target a specific search engine with a page designed to deal with that search engine's criteria. Although doorway pages should be carefully designed to target specific keywords for individual search engines, they should also provide customer-centric information and point the customer to the "guts" of your Web site. They should have the same look and feel as the rest of your Web site. When your doorway page adds to your customers' experience of your Web site, they will be more apt to appreciate and purchase your products/services.

Doorway pages can help you obtain a high ranking using the unique ranking algorithms of each search engine. On the average, a Web page that will be highly ranked by one search engine may not fare as well on another. The search engines that you want to cater to are: Google, Excite/WebCrawler, Go, Lycos, HotBot(Inktomi), AltaVista, and Northern Light. Ideally, you need one doorway page for each of these seven search engines for each keyword or keyword phrase that a potential customer might use to find your site. For example, if you anticipate that normally customers will search for your Web site using one of five different keywords/phrases, then you'll need 35 doorway pages — 7 search engines times 5 keywords/phrases.

There are three types of doorway pages:

- A page that invites the customer to continue on to your Web site's home page (at the same time it provides the specific search engine with a page that it will find highly relevant).

- A page that is semi-invisible to the customer through the use of a Java script redirection technique. The page that is submitted to the search engine is stripped down to the minimum so that the search engine finds it highly relevant but a customer will only see the page as a "flash" before the real page is presented to the browser. There are two problems with this method: If your customers' browser is not enabled for Java script, they will see the unattractive stripped down page. Then, some search engines are beginning to find the "redirection" code and are downgrading the relevancy of the page.

- A doorway page that is completely invisible to the customers using Agent or IP address delivery. That is where software like Ipush (www.ipush.net) comes in. Ipush is an IP based delivery and cloaking system designed to help you get the best possible search engine results and keep them. An oversimplification of this software is that it "cloaks" the doorway pages so that only the spiders from a specific search engine sees a specific page. This allows you to:

- never worry about your visitors seeing your doorway pages. Since they won't ever see them, you can design them strictly based on a particular engines algorithm. They may make no sense at all, but the engine they were designed for will love them.

- keep your rankings private, since they won't be able to see the HTML code that got the ranking

- design your regular pages freely without fear of hurting your rankings

- use multiple pages without the worry of hitting the limit in any search engine's criteria (go to www.ipush.net for details)

As a side note: Yahoo! does not accept doorway pages.

To find all the nitty gritty details necessary to design effective doorway pages, search the Web with one of the many search engines using the keywords "doorway pages." Or visit www.spider-food.net for extensive information on doorway pages and other search engine goodies. Another great site is www.spiderhunter.com where you can find a tutorial on cloaking techniques plus free cloaking script for your use, plus many other interesting details about spiders.

How to Register Web Pages

The best practice (there are exceptions) is to submit each page of your Web site, individually, to all of the search engines and directories. You may think that submitting each and every page of your Web site is not necessary since some pages may have, for example, investor information or contact information; however, every page that is listed is like an entry in a drawing — the more entries, the more chances you have.

You might opt to submit some of your Web pages by hand to specific search engines and automate the rest using Web positioning software such as Submitta (www.submitta.com), Webposition Gold (www.website-promoters.com) (mentioned previously), or check out one of the many Web site Promotion services available online. If you want to try it yourself here is a guide:

- Submit your main URL (i.e. http://yourdomainname.com) after you have finished designing your Web site.

- Submit other important pages in weekly intervals and in very small batches (no more than 10 a day) since search engines are very sensitive to what they consider spamming.

- A large Web site should submit its most important and customer-centric Web pages, keyword-wise that is, since it is easy for a Web site with 200 or so pages to hit their page limit (usually 50 or so pages) with search engines.

- Once you have submitted all of your Web pages, you need to not only re-submit each time you make substantial changes to a page but, also, once every three or so months re-submit the pages following the procedure set out above.

- Pages that are generated "on the fly" usually will not be indexed, so don't submit them.

- If you have pages with frames, don't submit them since most spiders will not crawl a page with frames (no matter what you might have read to the contrary).

- Test and check to see how your Web site rates with the search engines 6 weeks or so after your submission procedure is completed.

- Monitor your Web site listings regularly. Sometimes your listing can just disappear or some kind of error can cause the link to become bad, etc. When you find something wrong, re-submit that Web page.

Pay attention to how your Web site is listed on a search engine. Does it concisely state what your Web site is and the products/services provided? To assure that your search engine listing provides the proper information needed by the surfing public, use your title tag (e.g. TITLEBest Online Widget Store in the Universe /TITLE). Search engines then use as the descriptive paragraph one of the following, depending on the search engine: either your description tag (DEFANGED_META name="description" content="An online store with all the Widgets you would ever want.") or the first 250 words (or so) of visible text on your site.

Although it will take a little effort, it is important that you balance these tags. In other words, sometimes what you need to put in as a title or descriptive tag (to get a high ranking with a particular search engine) will not help you in your quest to have potential customers easily find your page through commonly used keyword searches.

Directories

Directories are differentiated from search engines in that information is categorized by real people instead of using a spider. Each directory has an in-depth submission form. Remember there are real humans manning the directories requiring lots of information to index your Web site. Note:

- It is vital that you carefully consider and choose your 25-word description and category that you want your Web site to be listed under. Once it is submitted it's very difficult to change your mind later.

- Find the best category listing for your Web site. The best way to do this is to go to that directory, search for a word or phrase you hope would be most used to find your Web site — the resulting category is the category for which you should submit your Web site.

- Provide an accurate, concise description of your Web site — using 25 words or less is the key to success. It is interesting though that if your Web site has graphics or photos and you state that in the submission form, your Web site will have a slight edge over other similar sites without graphics or photos.

When it comes to directories, since they are compiled by thinking humans, a good site, with good content, has a better chance of being listed.

Yahoo!

Yahoo! is in a category all unto itself. Yahoo! is a categorized listing that also has a search engine. Through an alliance with first Alta Vista and then Hotbot and now Google, when a surfer makes a search request, if no listing is found within Yahoo! then the search is automatically and transparently defaulted to the larger, spider-generated database. So even though you may think your Web site has a Yahoo! listing when you see your site in a Yahoo! results list, it may have, in fact, been generated from the search engine's larger database. This isn't the same as a true Yahoo! listing.

It is very difficult to get a good listing on Yahoo!, but it is well worth the effort since it is the most popular site on the Web. Much of the traffic to your site will be generated by Yahoo! — if you can obtain a successful listing.

Paid Listing Services

Even a paid listing service has its place. If you can afford it, your Web site can have one of the top rankings and you don't have to worry about meta tags, etc. The author must admit surfers do use them, just check out the popularity of GoTo.com. Other fee based search engines are findwhat.com, knoodle.com, onesearch.com, etc., if you are so inclined, check them out.

Conclusion

Understanding the peculiarities of search engines and directories is a complex subject. I have tried to cover what is necessary to give your Web site the best chance for success. But for those willing to delve deeper, an essential Web site is www.searchenginewatch.com. This is a good, quality site with wonderful information, use it often. Although it has an abundance of free information, if you join, as a member you will find an even greater wealth of information at your fingertips.

Note that the average time between your original submission to a search engine or directory and getting it into their database is about 5-8 weeks.

Finally, don't obsess over your search engine and directory listing and ranking, just follow what is set out above, and then move on. If you don't get traffic from one certain search engine, yes, check it out but if you can't figure out why, forget it and move on. There are many ways to market your new Web site, search engines and directories, although very important, are just part of the process.

ON-SITE MARKETING TECHNIQUES

How do you keep your customers coming back for more? On-site marketing of your Web site involves search engine submissions, strategic links, optimizing your copy, banner ads, opt-in e-mail, client retention services, affiliate programs, press releases and much more. In other words, it's whatever will work to draw potential customers to your Web site then convert them into paying customers. You want to build brand awareness, foster relationships with your customers, encourage repeat business and return visits to your Web site.

Established brick-and-mortars that have moved their business (or elements of their business) online must take care to reflect the essence of its brick-and-mortar brand, work with the brand, make sure that it takes the brand online appropriately. In other words, don't jeopardize your product by using marketing gimmicks online that you would not do in your traditional business.

To keep your customers coming back for more, include in your marketing plan strategies for:

- targeted opt-in e-mail which means that the recipients have specifically requested e-mail relating to a particular topic

- online newsletters

- content updates

- incentives, contests, and surveys

Some examples are a newsletter for registered visitors, a free gift for answering a questionnaire or for a referral, or a monthly drawing for one of your products. All of these suggestions (out of many that can be implemented) not only build traffic but also start you well on the road toward collecting data on your customers' demographics and offer the opportunity to amass your customers' e-mail addresses for use in future marketing campaigns.

Solicit Customer Feedback

Many astute business people don't understand how the aggressive solicitation of customer feedback can be a marketing tactic, but here's how.

Your first step is to create a short, say 25-question, customer survey that has a prominent position on your Web site. When customers take time to fill-out the survey, thank them by issuing a $5 gift certificate or some other "good" giveaway. Compile the information obtained from the survey and use it to fuel growth and change so that your site is always new and exciting. Also, using a survey allows you to find out what your customers' like and dislike about your site.

Another benefit from using the survey method is you get your customer's information — name, e-mail address and maybe even their snail mail address — all very useful for sending out future promotions. But be careful not to annoy your customers. It is advisable to mitigate the possible irritation caused by direct-mail (either e-mail or snail mail) by including something your customers will appreciate such as a newsletter or a certificate for redemption of a small gift or gift certificate; which can, in turn, result in customer appreciation.

Another way to use your survey form is for testimonial feedback that you can then use as content on your Web site. For example, if you offer a certain brand of shoes, in one of your surveys you can ask for opinions or comments about that brand. Use those comments on your Web site, such as, "I didn't need these shoes but they reminded me of when I was a child," or "I just wanted them because they were different."

Links

As mentioned earlier, numerous search engines use link popularity when ranking Web sites. This means starting a strategic linking program is a must for any new Web site. When a search engine sees a Web site that has a lot of other Web sites linking to it, it naturally assumes this profusion of links means it is a site with compelling content and is well-regarded in the Web neighborhood.

So what are you going to do? Immediately start working on negotiating reciprocal links, especially with Web sites that consistently appear in the "top twenty." Having a good base of incoming links from other Web sites is as important as providing links to the "top twenty" on your Web site. Remember this can also include your competitors' sites. Why? If any of your competitors' sites are among the "top twenty" returns when a search is done for "shoes" leading customers to that site and they don't find what they are looking for on your competitor's site, but see your link, guess what — they will end up on your site. You will be surprised how many of your so-called competitors will be very glad to link to your site in return for a link back. Why? Because the next time **your** Web site may show up in the "top twenty" when a potential customer uses a different search criteria.

Work hard to develop link partnerships with Web sites that are popular with your customers. How can you know what's popular? Use those surveys!

Quality links are the only links you should consider when developing your links strategy. Quality links are links that provide a valuable resource your customers will appreciate. Links give you the opportunity to provide a useful service for a potential customer even if there was no sale made at that specific time. The fact that you did provide the customer with information that was helpful will be remembered. A customer remembers the Web sites that enables them to accomplish their goal — even though the final purchase may not be made on your Web site. But you have provided value to your potential customers and that is crucial to bringing them back to your Web site.

There are many ways you can exchange links. Links can be banners, links can be placed in e-mails, links can be placed within informational text on your Web site, links can be an award, links can be provided within a buyer's guide or directory. Okay, now you get the idea, so go for it. Try any variety of these links or all of them — just do them tastefully and don't let the links distract from the presentation of your products/services. Links not only help with search engine ranking, they feed traffic to your site directly and they help to create name recognition. All good things!

Now, how to go about generating links? First decide:

- Which Web sites do you want as a link partner?
- Which Web sites would be of value to your customers? For example, ask your customers, in a survey:
    Where do you go for information and resources?
    Where do you shop in the traditional world?
    - What other Web sites do you visit when seeking the same product/service?

- Which Web sites offer a products/services that compliment your offerings?
- Which Web sites do you consider to be your competitors?

When vacillating on whether to establish a link relationship with a specific competitor, if you are offering a quality product that is competitively priced, a link to a competitor's site won't hurt you. It can actually help by providing your customers the information necessary to make a purchasing decision. Your customers aren't stupid, the Internet is a great venue for comparison shopping, so they will probably be visiting your competitors anyway. Make it easy for them, they'll appreciate it. Remember Miracle on 42nd Street — Gimbles referring customers to Macys and vice versa — same theory here.

Before searching for link partners, consider what kind of partner you want and what you have to offer the potential partner. Be diligent, be open to opportunities, be always on the lookout for a potential quality link relationship. If you are on a Web site that you think might have potential, act immediately, send an e-mail, use their feedback form.

Banner Ads

Banner ads are just small digital billboards that one Web site pays (in one way or another) to be placed on another Web site. When potential customers click on a banner placed within another Web site, they are sent to that Web site. Various studies have shown that the most powerful word in a banner ad is "free," that simplicity sells, and graphics enhance a message. If a banner is designed correctly, it doesn't distract from the message. Elements you need in a good banner design are:

- an attention-getting element

- a call to action

- a reason to click through

- content that ignites clicks, i.e., it tells them to give the banner a click

- placement of your Web site's logo somewhere within the ad

When a potential customer clicks on your banner ad to visit your Web site, it is called a "click-through." The ratio of impressions to click-throughs is called the CTR (click-through ratio). An effective banner ad design and astute placement on a compatible high traffic site contributes to the obtainment of a high CTR, which can double the click-through rate of your ad, thereby doubling your Return on Investment (ROI). A study by Doubleclick (www.doubleclick.com) found that:

- after the fourth impression, response rates dropped from 2.7% to under 1% (banner burnout)

- you need to focus on four important issues (creativity, targeting, frequency and content)

- the use of simple animation can increase response rates 25% just be sure that the animation doesn't slow downloading of the ad

- the use of cryptic messages can increase CRT by 18%, but probably do not attract potential customers or reinforce branding

- the use of humor is very effective

- using a question within the ad can raise CRT by 16%

- using phrases such as "Click Here" tend to improve response by 15%

- offering free goods or services generally improves CRT

- using bright colors in the design is more effective

- the use of a message that gives a sense of urgency actually decreases the CRT

If you aren't careful, banner ads often fade into the digital woodwork — even if you use animation and other special effects. If not managed right, banner advertising can be expensive and ineffective. Be very careful with your ad placement and make certain that you do not overpay for ad placement on Web sites that do not produce real customers to your site. Place banner ads on Web sites that you know your target customers visit. Targeting equates to better qualified customers, or potential customers that are more likely to complete the sale. How can you know — ask the question in your online surveys.

It is interesting to note that a study by ZDNet found that animated ads generated CTR at least 15% higher than static ads, and in some cases as much as 40% higher. However, animation does not take the place of response-driven copy and a creative idea. Avoid animation that takes a long time to download. But with simple, creative animation:

- more potential customers notice and pay attention to a banner ad if it has animation, even if they don't click on it

- potential customers are more likely to click for more information if the animation is done in an effective way (i.e. emphasize what product is about)

- the animated ad must have a strong, well-crafted message and a clear call to action

Frequency (the number of times a viewer sees an ad) is an important factor when planning a banner campaign to build your brand awareness. In addition to maximizing your ad dollar, controlling ad frequency can open up new creative doors by allowing you to create a custom banner package for your branding campaign. The correct delivery frequency is necessary for banner ad success and will help determine how successful your branding campaign will be. The right frequency is usually crucial for getting your message across since too few impressions and your message just isn't seen by enough potential customers, and with too many your banners just begin to fade into the woodwork. This is referred to as "banner burnout," i.e., a banner is no longer a good ROI. There are several companies that help manage your banner ad frequency rate. One such company is the previously mentioned DoubleClick (www.doubleclick.com) whose services allow you to control a sequence of banners that can be served to viewers in a specific order.

If you purchase banner space on a popular Web site such as Yahoo!, it will run around $20 to $60 per 1,000 impressions, i.e., the number of times surfers see a page that your banner is situated on. Ad placement services such as Internet Advertising Solution (IAS) (http://iaswww.com), L90 (www.l90.com), and Insidewire (www.insidewire.com) can assist you with specific, targeted placement of your banner ads in search engines such as Go, Excite, Lycos, Alta Vista, WebCrawler, HotBot, Magellan and other high-traffic sites. These services all work basically the same way. They have a method of determining the "known" number of searches performed based upon a certain keyword such as "widget." Then, if a potential customer goes to a search engine where you purchased the keyword phrase "widget" (and maybe others, budget permitting) and types "widget," that potential customer would see not only the normal search result, but also your Web site's banner on their computer screen. If all available impressions were purchased the potential customer would see the banner every time. If only a portion of the total impressions is purchased, the banner would rotate with other banners.

The industry average of CTR's is between 1.5 and 2.5%. If you purchased 50,000 impressions and received a 2% CTR, your Web site would receive 1000 potential customers. It is possible that with a well-designed and effectively targeted banner ad campaign you could receive a higher CTR, which is where a good banner design is important. When using services such as Doubleclick, IAS, L90 or Insidewire, you can easily rotate two or three banners during a campaign, which keeps a single banner from going stale. However, to receive the 1000 potential customers requires a substantial investment on your part, therefore, for small Web sites, it would probably be more cost effective to use alternative marketing methods and then supplement that with well-placed banner ads.

Another ad placement service, Webreference.com (www.webreference.com), did a study on effective ad placement. It found that the placement of the ad on the side of a Web page, next to the right scroll bar, increased click-through an average of 228% over placement at the top of the Web page. Of course, as viewers become accustomed to the ad placement along the side of a page, it might lessen its effectiveness.

Don't forget to factor in the costs of an agency that will be needed to create the banner ad and another agency or consultant to place the banner ad and plot your online strategy.

An economical approach is to develop reciprocal relationships with other Web sites that will cost you only your time (plus the cost of the banner itself). If you do pursue this method, follow these three rules:

- create a banner ad with the criteria set out above

- partner with Web sites that complement your site

- keep your expectations low

Consider using banner exchange services that enable you to easily advertise your Web site on a variety of other sites for free in exchange for hosting other member's banners on your Web site. Most of these services operate by membership and then provide the means for you to swap banner ads with other members. Some services you might want to check out are LinkExchange (http://adnetwork.bcentral.com), SmartAge (www.smartage.com), AdSwap (www.adswap.com), Exchange-it (www.exchange-it.com) and Great Banner Exchange (www.greatbanner.com).

Finally, once you have instituted a banner ad campaign, continually test and chart the performance of the banners from the very first day of placement using of your Log Analysis Software.

Affiliate Programs

To help drive quality traffic to your new Web site, consider setting up an affiliate program — sometimes called referral, associate, or partnership programs. No matter what term is used, these programs are attractive to many small Web sites that want to offset their costs by leasing space for a percentage of the sales made by sending traffic to other online businesses.

Affiliate programs are established by Web-based businesses to drive quality traffic to their Web site. In exchange for a host site sending a customer to your Web site, you pay the host site a commission based on the sales you generate from the referred customer. These commissions are all over the place and can range from 1 to 30 percent and upwards.

If you decide to establish an affiliate program you should provide one that can do online tracking, so your host sites can count the sales they have generated plus their commissions. The higher you can make the commission, the more likely your host site will actually promote your Web site in some way so it can send paying customers your way and earn additional income.

It also can work in reverse. With an affiliate program you can make your Web site more valuable to your customers, by offering them goods and services that are likely to interest them. You can also earn additional revenue from your site through partnerships with Web sites that will compensate you for the traffic, leads, and sales you send them.

There are services that manage affiliate programs by giving Web sites access to its own network of affiliate sites and measuring the sales each affiliate generates. A small sampling of the services you might find when you go to a search engine and put in the keywords "affiliate management" are LinkShare (www.linkshare.com), ConnectCommerce (www.connectcommerce.com), and Adbility (www.adbility.com), there are many more to choose from.

Newsletters

Newsletters (also referred to as: eNewsletters, ezines, e-mail newsletters or electronic newsletters) are an effective way to build goodwill, keep in touch with potential customers and obtain information about your customers since they must fill out a form to obtain the free newsletter. Through the combination of a little public relations, image-building and selling, you can provide your readers (customers and potential customers) with information they will appreciate and find useful. However, information is the key word here.

Through a newsletter (which can also be sent via snail mail) you can inform current and potential customers about different topics while *subtly* promoting your products/services. Your newsletter must contain a main story, which is informational, then the secondary stories can be targeted to your products and services.

Newsletters, when used as an opt-in/opt-out program, are a great tool for bringing customers to your Web site, cultivating repeat business and building customer loyalty. A good newsletter is entertaining, while providing valuable, worth-while information. It must be attractive, well written and relevant. Newsletters that are informative and rich in content can be just the reminder needed to bring customers to your site.

Before taking on the task of writing a newsletter you should ask yourself — do I have the time, aptitude and resources or the staff necessary to write a regularly scheduled newsletter? If the answer is yes, start your research. Find other newsletters that have the style and content that you like; read and study them until you know why each particular newsletter is effective.

Write your newsletter to a target audience. If your Web site serves a specific niche market, then you have no problems. However, if you have a more generalized Web site, you must dig into your customers' data to find a specific subject your customers will find of interest, and which provides enough material for a regularly scheduled newsletter. Once you have your target audience in mind and the niche subject matter, don't waiver. Stick to that particular subject matter, don't ramble. If your subject matter is collectible Barbie Dolls, don't also try to work in collectible Hot Wheels. That is another subject. What you could do is a survey and ask how many readers are also interested in other forms of collectibles, if you get a favorable response then start another newsletter for that niche market.

To establish a readership comfort level, create a distinctive style (both writing and layout) for the newsletter, which should be consistent in each issue. Establish a publication schedule (weekly, monthly, bi-monthly). Every issue should provide links to other sites of interest and/or reviews of sites about a particular subject of interest to your niche market. The text needs to be content rich. For example, you can review a new book and give links to sites with other reviews on the book and sites where you can purchase the book. Remember your readership wants a newsletter that informs, educates or helps them in their daily lives, not an "in your face" product brochure.

Create an easy-to-locate newsletter archive on your Web site so that your customers can find any back issue they might be looking for. Have links to your archive pages throughout your Web site. In each new issue of your newsletter refer in some way or the other to a back issue; this will lead readers to your archive pages and conversely to your products/services. Additionally, these back-issues can help build traffic to your site if you are diligent in registering each issue with the search engines.

A newsletter is a good tool, especially for the small Web-based business. Incorporate your newsletter into your overall marketing plan. If you produce a high quality, informative newsletter, and let other Web sites know about it, they will happily provide a link to your newsletter pages. You can also trade your newsletter for links, especially to other Web sites serving the same niche market (this will help build readership and, in turn, traffic to your site).

Benefits of publishing a newsletter, other than the obvious ones set out above are:

- Your newsletter is distributed via the one item everyone on the Web has in common — an e-mail address. E-mail is easy, free and works without a hitch. Readers can look at it at their leisure, print it out, save it, file it, and refer to it when needed.

- You can send potential customers numerous e-mails (the newsletter) chock-full of informative content about a subject the receiver has shown, not only an interest in, but a willingness to receive (along with a *little* promo for your Web site and its products/services).

- You promote not only your Web site but also its products/services. It is vital that you *subtly*, but relentlessly reinforce your Web site and its products/services brand(s).

- You build trust since familiarity fuels the comfort index. Every time your readers receive your newsletter wherein you have shared valuable information, you build and reinforce their trust.

- A newsletter can become an additional source of revenue. You can sell ads in your newsletter, but you first must build your readership to at least 5000 to make ads attractive to other businesses.

You will find that your customers and readers change their e-mail addresses more often than their physical address. You have to find a way to keep track of everyone's current e-mail address. One way is to use a listserv program like Majordomo. Also let your customers and readers in on the action, give them a simple form to fill out that allows them to subscribe, unsubscribe and change their e-mail address.

Market your newsletter, not only should you place your newsletter section with search engines but you should also list it in every applicable newsletter and/or ezine database available. For example, www.dominis.com/Zines/. This will bring in more subscribers, i.e., more customers.

If you continually publish a quality product, your readers will repay you for the help you have given to them through purchases on your Web site. Finally, ask your customers for feedback and always have an opt-out link in each newsletter.

List Management Software

Sending out your newsletter can be a daunting task unless you take advantage of e-mail list manager software. E-mail lists disseminate a single message simultaneously to a group of people. With e-mail lists, you can quickly and cost-effectively deliver thousands, even millions, of newsletter messages simultaneously over the Internet. Furthermore, through database integration, messages can be personalized according to each customer's demographic information and preferences. E-mail list management software makes it easy to manage your e-mail lists by automating tasks such as list creation, subscriptions, un-subscriptions, bounce handling of e-mail delivery errors, and the like. Look into an e-mail list management software solution such as:

LISTSERV (www.lsoft.com), the first e-mail list manager, and remains one of the dominant systems in use today. It lets you to create, manage and control your electronic mailing lists; maintain interactive e-mail discussion groups for customer service; technical assistance; and forums about any topic of interest; and distribute personalized direct e-mail campaigns with targeted information that the recipients have specifically requested.

Majordomo (www.greatcircle.com/majordomo/) is freeware distributed by Great Circle Associates. Although it does not provide technical support for the software, it does provide links to user support groups. Majordomo automates the management of electronic mailing lists through commands sent to Majordomo via electronic mail to handle all aspects of list maintenance. Once a list is set up, virtually all operations are performed remotely, requiring no intervention upon the postmaster of the list site. Majordomo controls a list of addresses for some mail transport system (like sendmail or smail) to handle. Majordomo itself performs no mail delivery (though it has scripts to format and archive messages).

With Petidomo III, CyberSolutions (www.cys.de/englisch/produkte/index) offers one of the fastest mailing list server solutions available along with extensive technical options. Petidomo III delivers all e-mail simultaneously rather than one-by-one.

Products such as LISTSERV also allow you to set up a discussion board or an e-mail discussion group on your Web site. This can enhance your newsletter offering by allowing your customers to communicate with one another.

E-Mail

Marketing, promotional materials, and methodology can be helpful in building a good customer base for your Web site, but be careful to not burn up your communication pathways. If used properly, e-mail is one of the best ways for a Web-based business to acquire new customers and grow and build long lasting relationships with current customers. Start with monthly e-mails then slowly increase the frequency and specialization of these e-mails by responding to your customer's requests — because you, as a responsible Web site operator, remembered to ask for feedback. It is possible to set up a list quickly by hand if it is small, or you can use specialized software (see below). Surprisingly good response rates to target e-mail campaigns are achieved because:

- e-mail hyperlinks allow recipients to go straight to your Web site

- the recipient has proactively requested the information and, therefore, is interested in the topic

- the recipient can opt-out if no longer interested in receiving specific e-mail

With the right e-mail tools, you can have a candid one-on-one audience to get customers to respond to an offer targeted to them. Check out Exactapro (www.exactapro.com), and, once again, DoubleClick (www.doubleclick.com) with it's DartMail, a comprehensive suite of online consent-based e-mail marketing solutions or you might want to use a service such as eTarget (www.trafficsurge.com/target).

One of the great values of a simple e-mail offer is that it has many of the advantages of the over-hyped push technology minus all of its complications. To effectively use an e-mail campaign you must request an e-mail address with each order, each new account, and each inquiry your Web site receives. It is best if you actually ask your customers if they would like to receive e-mail messages with special sales information and news about any new offerings.

Give your customers the option of getting their messages from you in the form of HTML-enhanced mail since this type of mail can deliver a more persuasive message than a plain-text e-mail. All of the newer e-mail clients can accept HTML e-mail, complete with graphics and layout, so use this technology wherever possible.

E-mail Netiquette: If you are going to use e-mail campaigns in your marketing efforts, it is imperative that you provide the e-mail recipient with a way to easily opt out of the e-mail listing. As an additional "trust" incentive from an online campaign designed to obtain e-mail addresses, state clearly that you do not sell your customer list to anyone without specific permission from the customer (although it is perfectly legal to sell your mailing list to others). However, if you feel it is important for you to have the option of selling a customer list you can provide a clickable button giving approval for the customer's information to be sold by you, but don't expect that button ever to be used. Use an e-mail campaign to increase your bottom line, not to alienate potential customers.

For some of the above-mentioned integrated marketing and advertising solutions, which can help to build profitable long-term customer relationships, look at Ezine Mail (www.ezinemail.com), a useful Web site for newsletters and e-mail campaigns. If you're interested in using opt-in e-mail campaigns visit www.bulletmail.com. The reliable www.doubleclick.com, with its many offerings, includes e-mail-marketing solutions.

DATA MINING

Data mining gives you a way to is look at trends and retrieve as much information out of existing databases as you can. Businesses have enormous databases holding various customer data (scattered all over the enterprise). These databases contain not only the customer's name, address, e-mail, but also data on their buying trends (what they're currently buying), their surfing habits, the technology they are using, etc. The key to success is unlocking and applying that valuable information. With the right tools you can send quick inquiries into the vast array of information found in your traffic logs, advertising reports, shopping cart, etc., and perform real-time analysis of that data, allowing you to instantly capture information about a customer's behavior. Using this technology, scouting through your various data sources, amassing the data, and then turning it into actionable information, allows you to use the data to deliver value-added marketing.

Properly used, data mining helps you to gain insight into the (evolving) requirements and needs of your customers through analyses of customer data throughout the entire customer life cycle: from identifying prospective customers to extending and maintaining customer relationships. Then use it for developing and executing personalized, customer-centric marketing programs — programs that truly optimize customer relationships and deliver the highest possible return on investment.

For example, your marketing people might want to know the number of customers who saw the new widget banner ad on your Web site's FAQ page exactly three times before they clicked on it. Maybe it would be useful to find out how many times a customer will search for something before it is decided that it can't be found on your Web site. If your Web site requires registration somewhere within the purchasing process or uses technology to differentially identify anonymous potential customers, the likelihood of using mined data increases exponentially.

There are many data mining tools available. Take a look at Data Distilleries DD/Marketer (www.ddi.nl/solutions/ccsintro). This product helps optimize the information extracted from your databases. Your database is explored from tens of thousands of different viewpoints with the aid of advanced data mining technology. This enables all the hidden information relating to customer behavior to be mapped out and highlighted. By using this new information your marketing department is able to adapt quickly and flexibly to the individual requirements and needs of each customer.

Another product to investigate is MarketMiner (www.marketminer.com), an automated, informative data mining tool that automatically produces a complete marketing analysis from, for example, customer demographics, sales, or response data from a past direct marketing campaign.

Finally, check out Unica Corporation's Affinium (www.unica-usa.com), a fully-integrated marketing automation suite designed to allow businesses to leverage customer information across multiple data sources and interactive touchpoints.

PERSONALIZATION

Personalization (one-to-one marketing) has the potential to completely revolutionize how a Web-based business markets its product to customers and maintains its customer relationships. What exactly is personalization? It is a compilation of detailed behavioral knowledge of individuals and/or groups of individuals with certain like-behavioral characteristics and the use of that knowledge to personalize a customer's online experience. To put it another way, personalization is the management of the customer relationship on an individual customer basis, but carried out in a mass production sort of way. For the most part, it is used in conjunction with some form of data mining. It is more than a MyWidgetPage offering, rather it is a personalized serving of ads and perhaps a re-ordering of a Web page's content which is accomplished in real-time to match a particular customer's behavior and shopping patterns. Personalization tools can be used to entice your customers to stay on your Web site, make purchases, click on ads, etc.

Planning

Proper implementation of personalization tools can lead to more sales, larger sales, more frequently returning customers. Customer benefits include easier access to products they care about — ease of shopping is something customers remember, so they will come back.

To implement an effective personalization effort on your Web site you must establish clear goals to point the way toward what to personalize. It takes planning. You must be able to predict the wants and needs of the individual customer and target what you want to accomplish with the implementation of personalization on your site.

Do you want to increase customer loyalty? If so, add personalization in such a way as to influence repeat traffic. Are your Web site's products/services something that customers usually feel that they need to research and evaluate prior to purchase (a refrigerator, automobile, etc.)? If so, personalize any portions of your site that can help in the customer's decision-making process. Of course, to do this properly you need to determine how your customers gather information before making a purchase.

Know your customers: Some will know what they want when they first click on your Web site. Others should be gently led into an information-gathering process that can aid them in their comparison shopping.

When implementing personalization on your Web site keep in mind the customers who are suspicious of personalization and all it entails. Privacy is a national right and is fiercely defended by some Internet users.

Customer Categories

Your personalization tools need to be able to trace the paths and gather information regarding individual customers who visit your Web site. In general, customer behavior breaks down into five categories:

- the impulse buyer (no research)

- the brand conscious customer (little research)

- the customers wanting the best value for the money (extensive research)

- the price conscious customer (extensive price comparison)

- the window shoppers

Be prepared to engage the customers in each of these categories so that they will stay on your Web site and eventually make a purchase. To do this you lay out a different motif for each customer category.

Products

Now you are ready to investigate which personalization tools are available to fit your needs. Here is what some of the software companies have to say about their own personalization products:

E.piphany Real-Time Personalization (www.epiphany.com) provides a robust, real-time marketing engine to personalize customer and visitor interactions. Our system is a powerful combination of real-time analytics, campaign management tools, and targeting capabilities. It ties together campaigns and offers across all your customer channels and touchpoints. The system incorporates the best aspects of rules-based and analytic personalization technologies to give you a single view of the customer. Real-Time Personalization builds a real-time profile for each visitor or customer with information drawn from many sources. The system can pull from clickstream data, customer databases, transaction systems, third-party data, and other sources. It selects the best offer for a particular person using up-to-the-second information. A self-learning engine observes each offer and, based on the response, dynamically adjusts offer targeting for future interactions. Customers receive the best product, incentive, or content offers. That means you can convert more of your visitors to customers. Because each and every interaction is intelligently personalized, customer loyalty increases.

DRYKEN's Storekeeper (dev.dryken.com/products) is the first and only eCommerce software product that dynamically generates high-fidelity buying predictions for each shopper based on all of the information available in that shopper's specific profile in real time. In particular, Storekeeper's proprietary predictive algorithms take into account the individual shopper's historical transactions and site navigation behavior. This is in sharp contrast to competitive approaches that simply classify shoppers into large affinity buckets where they lose their individual patterns and characteristics. Because Storekeeper's personalization granularity is the individual, the software can truly understand and cater to the needs and preferences of individual shoppers.

Manna's FrontMind (www.mannainc.com) is built with the e-marketer in mind, Manna's FrontMind is the only personalization solution that lets you understand your customers' needs, deliver precisely targeted offers, and continuously learn and improve on your e-marketing initiatives. FrontMind's unique approach combines self-updating customer behavior models, an easy-to-use "marketer's desktop", and in-depth pre-testing, ROI reporting, and analysis capabilities. Click-by-Click, Customer-by-Customer, Manna and FrontMind are changing the face of personalization.

Privacy Issues

The bad new is that personalization tools can and are being abused. Personalization has gotten a "bad rep" for violating an individual's privacy. These tools must be used with care, or you may find that you have alienated a serious percentage of your market share. Do not secretly profile the customer, do not send spam, and do not trade in personal information that you do not have the right to collect.

Personalization tools are a great asset if used responsibly. For example, to create a unique session focused entirely on an individual customer's needs, employing techniques to cross-sell, upsell, and perform goal-driven configuration on a one-to-one basis. Allowing you to present your products/services to your customers in terms almost too good to refuse. When you use personalization to understand your customers' interests, and provide them with solid unbiased information on those interests (without charge or obligation), then, if your customers like what you are delivering, you have a valuable commodity — a loyal repeat customer.

CHAPTER 16

Customer Service

*Technology: the knack of so arranging the world
that we need not experience it.*

Max Frisch, *Homo Faber*

Good customer service equals good customer retention and good word of mouth.

The explosion of e-commerce transactions brings tremendous opportunity to all kinds of businesses. Coming to the Web in droves are both the entrepreneurs looking for a new business model and the established brick-and-mortars seeking an opportunity to grow their revenues and expand their customer base through this rapidly emerging sales channel. Yet, all Web-based businesses are desperately trying to differentiate themselves from the competition. That presents a daunting challenge to most entering this new arena. The smart businesses realize that at least part of the differentiation will come from the quality of service they offer their customers. Web-based businesses must adopt customer service strategies so they can build customer loyalty, fulfill a broader range of customer needs, and increase the effectiveness of their sales and services.

Look at customer service like this — every contact a customer has with a Web-based business, its employees, Web-site, help desk, call or contact center and other business-related services influences that person's perception of that business. The technologies that the Web brings present a unique opportunity to create and nurture a special one-on-one relationship with every customer.

I can't say this enough — customer service is the best marketing tool a Web site has.

THE PROBLEM IN A NUTSHELL

You're business is increasing by leaps and bounds — that's good. But more customers visiting your site equal more customer inquiries and more online transactions, which means a higher burden on your order fulfillment systems and a greater load on the customer service department.

Numerous Web-based businesses are dilatory in their response to online information requests. Once a customer has been disappointed by how slowly their query has been answered, they are unlikely to try again.

Almost one-half of the currently operational e-commerce Web sites provide such poor customer service that they take more than five days to respond to an inquiry or complaint, if they provide any response at all! If a Web site ignores their online customers' inquiries, they are discouraging brand loyalty and driving traffic to their online competitor (who may be among the group that realize the importance of assuring customer satisfaction within the purchasing process). Who is the competition? It is the e-commerce sites that respond to their customers' inquiries within 24 hours.

Some sites leave their customers stranded where they can't easily find a way to ask for more information and/or send an e-mail request. On many sites, the "Contact Us" link (on those few sites that have them) simply launches a generic e-mail query screen — with no information about how soon they can expect a reply and/or where else to look for information. Other sites hide their contact information forcing the customer into a "hide and seek game" (a good example of this is www.net2phone.com), or give only a Webmaster's e-mail address. Many Web sites don't even give a telephone number for customers to use if they really need to talk to a human. This is not the way to provide quality customer service.

A CUSTOMER SERVICE STRATEGY

If a Web-based business doesn't develop a good customer service strategy it will lose customers — the same way a brick-and-mortar would lose them — by not responding to their needs. Efficient customer service is crucial for survival of any business.

In the past Web sites would often put an e-mail form or contact/e-mail link(s) on the site without any plan for handling the increasing volume of e-mail. A small Web-based business serving a niche market might be able to depend on only e-mail and the telephone for receiving and logging their customer queries and orders. However, most Web sites require an infrastructure that allows them to serve their customers through a combination of e-mail queries, online ordering and telephone support. At the same time, Web sites should encourage their customers to become more self-sufficient through detailed product/service descriptions, frequently asked questions (FAQs), and knowledge bases consisting of, for example, product specifications, articles, technical papers and manuals, white papers and case studies.

The first step in building a good customer service strategy is to ensure that the customer service department and/or call center knows how to handle every aspect of a customer's transaction. Although e-mail should be used as the main means of communication, telephone support (especially a toll free number) is also important. The customer service representatives (CSR) should be able to access and manipulate all the information involved in a customer's order, including tracking the status of an order through the fulfillment process until it reaches the customer's doorstep. If possible, the CSR should be able to communicate with the customers via e-mail, the telephone or online direct-connection software (chat) — all which are within the budget of most Web-based businesses.

The second step is to determine just what the Web-based business' continuing customer service strategy should address. Start with the minimum strategy set out in the previous paragraph, then plan ahead. To do this you need answers to the following:

- Can customers quickly find answers to their most frequently asked questions on the Web site?

- Can customers easily check on the status of any outstanding customer service issue?

- Does the customer service staff respond to all customer e-mails within one business day?

- Can the knowledge content on the Web site be continually updated in a dynamic and automatic fashion based on customer input?

- Is the most useful and/or commonly requested information presented to customers first?

- Do customers have an easy way to get to the human-based customer service?

- Do customers consistently return to the Web site to find information, and if so, is there any way of determining whether or not they do?

- Can the Web site generate reports detailing the support activities that have taken place on the site on a week-by-week basis? Do those reports help to determine the ROI of the site?

- Does the Web site give customers the option to have updates sent to them automatically by e-mail?

- Is the Web site constantly updating its knowledge base by publishing useful information that's maybe at the moment only in the minds of its best staff?

- Do customers ever praise the Web site because they found it especially helpful?

If the answer to any of these questions is a "no," "I don't know," or "maybe," it's time to get to work.

It's important for a Web-based business to monitor its customers' requests for information as they come in, since many of them tend to ask the same set of questions. Diligent monitoring of customer service inquiries allows a Web site to determine where to direct its efforts — allowing for much more efficient use of human and infrastructure resources. Also, it can use the information gathered to redesign Web pages to make them more responsive to customers' needs. Consider building an online knowledge base of product specifications, articles, technical specifications, white papers and case studies that can answer many of the customers' immediate inquiries supplemented with a comprehensive FAQ section. This empowers the Web site's customers to answer their own questions without human intervention, which translates into not only satisfied customers but also an eventual increase in a Web-based business' profit margin. An added benefit is that customers develop the perception that the Web site has a good grasp of what their questions and problems might be thereby strengthening their overall confidence in the site and its offerings. However, don't go down the road that some Web sites (www.microsoft.com and www.netscape.com, for example) have taken — don't leave customers in "self-help jail." Let product descriptions, FAQs and knowledge bases be the first line of service, but, in addition, offer easy-to-access e-mail support, chat, toll free number(s), and other forms of direct communication.

All Web-based businesses must find ways to make their sites more responsive to the constantly changing needs of their customers. Therefore, if they don't develop a comprehensive customer service strategy they will lose their customers to the competition, reap poorer returns on their investment and some might find themselves spending more money than is necessary on more expensive customer service solutions such as conventional call centers.

Ninety percent of the solutions discussed herein are costly. Many of the software and service companies have solutions that fall into more than one category, or overlap categories, set forth in this chapter. The customer service solutions can be software-driven, services-driven or a combination of both and they run the gamut from FAQ manager programs, to e-mail management systems that help you automate the process of sorting and responding to incoming inquiries, to full-blown customer relationship management systems.

AUTOMATE

Don't ignore the golden opportunity provided by an online, customer-initiated one-on-one relationship. Eliminate from the very start problems generated by an inability to handle the volume of traffic on a new Web site by putting into place systems that prevent the disorganization that arises in many Web-based customer service operations.

Everything needed to create a truly responsive site — monitoring and analyzing customer queries, creating the right content and posting it in a well-organized manner, handling e-mail communications, etc. — can be extremely labor-intensive. A Web site can be a victim of its own success if the volume of communications exceeds the resources dedicated to supporting that communication.

It's important to put in place effective, scalable automation tools. Such tools can automate time-consuming knowledge collection that, when neglected over time, will result in out-of-date content and dissatisfied customers. This can result in one of the differential factors that affect a Web-based business' profit margin.

Businesses that have a large volume of e-mail or find their e-mail growing should consider using an e-mail management system. However, most home-based or small Web-based businesses can, initially, rely on their internal e-mail system to process customer queries.

FAQs

Although FAQs are easily built simply by creating Web pages with questions and answers, the knowledge contained in an ever-growing FAQ section will, over time, become difficult for the customer to search and for you to maintain. Therefore, as a Web site grows, it should automate its FAQs to ensure that the knowledge contained therein can be rapidly searched and easily maintained. Software, such as, Askit Systems (www.askitsystems.com), FAQ Generator (www.cgi-world.com/faq_gen.html), and FAQ Manager (www.stason.org/works/faq_manager) can help with this task. If a Web site offers numerous products that require technical support, another solution might be something like Inference's k-Commerce Hosted Solutions (www.inference.com).

Chat

There are many live Web-chat solutions. Look into the solutions provided by Peoplesupport (www.peoplesupport.com), Liveperson (www.liveperson.com), Facetime (www.facetime.net) and others that provide live, human CSRs that are instantly available for a one-on-one chat session when a customer clicks on a "chat" button. These services are relatively inexpensive.

For example, LivePerson's setup fee is around $1000 plus about $250/month per CSR. It also has the advantage of being one of the many new Web-based application service providers (ASP). An ASP is a Web-based software hosting business that rents the software to you rather than selling it to you. In some cases, hosted apps may be cheaper than implementing a packaged CRM application internally. Just think, a completely integrated front-end and back-end where the applications are implemented and hosted by a single vendor — that's a model that's hard to ignore. For a small to medium size (SME) Web-site the ASP route, like LivePerson, is a good option since all that is needed is a few simple lines of HTML code and the button icon for its Web pages, and it's ready to go.

One caveat, do not use (at least not at this time) automated online personalities (robots) that supposedly can respond to a customer's live chat questions. They can't — they cause a lot of frustration, and until the technology has improved I would advise staying away from this type of solution.

A Web site could offer its customers that have multi-media capability (sound card, speakers, microphone and the right software) the ability to click on a button on a Web site to call a CSR over the Internet (a "Talk to Me" button). Once connected, the CSR can not only talk to a customer, but if the CSR's computer is equipped with the right software, he/she can even access the same Web page the customer is currently on. They can then browse the site simultaneously, solving problems and even filling out forms together. Customers like a personalized experience (the human touch), and it's necessary for Web sites to integrate one-on-one solutions into their offerings if the Web is to evolve into the e-commerce Mecca that's been so widely predicted.

Another cost saving is realized by routing calls across the Internet (Voice over IP). These calls cost much less than a traditional telephone call. So, using the "Talk to Me" option (which is Voice over IP) will also have a positive influence on a Web site's monthly toll-free number costs.

The huge enterprise software suites such as Servicesoft Inc. (www.servicesoft.com), Peoplesoft (www.peoplesoft.com), Wintouch (www.wintouch.com) and Right Now Technologies' (www.rightnowtech.com) RightNow Web are for only the largest e-commerce operations. A software suite itself is very expensive and to integrate it with a Web-based business' systems will dramatically increase the cost, sometimes ranging well over a million dollars. When investigating the feasibility of one of these suites, remember that a Web-based business must not only survive the procurement, installation and testing of the system; but, the costs of consultants and its own IT people who will integrate the system with the Web-based business' operations. Once everything is up and running you have the additional cost of maintaining a customer service center and its staff.

A Web site should treat its customers as the source of current and future profits, and not just as a series of individual transactions. It must develop and nurture relationships with its customers.

It seems that while many companies have been good at introducing passive Web sites they have not managed to come to grips with the practical procedures for handling customer service issues. There are basically two different strategic approaches:

The First Approach: Separate Technology

Even if a Web-based business separates its Web site and the CSRs (call center) it will still benefit from customer service automation to help it optimize the service provided to the customers.

When a Web-based business is in the start-up stage, separating the Web and its CSRs (call center) might very well be the most efficient. It could take the simple route (which isn't recommended) of designing the Web site so that the Web pages give a telephone number customers could call. Then either in-house staff or a call center would take product/service orders, handle technical support, customer service, etc. But, any Web-based business taking this approach should implement, as soon as possible, direct Web-based transactions such as online ordering, shopping carts, etc., followed with a FAQ section to answer the most common questions about the products and/or services.

When a small Web-based business is in the start-up stage, taking the first approach might very well be the most efficient. However, most Web-based businesses will continue to grow and prosper, putting an ever-growing burden on their customer service resources. As traffic increases automation will be part of part the solution. To keep customer service where it continually compliments the growth of the business (rather than hinder it), the first approach must be used for only the short-term.

Although the majority of the e-commerce sites in operation today are stuck in some phase of the "first approach" mode, don't let your site linger there too long. When laying out your blueprint, keep in mind that a Web-based business will need to include an infrastructure that allows it to adopt a more sophisticated technology when the need arises.

The Second Approach: The Entire Solution

Taking the second approach means that the Web site is no longer an island, but part of a multi-threaded contact strategy. To provide good customer service on the Web, you must open new lines of communication. E-mail is universal but must be well managed. FAQ pages and a dynamic knowledge base are easy to set up and, when managed properly and kept current (through help provided by the proper software), can consistently be an asset for a Web site. Web Chat can be especially effective for quick real-time queries, since it can be faster than a phone call.

There are advanced customer service solutions such as "Call Me" buttons, which allow the customer to schedule a call back by a CSR; and real-time query and response (some with co-browsing features), such as "Talk to Me" buttons — although best suited to high value sales and enterprise sites.

Some Web sites (large and small) that are currently using various degrees of advanced customer service strategies are www.landsend.com, www.medmarket.com, www.mecate-ch.com, www.ambrosiawine.com, www.fidelity.com, and www.casamilagro.com.

This approach may not be within the budget of the start-up Web-based business; however, most can implement some of the features, and gradually add others to increase its customer service functionality. There is some good news — a number of the customer service solution companies and customer relationship management solution companies are moving toward the ASP model which simplifies integration with a Web site and can lessen the cost for such a solution.

A "Call me" button on a Web site means that CSRs need to be on hand to call back a customer, either instantly or at a scheduled date/time/number. Customers seem to love this. This is a really powerful technique especially for a Web site that is selling high value products.

A "Talk to Me" button on a Web site requires that a CSR be instantly available when the customer clicks the button. This option uses voice over IP to establish an instant voice link between the customer and the CSR. However, Internet congestion, delays in the Web site's servers, the customer 's ISP servers, the call center's servers, etc., can mean that this method sometimes produces poor voice quality. One solution to this delemma might be Aspect (www.aspect.com), a product that can link voice over IP with Web chat so if the voice connection goes bad then text chat can take over.

Co-browsing requires that a CSR be instantly available to take over a customer's browser when requested to help with a form or to manipulate text or images on Web pages as the customer is viewing the same page. Only businesses offering very high value products (stock market investments), or perhaps businesses teaching customers to use complex products or who provide online schooling should look into this type of technology. However www.landsend.com and www.fidelity.com are using it to some success, so?. . . .

Web chat is a real time interaction between the customer and a CSR using text to conduct chat sessions. And, yes, this also requires that a CSR be available basically 24x7, but a single CSR can handle multiple chat sessions, perhaps as many as 8. This is good. Because it is highly productive it can be used for low end products.

Note that shopping cart abandonment rates dramatically drop when some type of "live" interaction is offered.

AUTOMATED CUSTOMER SERVICE

The unique combination of quality automated customer service systems (ACSS) and human customer service teams is one way that Web-based businesses can ensure profitability. The typical ACSS software is a Web-enabled suite which integrates sales, marketing, call center, help desk, field service, inventory procurement, and quality assurance operations.

Post-sales follow-up technology makes it easy for online merchants to offer superior customer service. These include FAQs and their answers, knowledge databases, and message boards. With the correct deployment, Web-based businesses can streamline their service offerings and costs, evaluate and target their key-customer. Now a Web-based business is on the road to building lifetime value and customer retention, for the long term.

When looking at the implementation of ACSS, take into account that many applications require specialized views of the customer data — predictive modeling tools, campaign management applications, call center packages, and Web applications — all which require different views in order to fulfill their role. The customer information architecture must support rapid delivery of customer data in a wide variety of forms suitable for application-specific requirements.

A properly implemented ACSS will find and identify essential bits of customer data that are located throughout a business' data infrastructure. Once found, that data is then imported into a common knowledge base that is shared by each arm of an ACSS to improve every segment of a business' customer service offerings. However, an ACSS must be scalable and flexible enough to operate effectively through any number of customer preferred channels, i.e., Web, chat, e-mail, fax, telephone or VoIP. The typical ACSS platform is a Web-enabled suite that lets a Web-based business integrate its customer service and marketing efforts. Research the products offered. To give you a place to start, try looking at Siebel (www.siebel.com), Quintus/Mustang (www.quintus.com), E-talk (www.e-talk.com) and Brightware (www.brightware.com).

E-MAIL

Customers not only want the ability to place orders for product and services, but they want to be able to obtain additional product/service information, resolve billing issues, track down shipments, or ask installation and product support questions. As stated previously, most of today's Web sites give their customers information on how to contact them by telephone, e-mail or by a form on their site. However, as customers become more "Internet Savvy," and as hold times at call centers increase (as they must with the e-commerce explosion), customers will become more inclined to send e-mails to the Web-based business (a boost to its bottom line). After all, why should they wait on hold to get information or place an order when they can just fill out a form or send an e-mail and then read the reply at leisure?

Many Web sites handle their e-mail traffic poorly. A customer may wait days for a response to an e-mail inquiry, and an automated response often doesn't come close to addressing their inquiry. A persistent customer might be able to obtain the answer they're looking for, but not without a lot of frustration. Although some Web-based businesses believe (wrongly) that automatic e-mail response can handle all direct customer queries, automatic e-mail response does have a role.

When responding to customer's e-mail inquiries I suggest the following as best practice, although you should pick and choose what would be suitable for your particular Web-based business:

- Issue a "thank you" auto-acknowledgement for each e-mail as soon as it is received with a time frame of when an answer can be expected (then respond within that time frame) along with an 800 number that the customer can call if they need an immediate solution.

- Have "click and drag" paragraphs available for CSRs to paste into the e-mail response.

- In some circumstances suggest a phone call (if the customer is willing) rather than be drawn into a long series of e-mail exchanges.

- Above all, be fast — make it your goal to handle 90% of e-mails inside 2 working hours, and want to be faster.

Should people who communicate with a company via electronic means receive less prompt service than those that use telephones? Remember, demographic studies indicate that people who browse the Web are usually more affluent than the general public, and are generally inclined to try new things. These are the very customers a company wants to attract and keep! Servicing customers through online methods is a proven cost-effective solution.

E-Mail Management Systems

The way to handle large volumes of e-mail is to give them the same quality of service as telephone calls. This is where a good, properly implemented e-mail management system (EMS) comes into play. Although costly, an EMS can provide the infrastructure, processes and methodologies that can handle online customer service issues in a manner comparable to, and sometimes as good or better than what is available through most call centers.

As a Web-based business becomes more and more successful, it must take the steps to ensure that the infrastructure supporting the Web site can promptly and efficiently handle the vast amounts of electronic communications it receives from its customers. One such solution is the e-mail management system (EMS).

As discussed previously, e-commerce is conducted in essentially one of two ways:

1. A customer obtains information on products and services through a Web site. (How extensive the available online information is can vary from product description to FAQ to an extensive, dynamic knowledge base.) The customer then uses the telephone to call a CSR to place an order and/or to ask for additional information.

   OR

2. A customer not only obtains detail information on products and services via an easy navigational path through a Web site but also can obtain additional information through various channels (chat, message boards, FAQs, knowledge bases, VoIP, co-browsing) and, of course, place the order — all entirely through the e-commerce Web site.

Many customers (especially the Internet savvy ones) prefer to take the self-help route (product/service descriptions, knowledge base, FAQs, message boards, etc.) then, if that doesn't work, they will contact the Web site via e-mail. If the customer has chosen to make contact via e-mail, then a Web site must make it as easy as possible for its customers by providing (at the minimum) a form on the Web site for its customers to fill out. A "Contact Us" Web page devoted to e-mail address links segregated by departments would be even better.

The advantage of e-mail (and online ordering) is that the transaction can be conducted in an asynchronous manner. Unlike a telephone call, the parties involved in the transaction do not have to be in the transaction at the same time. This is especially valuable to both parties when the interaction needed is minimal, and the need to complete the transaction is not immediate. For example, customers may want to get the tracking number of an order so that they can check the status of their order at their convenience. This desire by customers to use e-mail (and online ordering) represents a great opportunity for Web sites that have implemented a high-quality e-mail management system.

The value of a good EMS can be significant, for both customers and a busy e-commerce site. Clearly, one of the benefits of having an online presence is that customers can often conduct their own research on products and services, at their own pace. As discussed throughout this book, a well-designed e-commerce site makes it easy for customers to find what they want, and helps them get answers to most of their questions. Motivated customers will navigate their way through well designed Web pages, and will make a purchase decision or resolve a service issue on their own. This kind of self-service system offers tremendous leverage to a Web-based business that doesn't have the wherewithal to provide 24x7 call center capabilities. When implementing an EMS, study the Web sites of Net2Phone, Microsoft, Hewlett Packard and AOL, *learn from their mistakes* so that you can avoid making the same ones.

Requirements for a High-Performing EMS: The goal of all e-mail management systems is to get the right answer to the customers, using the right kind and the right amount of resources. This means that the EMS should be able to recognize the kind of inquiry initiated by the customer, determine what resource it will take to process that inquiry, and then apply those resources to get the answer to the customer. Let us examine each of these requirements in turn.

An incoming message must first be recognized by the EMS for what it is — the system must determine if it falls into a predetermined category of communications, such as a product question, an information request, a billing query, a complaint, or a follow-up to an earlier communication. E-mail tends to be free form in nature, so the EMS must have the ability to parse the communication, and determine the category from the message itself. The EMS must then determine if it can be handled in an automated manner. A majority of customer queries fall within a few categories. For example, a company that sells headsets may receive a large number of installation questions, but the questions themselves may fall into a few categories (e.g. sound card questions, volume requirements, operating system compatibility, etc.) and the company already knows the answers to most of these questions. With access to a comprehensive knowledge base of answers to these frequently asked questions, a good EMS can match a customer's request to the appropriate answer in the knowledge base. Not all e-mail can be processed automatically. Some messages may require customization and personalization of answers selected from the knowledge base.

An EMS must have the ability to identify e-mails that don't fit into a known category and route them to a knowledgeable CSR. That CSR can then respond using the knowledge base, one or more phrase banks that contain standard language that reflects the company's style, and their personal knowledge and experience. The EMS should then provide the ability for the CSR to use approved phrase banks and a spell check function to enhance quality prior to forwarding the response back to the customer. It should have the functionality that enables CSRs to annotate notes to either the customer's message, or to the customer's profile. Other CSRs can then use these notes to ensure superior customer service. For example, a CSR may use the annotation capability to record why the customer was not charged for shipping if the company policy is "no free shipping."

A CSR may not be able to completely handle all customer communications allotted to him or her. For example, the CSR may prepare a response but want to forward it to a co-worker or supervisor for review before sending it. Another customer message may require a response from someone with more knowledge. To facilitate this, the EMS must provide a workflow capability that allows a CSR to hand off a message to another CSR, or a supervisor.

A supervisor must be able to monitor in real-time the state of all messages currently open, just as a call center manager can look at the state of all telephone calls being handled by the call management system. This allows supervisors to manage workloads, personnel needs, training needs, etc. Supervisors can also use this information to quickly identify any potential problem areas, and prepare to handle those areas. For example, a favorable product review on CNET or the mention of a product by Oprah or Rosie O'Donnell on one of their daytime television shows may at first cause a trickle then a torrent of information requests. Just like in a call center, an alert supervisor can observe the initial change in the incoming workload, and make adjustments to assure the best quality service.

The EMS should also provide a reporting capability that helps supervisors measure and manage the performance of their CSRs. A good EMS will further provide the capability to survey customers on the quality of service received, and manage the results of the survey.

The database used by the EMS should be easily accessible so that custom reports can be developed as necessary.

A big benefit of electronic communications is that they are recorded on media and therefore the details of every customer interaction are retrievable. (This is often not the case with telephone calls). This means that the entire e-mail history received from a customer in the past can be presented to the CSR every time they send in a new message. This provides a complete context for the CSR. A good EMS should provide not only the ability to preserve and present context, but also give the company a valuable database of interactions that can be mined for marketing purposes in the future. For example, the database of all customer interactions may reveal that customers who ask questions about one particular product often start by asking about a certain feature. This may indicate a need to change the product in some way, or it may even present a revenue opportunity for a complementary product.

Finally, a good EMS should be easy to use, install, and manage. It should not require a significant training effort. It should be adaptable and flexible enough to fit into the way you do business and not require you to change your business models or processes. Lastly, the system should leverage the Web site's existing technology infrastructure by seamlessly integrating with its current e-mail, e-commerce, and front-end and back-office systems.

Although expensive, an investment in a robust, scalable EMS provides returns in many ways for a large or enterprise Web site. An EMS can reduce the costs associated with handling customer service requests by up to a factor of five. A Web site can avoid building or contracting with an expensive call center. The CSRs can easily telecommute. A Web site can assure a consistent quality of service to its customers, by ensuring that all customer interactions use the same base of knowledge and communication styles. It can increase revenues by including new product information with outgoing messages (which the Marketing Department will love). Most importantly, it can improve customer satisfaction and loyalty by giving customers a reliable way of communicating with you.

A Web-based business should consider investing in an e-mail management system if its Web site:

- handles more than 1000 e-mail requests and online orders each day

- has more than five full-time employees handling online communications

- has customers that expect 24 x 7 service and the same (or better) level of service as they get from a call center

- receives many "routine" e-mail requests

- has found that online communications are becoming the bane of its existence

Begin by looking into eGain Mail (www.egain.com), Lotus' Online E-mail Management System (www.lotus.com), Calypso Message Center (www.calypsomessagecenter.com), Transform Response (www.transres.com/response) and Kana Response (www.kana.com). There are many more, but this should give you a starting point.

OUTSOURCING

Most Web-based businesses use some level of technology to increase their customer service offerings. But, technology can't do it all — timely responses are impossible if the human resources are not available. Throughout this book the author has preached "scalability." Well, scalability not only applies to technology; it is also relevant to staffing needs. As online sales increase it will become necessary to increase the human-based assets in customer service. Not only will these needs grow throughout a business' life cycle, they will also ebb and flow with the seasons (for example, holidays, back-to-school, snow season if a Web site sells snow blowers or mild weather if it sells boating equipment).

As customer service resources become strained to the limit during peak periods, the ability to quickly and cost-effectively scale to meet these demands is essential. One way to assure scalability is to outsource. But you need to be prepared — do your homework and find the call center or customer service solution provider that will meet the needs of your Web-based business. If any integration is necessary, have it well in hand before the necessity arises. A Web-based business will want a standby customer service solution to have the same access and timely visibility into customer orders as its ongoing customer service solution.

CALL CENTERS

Significant portions of real world transactions are conducted over the telephone and many of these customers are routed to call centers filled with CSRs who handle various customer interactions. Using the telephone for commerce and associated customer service functions is widely accepted by the public. The brick-and-mortar businesses that have migrated to the Web probably have existing call center relationships, but will still need to address the world of the Web. Can their current call center do this? If not, what steps should they take? Should they use a hybrid system with some matters handled by the call center and some in-house? Most e-commerce sites will find that they have the need for the services of a call center.

A call center is a combination of employees (CSRs) and hardware and software designed to aid in the efficient processing of large volumes of telephone calls. It is where a high volume of calls are placed or received for the purpose of sales, marketing, customer service, telemarketing, technical support or other specialized business activity. To take it a step further, a call center is a place for doing business by phone that combines a centralized database with an automatic call distribution system. However, a call center can be even more than that, it is:

- a fundraising and collections organization

- a help desk, both internal and external

- an outsourcer (better known as service bureau) that uses its resources to serve a number of companies simultaneously

- a reservation center for airlines and hotels

- a customer service department for catalog retailers and e-commerce sites

- an e-commerce transaction center that doesn't handle calls so much as automates customer interactions

A self-service Web site has its limits. No matter how well designed the Web site may be, not all customers can or will navigate their way to the correct information or they may just not have the time or inclination to sit through an extended browsing session. A Web site should offer alternatives to these customers. Give them the option of picking up their telephone and calling a CSR. Although this kind of immediate service adds to the costs, it can be extremely valuable to an e-commerce Web site that offers products and services that require a lot of research or has complicated installation requirements.

Call center technology and the solutions it provides is a dense subject and beyond the scope of this book. For additional information on call centers go to www.olccinc.com, www.the-resource-center.com (2 great sites, bookmark them), www.callcenternews.com, www.callcenterops.com, www.callcentres.com, to just name a few — there is a lot of information on the Web about call centers and outsourcers. Or perhaps purchase one of the many books that are available on this subject. One of the author's favorite is *Designing the Best Call Center for your Business* by Brendan Read.

MULTIMEDIA AND WEB-ENABLED CONTACT CENTERS

Some of the most exciting trends in call centers are the multi-media contact centers and/or the Web-enabled contact centers. Web-based businesses will increasingly find that their customers want to conduct business in a variety of ways: text chat, e-mail, VoIP conversation ("Talk to Me"), "Call Me", and the toll free number. If a Web site is offering a variety of options to its customers it needs to be sure that the call center it contracts with has the resources to answer phone calls, reply to e-mails, conduct real-time chats, and speak to customers via a multi-media computer.

Why would a Web site want or need a multimedia or Web-enabled contact center?

The Web appears to be a self-contained entity where a customer can surf the Web, get information, and buy products and services; and although it is a great channel or conduit for all kinds of things, it is a passive channel. An e-commerce site needs a way to handle customers and potential customers who want a dialogue, whether through e-mail, chat, telephone or VoIP.

A brick-and-mortar has a superlative, multi-functional sales tool — the human being. For Web-based business to emulate this same type of service, it needs a Web-based call center. You're on the Web, let the Web do what it does best — automate. But at the same time keep the human element — which is where call centers enter the picture.

The fact that call centers offer a personal and immediate response makes it an easy choice for customers — it is also your most expensive one. So you must make it easy for you customers to find quick access to other customer service channels — FAQs, e-mail, a knowledge base, message boards, chat, etc. A well thought out and designed Web site can help build a contented customer base and at the same time reduce its annual call center expenditure.

Most of the multimedia center and/or Web-based call center applications work on the same principle — the Web site's customers click on a "Call Me" or "Talk to Me" or chat button placed on the Web site to communicate directly with a CSR. With any of these three options, the CSR and customer engage in a real-time two-way chat — voice or text. Of course, for it to be voice-based the customer needs a microphone, speakers and an IP-based telephony application, such as Microsoft NetMeeting. Some of the applications even allow collaborative "whiteboarding" or "co-browsing," i.e., the CSR can browse along with the customer, each viewing the same Web page at all times — the CSR, in effect, takes over the customer's browser for a short period of time. In addition, the applications can also usually automatically track, store and intelligently queue e-mails to appropriate CSRs or route electronic messages to the correct destination, so customers don't have to wait hours or days for a response.

PeopleSupport (www.peoplesupport.com) is a solution that many of the SME Web-based businesses might want to look into since this company offers a sundry of options. This is an online customer service outsourcing company where CSRs do everything from managing e-mail to offering real-time text-chat type of customer service. PeopleSupport offers many flexible services. For example, a Web site can contract with PeopleSupport for their CSRs (who answer questions as though they were the Web site's employees) to provide live chat support to help customers perusing the site, but opt to handle all e-mail inquiries in-house. Or a Web site might want to only use PeopleSupport's technology (its software is transparently accessed from its application service provider) and have its own in-house CSRs interact with its customers. PeopleSupport provides many different scenarios within which it can provide customer service support.

Go to their Web site and click on their live demo where you can test their chat services through a chat session with one of their CSRs.

Look into LivePerson (discussed previously in this chapter) or check out HumanClick at www.humanclick.com. With this product/service when the customers need support, the 24/7 support staff at HumanClick.com is always ready to help and it is easy to use.

THE SITE EXPERIENCE

The Web's key appeal to the general public is its perceived ability to provide immediate gratification. When customers come to a Web site they expect to immediately find information or products, then to solve the problem or purchase the product — fast! Consequently, the Web user is sensitive to any delay. It takes about 8 seconds before a customer gives up a quest for a product and/or service and goes to another Web site or abandons the search entirely. Web-based businesses, therefore, operate under tremendous pressure to anticipate every possible need of every customer. This expectation is passed on to the Web designer, the people who contribute to the development of the Web site's content, the marketing department and customer support staff. Since the customer is hypothetically everyone in every geographic region, the range of information that may potentially be requested is staggering. Solution? Prioritize — rather than getting stuck in limbo because of the enormity of the task, get the most important information and services on your Web site first, and then add to it over time, as your customers' needs direct.

The same customers, who expect instant action and gratification, expect better customer service from a Web-based business than they expect from a brick-and-mortar business. To maintain a high level of customer satisfaction the Web-based business must realize that "site experience" is actually more important to an online customer than "product experience," and build the Web site and customer service solutions around that fact.

Good marketing can be for naught if there is poor customer service.

CHAPTER 17

Logistics and Order Fulfillment

Better later than never, but better never late.

Sometimes Web-based businesses forget that the Internet is just another channel from which business can be conducted. Granted it is unique in some ways, but many of the same rules apply, especially when it comes to logistics and order fulfillment.

One of the last functions in the chain of customer-centric processes is the fulfillment of the customer's order. Ensuring that the customer's order is picked, packed, and shipped accurately is the final step in the online shopping process.

As online sales continue to explode three factors put new pressures on a Web site's order fulfillment systems:

- the expansion of the product line offered to the online customer

- the necessity of moving a large volume of small packages at breakneck speed

- the task of meeting ever growing customer expectations

Web sites that don't address order fulfillment with the same energy as they jumped into the role of online selling will find themselves fighting an uphill battle for customer loyalty. Web-based business can meet these demands by taking the steps to **immediately** begin developing a fail safe fulfillment system that delivers end-to-end logistics, i.e., package visibility and service continuity from buy button to final destination.

End-to-end logistics consist of three basics:

1. Empowerment of the customers by keeping them informed and providing self-service solutions that apply to common fulfillment issues.

2. Staying focused on the quality and availability of the product.

3. Speedy delivery of the product to the customer.

Running a sophisticated e-commerce site often means (on top of everything else) operating a warehouse, pulling inventory from shelves and packing it for shipment, retaining a delivery service, helping customers track an order until it arrives, and dealing with returns. To do this successfully a Web-based business must rely on automated logistical solutions.

Customers have been led to believe through marketing and media hype that the Web is all about convenience. They come to the Web with the expectation that online shopping will be quick and easy. Sadly, that is not the reality.

Whether you are a small start-up business or an enterprise site, coordinating and delivering at Web speed is a tremendous challenge. But if a Web site does succeed it has a tremendous competitive advantage.

IT'S STILL ALL ABOUT THE CUSTOMER

Hopefully, the reader did heed what was said in the previous chapter — customer service is the best marketing tool you have — and logistics is an arm of customer service. To guarantee the best customer service, a Web-based business can't separate the warehouse from its order management. This is true no matter what the size of the Web-based business.

A small entrepreneurial startup may have little experience with shipping product. A click-and-mortar through its counterpart has an infrastructure that is, in all probability, geared toward shipping palettes or cases to distributors or stores — not quantities of ones and twos. Web sites have customers with high expectations, they want their products fast, and they may expect shipment of different products to different addresses, and ask for instant credit for returns.

MIRED IN THE SMALL PARCEL DILEMMA

Although online shopping is exploding, less than one-half of the Web sites make a profit on a one-item product order. Profit comes when the customer purchases more than one item, but even then it is dependent upon efficiencies in the Web site's logistics and fulfillment processes.

If it is designed efficiently, a Web site can keep the cost of receiving, storage and picking down to less than a dollar per product. But when the cost of packing (labor, the carton, and packing material) and delivery is added in, the total distribution cost can increase from to between $6.00 and $8.00 per product.

A Web site also has to find a way to overcome the cost of continually shipping out small packages where the shipping sometimes is at least one-half of the overall value of the product purchased.

This high distribution cost is one reason why the Web has not progressed past the "rapidly emerging sales channel" stage, except in a few specific areas — books (where 20-50% discounts are given on popular books), high ticket items, and virtual products (software).

Unless the customer is shopping for a specific hard-to-find product or finds the convenience of shopping online outweighs additional costs — the Web site has an uphill battle. For many products, it is much less expensive to go to the local retail store, even when the cost of gas and the time to drive and shop is factored into the equation. Of course, the Web site also has to overcome the fact that shopping at a local retail store brings immediate gratification — the product is in-hand and the customer is not forced to wait for its arrival.

LOGISTICS

Taking an online order is the easy part. Getting the product to the customer is tough. That last yard — completing the sale to the satisfaction of the customers so they return and order again — takes planning and organization. The key word is "completing" and the sale is not complete until the product is in the customer's hands and the customer is satisfied. It's the least glamorous part of operating a Web-based business and it's the hardest to get right. The complex process of getting a product from the Web site's virtual checkout counter to its customer's doorstep is what order fulfillment is all about.

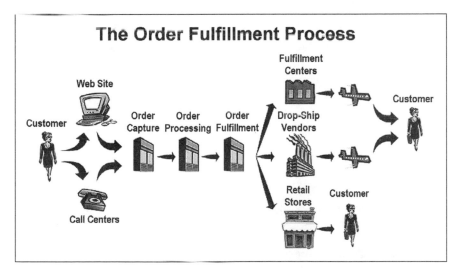

Logistics moves the right product to the right place at the right time. For a Web site to become more efficient and, therefore, profitable, it must reduce inventory costs and logistical costs, i.e., order fulfillment costs. Fulfillment is a logistical challenge for the whole e-commerce community. This is why many of the major brick-and-mortar Web sites offer only a limited number of products. But, to stay competitive in today's market, these e-commerce sites must expand their online product offering.

A Web-based business' e-commerce logistics requires integration of systems that run from the Web site's shopping cart clear through to the shippers tracking system so that the Web site is notified when the customer receives the package. It also requires managing the complexity of delivering thousands of mostly small packages daily to their unique destinations. With few exceptions, Web businesses have simply ignored the necessity of integration with inventory and distribution systems, the warehouse and its value chain.

Before making any fulfillment decisions, consider how your business will:

- process orders

- manage multiple suppliers seamlessly

- provide a comprehensive exception-handling process

- handle the issue of returned products

The Issues

Thankfully, a Web-based business needn't become an immediate expert in fulfillment. Someone in the value chain must be an expert in fulfillment, but it doesn't have to be the Web-based business. It is quite easy for new Web-based businesses to outsource virtually all back-end logistical functions including:

- order management

- warehousing and inventory management (including forecasting)

- IT systems integration to connect the front and back systems

- fulfillment

- post-sales services like warranty repair, returns management, customer care centers, spare parts fulfillment

Nonetheless, Web-based businesses that outsource their entire fulfillment needs must be concerned about the possibility of isolating themselves from their customers. An emerging pattern in the outsourcing area is that a Web site first outsources its fulfillment needs, followed by moving the process in-house as it decides to make logistics a key part of its internal business process.

But should a Web site outsource its fulfillment and distribution process or keep it in-house? First ask whether it makes good business sense to fill orders in-house or hire a fulfillment service. Another option might include contracts with drop shippers using a third-party logistics partner like OrderTrust (www.ordertrust.net) to handle the process. Assess your order fulfillment requirements and balance them with the resources available in-house. Once that task is completed, you will be in a better position to determine which approach will enable your business to fill orders and provide quality customer service at a price that leaves room for a profit.

Instituting the systems and rules that govern inventory management, sales forecasting and efficient delivery of products are the key items the majority of Web-based businesses need to work on, but just as important is sharing information about the fulfillment process with the customer. Keep customer's informed — when an order will be delivered, if a product is out of stock, whether it is backordered, or if the order has been cancelled.

To be successful, Web sites (in particular the large and enterprise sites) have to automate as much as possible and as soon as possible. Smaller Web sites should build a scalable back-end system so they can implement the automation of these processes in the future.

The real magic is what's going on inside the fulfillment processes and the systems that are connected to them.

- Mining data to project inventory and demand.

- Tying the customer's ordering process tightly to the supply chain, which in turn, gives Web-based businesses a better understanding of what inventory is available and when the next product shipments are due, so that it can inform customers when to expect delivery.

- Integrating systems from the time a Web-based business' customer clicks the "buy" button to when the product(s) is delivered to the customer's doorstep.

- Enabling the Web site and its customers, to track product and purchases.

- Respond to exceptional circumstances — like broken products, damaged boxes, or misplaced items in an order, backorders, returns, etc.

• Keep processes such as filling orders and shipping efficient, to avoid cost overruns.

Many operational Web sites find that they are saddled with either an e-commerce packaged solution that they can't integrate with their fulfillment processes or they are still in the brick-and-mortar mode of fulfillment. New startups can avoid both of these situations with proper planning.

The entrepreneurial Web sites trying to solve their fulfillment issues may find that their existing e-commerce system is the problem. If so, they can temporarily outsource their fulfillment, though there will probably still be problematic integration issues. However, somewhere down the road they will have to bite the bullet and make the necessary changes so they can bring fulfillment in-house.

The brick-and-mortars making their move to the Web have many choices. If their sales channel consists of retail stores and/or distributors, then in all probability their in-house back-end won't be able to manage the demands of an e-commerce Web site. To handle this problem the new click-and-mortar needs to build out a new fulfillment center (or establish a relationship with a fulfillment service provider). This way the current in-house systems can still have a role in the fulfillment processes, avoiding some of the costly technical and integration issues.

The software and middleware that is necessary to make all the "magic" happen is a complex and extensive subject which is outside the scope of this book. The author suggests you look at www.elogistics101.com (subscribe to the newsletter). Also, www.workz.com has some very good articles on fulfillment plus it's another good Web site to bookmark. Another site with some interesting articles on fulfillment is www.internet.com (just type "fulfillment" in the search box). For some more helpful articles go to www.opsandfulfillment.com and don't forget to subscribe to the magazine. Keep an eye out for the author's new book written on the subject.

As OrderTrust states on its Web site, "the 'messyware' involved with connecting your sales channels to the multiple vendors in your commerce community, suppliers, fulfillers, customer service centers and more" is a complex subject requiring expertise in innumerable diverse areas.

Logistics Plan

A logistics plan lays out the chain of events from receipt of the customer's order through delivery of the product to the post-sale processes. It should be a guide upon which all fulfillment decisions are based. A formal logistics plan will ensure that everyone (you, relevant employees, partners, consultants and outsourcers) consider not only the Web site's requirements, goals and objectives, but also what each player can bring to the table. This will help to assure that everyone is on the "same page."

There are questions that a Web-based business must ask before it can solidify its order fulfillment solutions. Once the answers are in hand, use them as the starting point in the design of a good logistics system to ensure that a Web-based business' order fulfillment processes will efficiently serve it and its customers no matter what fulfillment method is used.

Product and Packaging

- What are the physical characteristics of the Web site's products and how do they vary in size, weight, and packaging?

- Does the Web site offer products that will require special handling and/or packaging (breakables that will need repackaging, different size items in one box or a separate box per item, signature on delivery requirement, etc.)?

- Will the Web site offer products that will need a number of different components or accessories to be in the same box (a printer, printer cable and spare ink cartridge or a DSL Modem, a telephone cord, line filters, etc.)?

- Do any of the products require sub-assembly?

- Are any of the products "over sized" or "heavy weight" so that they may require a different carrier from the norm?

- Are any of the products perishable or fragile, requiring a specific transportation mode?

- Do any of the products require special licensing for transport (i.e., alcohol, pharmaceuticals, etc.)?

Average Order

- What is the size and value of the minimum, maximum and average order?

- What is the Web site's current volume of orders?

- What volume of orders is expected 6 months, 1 year, 2 years and 5 years from now?

Shipping

- What carriers do the Web site and its suppliers use and what system is in place to track shipments? Is the tracking system easily accessible to everyone including the customers?

- Will the Web site offer online tracking and tracing to customers?

- Will the Web site offer its customers a choice of carriers?

- How will shipping rates be determined? Can the Web site accommodate customers who already have a UPS/FedEx/other carrier account number and want to be billed directly? Is COD an option?

- Can customers ship to multiple addresses from a single order?

- If the Web site does ship in branded packaging, will this external branding affect security as far as delivery is concerned (i.e., will it encourage theft)?

- What is the back-up plan if notification is received that a shipment has been delayed/lost/damaged?

- Is the Web site willing to absorb any of the shipping and handling costs? If so, under what conditions?

- What is the acceptable level of shipping costs compared to the order value (from both the customer's perspective and the Web site's)?

Delivery Quality Control

- What is an acceptable time period to get products to the customer?

- What are the criteria for on-time delivery, damaged claims, order accuracy, supply availability?

- How will quality checks be performed?

Inventory

- How are orders for out-of-stock products handled? If the product is expected to be available in a short timeframe, does the Web site still take the order and risk having to upgrade the shipping to meet the promised delivery date?

- How much inventory is needed to ensure product availability?

- Can suppliers respond adequately to a sudden increase in orders?

- How will replenishment be triggered once an item is picked from storage?

Returns

- What is the percentage of anticipated product returns?

- How are returns to be handled (dispose of them, use a secondary market, refurbish and put back into inventory, return to supplier)?

- What are the arrangements with suppliers for returns?

- How will customers return the products? Do they require authorization or special packaging/labels for return? Are there any return restrictions, and if so, does the Web site have the documentation posted to support that policy?

- Who is responsible for inspection/valuation?

- When does ownership shift to the customer or back to the supplier?

- What records are required to keep track of potential tax write-offs or supplier credit?

- How are tracking records integrated with inventory management and shipping records to produce necessary documentation?

- What financial arrangements are in place with suppliers for return credit?

- What documentation is required from the receiving department?

International Orders

- Is the Web site selling products for international shipment? If so, how are currency transactions to be handled?

- Who will fill out international documentation?

- Who will be responsible for duties and taxes/customs clearance?

- Are these costs included in the shipping cost quotes?

- Has the Web-based business planned for the additional costs elemental to international shipping/transactions?

Seasonal Considerations

• If the Web site offers products that are seasonal, how will that affect the warehousing/inventory requirements?

Suppliers

• Are suppliers willing to ship direct to the customers upon request?

• Can they ship daily, if necessary?

• Are suppliers willing to change from a "pallet" or "bulk" shipment basis to a smaller count shipment?

• Will suppliers accept small orders?

• Will the supplier be responsible for transportation costs to the fulfillment center?

• If the Web site is using drop shippers (see later in this chapter), are its suppliers willing to repackage their product in the Web site's branded boxes and use its branded labels, promotional material, etc.?

• If the Web site is using drop shippers will they insist on using any of their branded products? If so, what and how will it affect the Web site's brand?

Infrastructure

• How will the Web site send order information to the fulfillment service provider, how often (real-time, hourly or daily) and separately or in batches?

• How will the Web site handle package tracking and provide the information to its customers?

• How are the Web site's order entry systems integrated with the fulfillment, inventory management, returns management and shipping systems?

• Do some orders get priority over others, if so, what are the criteria?

• How are the Web site's financial systems integrated with its inbound shipping, inventory management, orders entry, delivery and return information systems?

• Can suppliers, order entry, inventory management, fulfillment, accounting, shipping department and carriers all "talk to each other" to trigger coordinated action?

- What online "alert" systems exist for replenishment, delivery delays, order inaccuracies, erroneous shipping addresses, incoming returns, etc.?

- What system is in place to keep track of all products as they move from supplier to customer (item by item, not just by order)?

- How does the shopping cart technology link with the warehousing/distribution operation?

Warehousing and Fulfillment Centers

- What are the warehousing requirements (area needed for inventory, supplies and shipping prep; docks; fork lifts; racking and sorting bins; conveyors; pick-and-pack systems; radio transmitted bar coding; software; shipping and labeling equipment; etc.)?

- Is the inventory storage area designed for easy and efficient order picking?

- What are the preferred geographic locations of the fulfillment center(s)?

- Is a dedicated facility needed or are the products to be put into a warehouse/distribution operation that others also use?

- Are sophisticated services and space needed or would a direct mail company or public warehousing space be satisfactory?

- How well does the distribution facility accommodate multiple carriers for inbound/outbound shipments? Who will handle scheduling?

- What is the trade off financially between outsourcing logistics vs. the Web-based business operating its own warehouse and distribution facility?

Insurance

- What is the Web site's policy regarding insurance coverage for loss, damage, and theft? What is the carrier's and what is the customer's responsibility?

- Is the insurance information clearly posted anywhere on the Web site?

Exceptions

Just as in the traditional sales channel, there is the need for handling exceptions. If a Web site is using the drop-ship model (explained later in this chapter), what does it do when an individual customer order includes products from multiple suppliers and one of the products ordered is out of stock or backordered? Or perhaps it handles its own shipping and inventory and it is out of stock and it doesn't know when it will be replenished.

- How does a Web site handle a partial shipment?

  Hold the shipment for all the items, ship all ordered items that are available and cancel the rest?

  Does it request the customer's input prior to making a decision?

  Does it hold the order until it receives a reply from the customer?

One solution is to have the Web-based business' order fulfillment system include event-based triggers that are modeled on specific business rules. To implement such a rules-based system requires that you to sit down with the appropriate personnel, suppliers and, if necessary, the fulfillment provider, and correlate the business rules.

Management of Suppliers and Channels

Most Web sites will have multiple suppliers providing a wide array of products. Again, the drop-ship model (although, in some instances, it is the most efficient) poses the most problems to the Web-based business. However, situations can arise with any fulfillment model, and Web-based businesses should have the ability to accommodate customer orders that include products from a variety of suppliers. The Web site must be able to apportion each order appropriately and track it through each supplier, and at the same time give its customer a seamless view of the shipping data. If a supplier messes up in product delivery, the customers hold the Web site responsible, not its supplier. A Web site must keep on top of its entire supply chain.

BACK-END INTEGRATION ISSUES

A Web-based business must have a clearly defined process for moving an order from its Web site to its fulfillment center, whether it is in-house or outsourced. This process will tie the order to its payment and fulfillment processes — this is where integration with its back-end systems becomes critical. The large and enterprise Web sites will also find it necessary to tie into back-end applications, such as enterprise resource planning (ERP), inventory management, and financial applications.

A brick-and-mortar that is making its move to the Web may already have pieces of the fulfillment process in place, but the in-house operations may not be familiar with the one- and two-item shipments that will, in all likelihood, become the norm for its Web operation. The brick-and-mortars will be tempted to build out their existing "bulk" distribution center to handle its Web site's fulfillment needs — this is not always a good idea. But, depending on the legacy infrastructure, this method could provide low on-going costs and greater operational control with easy stock status information and higher product availability. On the downside, there may be a risk of confusion to current operations, and the ability for existing personnel to adapt to change should be a consideration. The transition could generate a long period of inefficiencies due to the necessity of building a complex system of individual software components that require integration, customization, and management in order to merge the Web-based business with the traditional business' systems.

An alternative solution is to find a fulfillment provider to handle the click-and-mortar's logistical processes. The decision should be based upon scalability — does the brick-and-mortar (and its Web site) have the budget and time necessary to build and maintain its own customized solution? Or can a fulfillment provider more effectively furnish a solution to fit either or both of its e-commerce and traditional channel needs.

All Web-based businesses will find that integration with their back-end systems is a challenge (and costly), but it is absolutely necessary since it is the key to imposing order in fulfillment chaos. A Web site must be able to integrate not only with content management systems but also customer management systems, customer service systems, order fulfillment systems, inventory management systems, and financial systems, to name a few.

SHIPPING

For the Web-based business, selecting the right carrier can be a difficult chore. So many options are offered that the best choice is not always clear. When looking for a shipping partner-type relationship ask:

- Do they offer a full range of shipping services, i.e., same day, next day, ground, air, etc.?

- Do they have online real-time tracking and tracing that can integrate into a Web site's back-end and its warehousing systems?

- Do they have automated, easy return service that is consumer friendly?

- Do they offer complete transportation management services, including palletized inbound shipments as well as small package services?

- Can they offer the same connectivity and tracking services if shipments move outside the shipper's network (a commercial airline or a train or ocean container)?

- Can they handle orders 24x7? If not, what is the latest they will except a package and what is the latest they will pick-up a package?

- How late can a package get into their hands and still be delivered the next day?

It is essential for a Web site to integrate tracking information into its systems and make that data available to customers. For example, Federal Express has a customized shipping system that allows qualified Web-based businesses to track deliveries once every hour. This allows a Web site to not only check when a package was delivered and who signed for it, but also the orders that were returned because of a problem with the delivery itself. Then this information can be sent to the Web site's customers via e-mail.

Shipping is one of the most costly factors of order fulfillment. Keep in mind that shipping rates are determined by three major factors: travel mileage, package weight and delivery times. Let's say you're shipping a package from San Francisco to New York City and the weight of the package is five pounds or less. Using FedEx Standard Overnight or UPS Next Day Air Saver would cost approximately $30 (FedEx being a few pennies more), Airborne Next Afternoon Service runs approximately $21, and the U.S. Postal Service Express Mail runs $24 dollars. Second day service is a more reasonable, although still expensive — FedEx and UPS both running around $16 (again FedEx is a few pennies more), Airborne runs a little over $10 and the U.S. Postal Service charges $6.50 for its Priority Mail service.

Now lets look at what the shipper does to earn the $6.50 to $30:

- transport the package whether it is 5 miles or 5000 miles

- provide tracking information so you and your customer can know exactly where in the shipping cycle the package is located

- deliver the package to the customer's front door

- record when the package is delivered to the customer's front door

Speed is an expensive commodity — however the Internet is all about speed and so many Web-based businesses are in a catch 22 situation — a speedy delivery of products but inexpensively — eek!

If you choose to offer your customers shipping options, post clear, concise and fair shipping choices and policies on your Web site. If overnight service is offered, clarify what time orders must be received for same day shipping and that orders placed on weekends and holidays are shipped the next business day (unless that is not the case).

There are several online sites that provide information on the best shipping options based on origin and destination of the package as well as the weight and dimensions. Check out www.iship.com and www.smartship.com, they both offer templates that allow a Web site to find the best options for shipping a package based on delivery times, weight and destination with a comparison of UPS, FedEx, Airborne, and the U.S. Postal Service. Just fill out the online form with the appropriate information — shipment dimensions, postal codes and loss-protection options. It even has a place for a Web site to add its handling charges (if any). Both Web sites also offer an integration tool that will allow a Web-based business to provide the service directly on its Web pages as a convenience for its customers.

A more sophisticated alternative is www.InterShipper.net. This site also provides comparison of rates among multiple carriers (domestic and international). But it goes further with tracking, drop-off locations, pickup scheduling, ZIP code lookups, along with an integration tool so a Web site can provide the service to its customers.

FULFILLMENT

Although most Web sites currently receive fewer than 400 orders per day, as the buying public gains trust and comfort with Internet purchases, Web sales should increase exponentially. Inventory and fulfillment issues resulting from increased orders will continue to catch many an unwary e-commerce site unprepared. Now is the time to perfect the fulfillment systems and services needed so that when a Web site's business starts to take off, everything is in place.

When a customer orders a product from a Web site, that customer is trying to achieve one or more of four objectives:

1. Save money on product cost (which is partially offset by the addition of shipping costs).

2. Avoid the additional expense of state sales tax.

3. Purchase specialty products that are not available locally.

4. Convenience: avoid a time-consuming trip to a mall or specialty store.

What the customers fear most about buying from a Web-based business is the uncertainty of whether their purchase will be delivered when promised. Web newsgroups are full of tales about products ordered and not received when promised (sometimes never).

There comes a time when every Web-based business selling a physical product as opposed to a virtual product (such as software that can be downloaded over the Internet) must decide how to pick, pack and ship the product to customers in a timely manner. As stated many times in this book, online customers have zero tolerance for delays and poor service. What can a Web site do to provide superlative fulfillment services?

- Have the Web site linked directly, in real-time, to the fulfillment center (in-house or otherwise).

- Build a real-time inventory management system so that its inventory is constantly verified — if a customer sees it on the Web site, the product should be in stock and instantly available. If it is out of stock, but on order, have a system on the site to advise the customer that the product is backordered and when the customer can expect it to ship.

- If the customer places the order by 5:00 p.m. (local time), the product should be shipped to the customer that day.

- Orders should be bar coded and scanned during picking and check weighed at the manifesting scale to insure complete picking accuracy.

- If an order will take more than 2 days to deliver, special low rates on 2nd day shipping should be offered to the customer (i.e., fulfillment center is in Vermont and customer is in Hawaii).

- If an order placed prior to 5:00 p.m. (local time) cannot be shipped the same day, it should be shipped the next day with free upgrade to "next day" delivery to insure it is received within two days.

- As soon as the shipment is manifested, an e-mail should be sent to the customer, showing shipping date, expected arrival date, final costs and tracking number. If the order is to be shipped from multiple sites, an e-mail should be sent for each part of the shipment.

- Another e-mail should be sent the day after expected delivery for verification that delivery was made and accurately fulfilled.

- A bar coded "return" label and document should accompany each part of the shipment for use if any part of the order must be returned.

Outsource what can't be done in-house. Re-visit the situation regularly and when the return on investment (ROI) shows it is feasible, integrate the process in-house with the necessary technology, personnel and facilities in place.

Keeping the Customer Informed

What customers don't **see** on their favorite e-commerce site is its behind-the-scenes rapid and efficient ordering and fulfillment process. The e-commerce site that understands the importance of the logistics involved in **timely** order processing, **notifying** customers of unavailable items, **providing** real-time order tracking and status information, **implementing** billing procedures and inventory-tracking procedures will soon become a customer's favorite site. While the customer could care less about the underpinnings of the site and how it works, they know it works for them.

This is where a Web-based business' back-end transaction management takes center stage. Order and shipping confirmations delivered to the customer's e-mail in-box at the time that the order is processed should be a common practice. Keep the customer apprised of where their order is in the pick, pack and ship process.

Order confirmations should contain enough data to give the customers confidence that their order will arrive on time. Once the Web-based business has confirmation that the order is on the way to the customer (it is in the hands of the shipper), it may wish to follow with an e-mail to its customer. The e-mail may say something like "Just thought we would let you know your Order Number 12345 is on its way." (Also provide the shipping and tracking information plus a link to use if they want to check on the status of the shipment). When the Web site obtains confirmation that the package has been delivered, a rigorous customer service will follow-up with another e-mail to the customer verifying that delivery was received and the product(s) met their expectations

If the Web-based business has opted for the drop-ship model without an integration process, it may find that providing this service will be difficult and time consuming. Order management companies can help such as OrderTrust www.ordertrust.net, Netship (www.netship.com) and Dotcom Distribution (www.dotcomdist.com).

The confidence a Web site instills in its customers will be worth the struggle that it went through to provide the information. And the Web brand will be paid ten-fold in ongoing consumer loyalty. A lack of shipping confirmations will result in worried customers interacting with CSRs to obtain assurance that the order is on its way (an avoidable expense).

The "Holy Grail" of customer confirmation is to keep the customers in the loop by providing a confirmation that outlines the order details with everything from the recipient's name to cost and billing information. Include:

• a personalized greeting

- the order number and summary with charges

- estimated shipping and arrival date

- bill-to and ship-to addresses

- customer service contact information

- special request information (gift wrap/gift messages, special delivery instructions)

- links to order status and order history

- links to return information

The shipping confirmation should include all of the above information plus tracking numbers (when relevant) and links to the Web site's package tracking service.

Again, a Web site's customers expect a lot of information — ideally shipping costs, delivery times, order status, product availability, real-time online customer service — and they want easy access to it on the Web. Providing what they want on your Web site — versus the fulfillment provider or shipper providing the information — is preferable for branding purposes. All of this may require a large investment in what may seem like an over aggressive Web-based supply chain management technology, but as the Web site prospers it will become a necessity.

Fulfillment Models

The "back-office" subsystems of e-commerce sites — those that provide the link between the customer experience and the actual physical delivery of goods to the customer — continue to be a challenge for Web-based businesses. These parts, which include inventory management, order capture and management and reconciliation, often prove to be more difficult than the construction of the site itself.

But all fulfillment is not equal — online stores generally fit into one of six order fulfillment models, each with distinctive benefits and faults.

The Single Web Site Order Model: The product is ordered off the Web site and shipped from an in-house fulfillment center (a basement or a garage for a home-based business — a warehouse or distribution center [possibly automated] for larger businesses) to the customer in one shipment. This model has one great advantage over the other models — easy returns — since it gives the Web-based business an increased level of control over every moment of the brand experience. This is what the mail order catalog business has been doing for years. However, it does require know-how, labor, facilities and often, special equipment and software, all of which may be outside the area of expertise and budget of the average Web-based business. The disadvantage is that there is usually only the one shipping location, which means that same-day delivery is impossible (except in a small geographical area) and next-day delivery is expensive.

Kiosk Order Model: More and more brick-and-mortars are beginning to use this model (and in the future you will find pure-play Web-based businesses in this space). The customer orders products, using a Kiosk with a computer and high speed connection, located at a store or mall. With this model the customer doesn't need a home computer and most of the time can even pay in person for the products ordered. In this way it is possible to order products offered online and pay in cash. The customers also have the choice of picking up the order on their next trip to the kiosk location or having it shipped to a specified location. One advantage of this model is a possible increase in customer loyalty — there is human interaction (the store clerk that takes the payment and hands over the products). Also, an almost unlimited range of products can be made available at a neighborhood store, provided the customer can wait a couple of day (if they are not willing to pay for next day delivery). Soon Internet Kiosks may be as prevalent as ATMs, so you may order your favorite books, wine, clothing and gourmet food at your corner coffee shop or dry cleaners and pick up the order a few days later.

The Drop-Ship Model: This model is popular with some small Web-based businesses, particularly because it reduces initial capital expenditures. With this model a customer clicks the buy button on a Web site, the Web site then forward's the order to it's drop shipper(s) (a wholesaler or distributor that owns a variety of products). The drop shipper then fills that order by shipping product directly to the Web site's customers. The Web-based business owns the customer database, while the drop shipper owns the products. The drop shipper pays the Web-based business a sales commission. The drawbacks of this arrangement are that there is little or no control over how the products are packed and shipped. Unless negotiated in advance, your products can be shipped with the drop shipper's name on the packaging instead of the Web site's brand causing difficulties in retaining a loyal customer base. The drop ship model generally functions best if a Web site offers a wide range or generalized base of products but does not want to worry about managing the entire chain of the order fulfillment process.

The drop-ship model requires that the Web-based business give up much of its control of the fulfillment process. Although a Web-based business may determinedly establish rigid guidelines for its drop-ship suppliers, it is still putting its brand in the hands of strangers. This includes everything from quality of product, delivery to the customers, communication with customers concerning tracking, shipping, delivery dates, returns, and so forth.

When it comes to integrating the front-end customer experience with the drop-ship fulfillment process the disadvantages of this model become apparent.

- A Web site probably won't have any control over when the order will be shipped to the customer or in how many packages. It might not even know if the product the customer ordered is in stock.

- A Web site may not have a way to provide customers with tracking or shipping status information.

- The products ordered from the Web site may be shipped with the drop shipper's own name on the labels and packing lists, negating the Web site's branding efforts and causing customer confusion on receipt of the package.

This model isn't hopeless. If a Web site does decide to use the drop-ship model for some or all of its products it needs to iron out these peccadilloes prior to entering into any written contract. If a Web-based business is determined to make the drop-ship model work, then it should consider utilizing a service for its order management — OrderTrust (www.ordertrust.net), Netship (www.netship.com) or Dotcom Distribution (www.dotcomdist.com) — so it can regain some control over the fulfillment process. Or some of this can be accomplished by establishing internal monitoring processes, assigning employees to drop-ship monitoring, and leveraging technologies that will help to integrate the Web site with the drop-shipper's systems to aid it in keeping the customer informed.

Same-Day Home Delivery Model: The products are ordered online, picked and packed at a local distribution center, and delivered the same day to the customer. This approach offers the convenience of local shopping with an added benefit of being a timesaver. However, to provide same day delivery is always more expensive, both for the Web-based business and its customer. The customer may feel it is a good tradeoff — personal time for money. It requires a very complex distribution and delivery network. Because of this it must be limited to specific geographic areas (how is a Web site going to give same day delivery to a farmer in the outreaches of Minnesota or a customer in the mountains of New Mexico).

Fulfillment Service Provider (FSP) Model: This model is a cost-effective alternative, the Web-based business can outsource its warehousing and distribution services to a third party. The companies offering these services are called third party logistics providers, fulfillment service providers, or fulfillment houses (they will be referred to as fulfillment service provider or FSP in this book). This model could utilize one or multiple distribution centers strategically located nationwide or worldwide, each center carrying inventory levels relative to their regional market. This model gives the Web-based business a good deal of control over all aspects of product quality, distribution and messaging.

The FSP receives merchandise from the Web-based business and numerous other businesses and it stores the merchandise in its warehouse(s). It picks and ships the orders received by its clients. Since the FSP provides this service to numerous businesses, it can spread the costs of the operation across a large base. However, Web-based businesses may find that maintaining the optimum service levels will require adjustments — just give everyone at least 4 or 5 months to work out all of the bugs. In particular, many of these providers make it difficult for a Web-based business to obtain real-time information about inventory status and order status. So don't sign a contract with a new FSP just a month or so before the Christmas buying rush.

Many large Web sites are currently using this model. There are Web-based businesses that feel (and rightly so) it's good business practice to concentrate on their core strengths and contract with experts, such as a FSP. The FSP will, for an up-front agreed price, provide whatever services are needed. The FSP will receive a Web site's products, warehouse them, and when customer orders are received, it will pick and fill the customer orders, and pack and ship each order to the customers by the method that the Web site and/or its customers choose. The provider works for the Web-based business and therefore the labels and packing lists carry the Web site's name and logo.

The fulfillment service provider model is frequently identified as the future of e-commerce, but it's not there yet. While, many Web-based businesses try to deliver on this image, they find the cost of fulfillment can dwarf the cost of the product.

In-store Fulfillment Model: This is a click-and-mortar model. When an online order is received by a click-and-mortar it is fulfilled by employees who pick stock from its counterpart's, traditional retail store shelves. Then the product delivery process is basically the same as any other model. This model does incur less startup costs in the short term, and some brick-and-mortars use this model to "dip their toe" in the e-commerce arena. In the end though, this model can be very expensive due to overhead and the complexity in tracking and pricing the same inventory for store and Web sales. How do you bill costs to each entity?

Before you read any further, ask:

- What type of fulfillment model would best suit your Web site?
- How dependent on high-service levels are your Web site and its customers?
- Are the customers more concerned with cost or slow delivery?
- How is your Web site planning to process returned products?

IN-HOUSE SOLUTIONS

Controlling the entire customer buying experience, from beginning to end, will give a Web site a competitive advantage. However, the Web sites must learn how to make a profit on each shipped package. If you ask almost any Web-based business, "what is your cost of fulfillment?" The reply will be "I don't know." Demand for order fulfillment solutions is reshaping the existing e-commerce landscape. Web sites are growing up and forced to face the hard fact that fulfillment is a serious issue. While most Web businesses initially survived by offering a limited number of products they now must expand their product range to compete.

Large and Enterprise Size Web Sites

Any Web-based business with more than 1,000 orders per day should bring its e-commerce fulfillment in house for three reasons:

- It gives more control of the operations,
- It leverages economies between existing and online channels, and
- It allows differentiation of customer service.

API (Application Programming Interface) - Software that an application uses to request and carry out lower-level services performed by a computer's operation system. In short, an API is a hook into software. An API is a set of standard software interrupts, calls and data formats that applications use to initiate contact with network services, mainframe communication programs, etc. Applications use APIs to call services that transport data across a network.

Evaluate Your Existing System: For a brick-and-mortar making its move to the Web one of the first steps to take is integration of its back-end systems. Until now, Web site integration issues were limited to the applications residing within the Web-based business' own domain. However, logistics technology requires that integration now extend outward toward the 4 corners of the world and application program interfaces (APIs) are the passports. Most e-commerce systems have APIs but they vary widely in capability. Some legacy systems have APIs with varying capabilities. There are even custom-built legacy systems without APIs but there might be a way to modify them to directly use the Web site system's APIs.

EDI (Electronic Data Interchange) - A series of standards which provide computer-to-computer exchange of business documents between different companies' computers over the Internet. EDI allows for the transmission of purchase orders, shipping documents, invoices, invoice payments, etc. between a Web-based business and its trading partners.

XML (eXtensible Markup Language) - A system for organizing and tagging elements of a document. XML has the ability to structure exchange of data between computers attached to the Web, thus allowing one Web server to talk to another Web server. This means manufacturers and merchants can begin to quickly swap data, such as pricing, stock-keeping numbers, transaction terms and product descriptions.

If it is determined that taking the API route is too pricey, risky or inadequate, the next course to take is Electronic Data Interchange (EDI) and Extensible Markup Language (XML). Both can provide integration between systems. EDI is a well-established standard — the EDI messages are normally transmitted between businesses by Value-Added Networks (VANs). XML is an emerging standard for describing information and can be transmitted directly between businesses over the Internet, but translation will be required between the legacy system and the e-commerce system.

Options: After evaluating the present back-end systems and the current needs, a Web-based business usually has the choice of three options for its e-commerce platform:

A custom solution: This is a good choice if you have the capital and the time to design a comprehensive solution to give your Web site the integration it needs.

A packaged solution: This can, at times, be less pricey than a custom solution. A packaged or product solution is not the typical "out of the box" product (this solution can't be bought in a retail store). A packaged solution still requires specialized integration incurring the expense of "professional services." A Web site will have to find the right packaged solution that can integrate with its existing systems since not all APIs are equal. Find out how the APIs operate with remote systems and with the Web site's specific fulfillment needs and existing systems, and don't forget the security issues.

Many high-end packaged solutions offer APIs, EDI and XML capabilities. But it pays to be careful, a product that states it offers EDI capabilities, could only mean that it simply sends an EDI850 purchase order message in response to an order. This falls short of the kind of meaningful interchange needed to support a Web site's fulfillment needs. Finally, if the existing e-commerce system is currently running on a packaged product, it may be that the necessary usable hooks and tools to integrate the product will cost many times more than the original cost.

An application service provider (ASP) solution: It seems every day a new application service provider (ASP) offering a specialized service opens its doors for business. This may be a good alternative solution for some Web sites. Since ASPs maintain software and infrastructure for many clients, the cost can be spread across the landscape, resulting in lower costs for the clients. The cost of software and integration are often built into a long-term contract and amortized. A good ASP can provide an e-commerce solution that seems like it is customized but without incurring the huge development, maintenance, and infrastructure costs.

ASPs usually offer third party or proprietary software. If the ASP is offering third party software then there might be a few complications: The ASP may have built-in cost factors that could limit the value proposition to a Web site. The ASP is forced to rely on the third party vendor to fix bugs or provide answers to technical problems.

An ASP that offers its own proprietary software usually can provide a lower ongoing cost factor and greater flexibility. These ASPs also seem to be more flexible in their pricing policies. A Web site also might find the ASP is more responsive to adding product features or fixing bugs.

The shared infrastructure provides architectural advantages, which can reduce the cost and time required for setup and integration. Just be sure that your IT people go over everything with a fine tooth comb to verify that the ASP can meet the Web site's specific needs.

Once everyone is satisfied with the decision — be it custom, packaged or ASP — get those legal eagles involved and set it down in writing — how integration is to be addressed, what the costs will be, and how long it will take. Get warranties and guarantees with penalties for overruns.

What Must be Overcome: Although customer-centricity is the key for the rush to upgrade fulfillment capabilities, some Web sites are wondering whether they can simultaneously update their fulfillment process and avoid compromising the customer experience. The astute Web-based business knows that to maximize efficiencies and benefits it cannot afford to make fulfillment an "either/or" decision. What a Web-based business could do when selecting the methods and tools to optimize the fulfillment process, is to not immediately do a integration of the entire customer experience. However, each component should be fully knowledgeable of the other so that the response to the customer's needs can be personalized and delivery made to the customer's satisfaction.

Even large Web-based businesses find it difficult to master direct-to-consumer fulfillment. It takes a lot of guts for one of them to set up their own fulfillment center, especially since most of them make the majority of their gross income during the November and December shopping season. If they haven't done everything right, their fulfillment operations will fail under the holiday crunch. Nevertheless, a huge plurality of the large and enterprise Web sites (mainly click-and-mortars) are adamant about bringing their fulfillment processes in-house.

The deciding component of a Web site's success in building an in-house fulfillment system will be its willingness to view the entire fulfillment process as a realm without borders. When it is optimizing its fulfillment processes it must examine everything from the customer's initial product order through the delivery to the customer's door. This means a Web site cannot restrict its view to internal operations alone.

The biggest problem everyone faces is the lack of a "single" solution that can help integrate all of the back-end order processing operations to facilitate finding products from alternative suppliers, expediting orders, keeping customers informed, and processing the financial end. Even with a good logistics plan, all of this involves a mess of prickly specifications:

- taking care of credit-card authorizations

- routing one order to multiple suppliers

- routing status updates from those suppliers to customers

- handling order cancellations and product returns

- keeping up with the availability of inventory and the forecasting thereof

- shipping specifics, and the list goes on

The main dilemma is that all of these applications have no *de facto* communication standards. One solution might be to bring an extensive library of pre-built connectors into play; the connectors could reside at the Web site's hub, speaking the language of and translating between the various applications that must communicate with each other. Keep in mind that a comprehensive integration project can be a long, resource intensive process. Most Web sites will find that the complication of building out customized solutions is their only alternative.

Many Web sites will recognize that developing the needed expertise internally is not cost-effective. For most, the faster, more efficient option will be to contract with one of the new breed of consultants and software vendors who can help a Web-base business forge a trail through this technological briar patch. But first a Web site must assess its current fulfillment needs and capabilities and compare that with its long-term goals. Then, determine what is missing in terms of operational and functional processes, strategic direction, technology and organization. Once everyone has grasped that it can be done, then the task is to set out the tactical steps to fill in the missing pieces and begin moving toward complete implementation. It's easy to agree on a strategy and identify what is missing but the sticky wicket is defining the tactical operational requirements. If a Web-based business can set out a feasible plan that cuts to the nuts and bolts of the process, then it has a fighting chance.

A smattering of companies a Web-based business might want to talk to about their integration issues are: Swift Technologies (www.stecnet.com), CommerceWare (www.commerceware.com), Target Database, Inc. (www.targetdb.com), Industri-Matematik, International (www.im.se/im_home), Yantra Corporation (www.yantra.com), Modus Media International (www.modusmedia.com), Oracle Corporation (www.oracle.com) and Onesoft (www.onesoft.com).

Web-based businesses that are willing to do their homework will succeed faster. Once work has begun, everyone on the team should be available for daily or thrice weekly conference calls to avoid duplicated effort and to assure that everyone is in adherence to the logistics plan and timetable(s). Everyone must stay focused on the unequivocal requirement for a system flexible enough to grow over time.

When a brick-and-mortar is planning a move to the Web, it assumes the easiest and most economical route is to keep order fulfillment in-house. But as its Web-base business grows, it must come to grips with the fact that its distribution system is based on pallets or many-item orders, and 9 times out of 10 it can't handle the one- or two-product, small-package shipments that a Web-based business encounters.

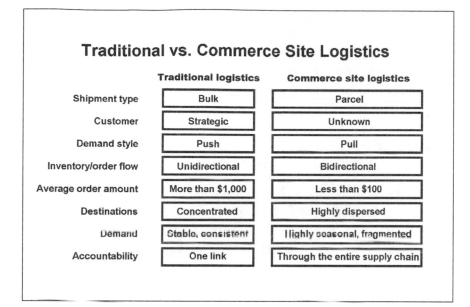

One option for enterprise Web sites choosing to keep their fulfillment in-house is to look for either a direct-to-consumer competency buried somewhere in-house (such as a small catalog operation) or buy a logistics firm or a competitor with e-commerce fulfillment capabilities already in place. Either alternative can make it easier to implement technologies to handle basic e-procurement or elementary e-commerce tasks. But this course won't give a Web-based business complete integration of internal and external systems across the entire value chain. Click-and-mortars that integrate these systems to support real-time two way flow of information throughout the value chain (the entire supply chain, customers, internal applications, and financial) require custom solutions.

Another consideration for brick-and-mortars: From an economic standpoint, many traditional brick-and-mortar businesses should keep their Web-based business separate from their traditional business to enable them to keep track of actual costs — especially if the Web-based business experiences early losses.

Small to Medium Size Web Site

Small Web-based businesses should not lose hope. It's true that the home-based Web site and the SME sites can't afford the infrastructure that the enterprise Web-based business should put in place, but it's not absolutely essential, if there isn't a large inventory. Look at your logistics plan, it should give you a good idea of what you need to do.

Order processing can be tamed if the volume is within a manageable range. As orders come in it is prudent to send e-mail acknowledgements to the customers. Then, process the orders through the payment authorization process, generate invoices, log all information into the accounting and inventory software. With such a system a Web site can know how much inventory has been sold, to whom, and at what price. Once that is completed, it is time to pick the orders (find the physical products in your inventory), package them along with packing lists, invoices, return information and return labels, and any promotional materials. Now they are ready to be delivered to the shipper — all of which admittedly can be both time- and labor-intensive.

Once the packages are in the hands of the shipper, then there are the follow-up e-mails to the customers containing the total charges, shipping information including tracking information (if available) and estimated delivery date. Once confirmation that a package was delivered to the customer (and it is up to the Web-based business to keep on top of this), send a quick e-mail to the customer to verify that delivery was received and the product(s) met the customer's expectations.

Software, etc.:

Inventory issues can lay waste to a Web site that is "starting to take off." To alleviate this problem, many e-commerce software packages provide a full-featured inventory control system, including out-of-stock and low-stock notification by e-mail. If the e-commerce software your Web site uses doesn't offer this feature, see if there is an upgrade available. Or your Web hosting service may offer an online inventory system which will need to be synchronized with the Web-based business' off line inventory system — a flat file database, Corel Paradox, Microsoft Access, Microsoft Works, etc. If the latter is the system that will be used, test the Web hosts order-activity file formats to see which has the least compatibility issues.

Another suggestion is to use off-the-shelf software like Quicken QuickPOS, Intuit's QuickBooks or PeachTree Accounting and Microsoft Excel since all have good inventory management packages which can help a small Web site manage their inventory and track orders.

Finally, a small but active Web site might want to take a look at Hallogram's IntelliTrack Inventory module (www.hallogram.com/barcodes/software/intellitrack/inventory) that maintains inventory with physical inventory and cycle counting capabilities.

Whatever inventory system is used, carefully monitor the sales activity of each product in the inventory and set realistic reorder levels (so the Web site doesn't run out of its best sellers). If you do run out of a product have a system where it is possible to place a "temporarily out of stock" notice adjacent that product with approximate replenishment date. Also insert additional information (cross-selling) about another product that may "fill the bill."

If the Web site's volume of orders is such that some type of additional automation is advisable, help might be available through:

Haven Corporation's (www.havencorp.com) various software offerings should be of interest to a Web-based business who is handling its own order fulfillment.

TDM Logistics' (www.tdmlogistics.com) Distribution Manager allows you to easily manage thousands of shipments in a single day, right from your shipping department.

Bonafide Management Systems' eResponse (www.bonafide.com) order fulfillment software that works for all sizes of Web sites from the small startup to the large, high volume e-commerce sites.

Another system worth a look, especially for small to medium size Web sites, is Order Desk Pro (www.odpro.com). This is an order entry, order tracking, sales performance analysis and customer database management tool specifically designed for companies that receive orders over a Web site.

For the busy medium size Web site there is Verian Technologies's (www.procureit.com) ProcureIT order processing and inventory software that works with an ODBC database.

And last, there is also, of course, order management services such as OrderTrust (www.ordertrust.net), Netship (www.netship.com) or Dotcom Distribution (www.dotcomdist.com), which allow a Web site to keep some of the physical fulfillment duties in-house and outsource some of the more expensive technology driven aspects.

Shipping Procedures: First, the customer's view. Decide if you are offering shipping options to your customers. If the Web site offers multiple shipping methods, give your customers the tools to pick their shipper of choice and the method (i.e., overnight, 2nd day, standard), and calculate the cost of shipping. A good practice for small Web sites is to offer links to each shipper's site on the Web page where the shipping information is provided. This way the customers can easily calculate cost and track their package (assuming it is sent with a tracking number). Your shipping page should include the Web site's shipping policies set out in a clear, concise manner, sample weight/price shipping charts, and perhaps a note about the amount of time that the average package will spend in transit. Educate the customers, make them aware of all shipping options. Many will opt for second day service when they realize the difference in cost.

Now: getting the product to the customer. Check with the customer service representatives at the larger courier services, including the US Post Office. Ask about rates and services for new business accounts. Compare times for last drop off and delivery times, if they offer guaranteed delivery, refunds, insurance and free supplies.

The U.S. Postal Service provides Express Mail Corporate Accounts, which are a big help since they let patrons avoid weighing packages, affixing stamps and battling with postage meters. To set up an account, complete the application on the Postal Service's Web site, http://new.usps.com, and either mail it in or take it to a local post office with the initial deposit.

Note that because of heightened security restrictions by the Federal Aviation Administration, any domestic mail other than Express Mail weighing 16 ounces or more and bearing stamps must be given in person to a retail clerk at a post office or given directly to a letter carrier.

The U.S. Postal Service, either through its Web site or at the local post office, offers many of the supplies needed by a fulfillment center. For example, Express, Priority, and Global Envelopes, rolls of Priority Mail tape, sturdy boxes for shipping fragile items, padded envelopes for small items, pre-printed Express forms and self adhesive Priority Mail labels with the Web-based business' return address.

The courier services make it easy to set up an account online. Federal Express, Airborne, and UPS will schedule a daily pick-up for the Web-base business. UPS charges a small weekly fee for pick-up service, while Federal Express and Airborne do it for nothing. But, Federal Express' shipping fees are usually a bit higher than UPS's. If the shipping facilities are located near any of the major couriers' drop off points, or near one of their drop boxes, it might be easier to just drop off the packages.

FedEx offers several software packages to ease its customer's shipping chores. **Airborne** offers a number of software packages to help customers to better manage shipping products through its service. **UPS** offers its Online Office software to help its customers process shipments, print address labels and pickup records, and track packages. **DHL** has Easy Ship software that it provides to customers that meet specific criteria.

Negotiate with the shippers — it can't do any harm and most of the time, it is possible to obtain volume discounts, especially if the rates offered by their competitors are brought into play. Then pass on any savings obtained to the customers. As orders increase, re-open the negotiations. If done right, it is possible to optimize the Web site's shipping solutions by exploiting each shipper's strengths while getting the lowest rates possible.

Visit these services' Web sites for more information. Federal Express (www.fedex.com/us/welcomecenter), UPS (www.ups.com), Airborne (www.airborne.com) and DHL (www.dhl.com/main). Also visit your U.S. Postal Service's Web site at http://new.usps.com for Priority Mail information including its "e-merchandise return" service

All items with a retail value in excess of $100 should be insured. The standard insurance provided by courier's usually cover the first $100. Simply fill out the corresponding space on the air bill and there will be a small fee charged for each additional $100 beyond the first $100.

It is important to stay on top of the delivery time of all shipments. If a certain courier offers a guaranteed time (or day) of arrival, and that guarantee is not met, ask for a refund. In all probably the Web site will have a disgruntled customer when a package arrives a day later than expected, and your business will be the whipping boy, not the shipper. Passing the refund on to the customer not only assuages that anger, it builds the Web site's reputation as an e-commerce site that offers outstanding customer service.

OUTSOURCING

The goal of outsourcing fulfillment should not be one of short-term cost reduction, but rather speed to market. Outsourcing in the long run, usually costs more than an in-house system. The benefits of using a FSP is that it provides a reliable method of getting the product to the customer while keeping in-house control of important data such as inventory, reorder levels, and delivery confirmations. Outsourcing fulfillment can allow a Web-based business to focus its energy and resources on marketing, product development, sales, and building its customer base.

You've read a bit about the outsourcing choices; this section is going to really dig into the subject. While outsourcing can make fulfillment and distribution simpler and more efficient it does have limitations and drawbacks.

- Outsourcing is not cheap.

- Many FSPs will not service a Web site with small shipping volume.

- An inventory that consists of a large variety of products can also affect service and price. level. For example, it's more costly and time-consuming to prepare packages that contain different combinations of items than it is single-product packages.

- Some FSPs will only respond to inquiries regarding the status of an order while others will provide full product support.

- The level of services in warehousing and inventory management may also vary from company to company. In some cases, the FSPs will order stock directly from the manufacturers while others will expect the Web site to ship the products to their main warehouse for packaging and delivery.

- The drop shipment option may result in multiple shipping charges for some orders.

- Web sites using drop shippers will have to deal with customer confusion due to packages arriving at different times from different shipping locations sometimes without the Web site's brand anywhere in site on the packages.

- The drop shipment option requires complex tracking and returns procedures compared to FSP shipments.

When Should a Web-based Business Outsource?

Admittedly outsourcing to a FSP offers quick access to proven state of the art technologies. This can be a good starting point for a new Web-based business. Lower start-up costs preserve scarce start-up capital. These initial savings however mean a higher per product cost during the operation of the Web site. Then there is the concern that any outsourcing model presents: How to keep control of the management of quality, accuracy, accountability, and customer service priorities, as well as integrating back-end systems.

Outsourcing to a FSP **only** makes good financial sense for a startup Web site if, in its day-to-day operations, it has **more money than time**. When it needs every penny, it should keep its fulfillment in-house. If the Web-based business' competency lies elsewhere and it can earn more utilizing its staff's elsewhere, look outside. If an established Web site is currently handling fulfillment in-house, it should look at outsourcing **only** when it has reached the limits of its current facilities and infrastructure and the incremental cost of expansion would be a prohibitive expense or it can't have the disruptions that a rebuild of its infrastructure would bear on its business.

A Web-based business might consider contracting with a FSP for the same reason it chose to outsource its Web site to a Web hosting services — a FSP can afford the very best software and hardware solutions, because its costs are spread over many customers. Outsourcing then gives the Web-based business an additional benefit of having a cutting edge fulfillment process at its fingertips.

Regional Distribution Centers

Suppose a FSP ran a network of distribution centers, and each center could ship product for dozens of large and small e-commerce sites. A Web-based business could contract with of the FSPs with multiple distribution centers, giving it a presence in many regional areas.

Using the regional distribution center model allows a Web-based business to use just-in-time (JIT) inventory management, thus saving on inventory holding costs. When a business has only one distribution center its products are usually received in large quantities and stored in pallet racks until needed. As items are picked, more products have to be dropped from the pallet racks to replenish the picking area. This receive-store-replenish-pick cycle is a repeated expense, and, if replenishment is too slow, out-of-stock notices may occur even when product is in the building.

If a Web site is going with the JIT inventory model, it should look for a FSP that has supply chain management software to accommodate just-in-time shipping; thus allowing products and orders to flow smoothly from manufacturers and distributors to regional distribution centers and finally the customers. Adoption of a JIT model can result in increasing the frequency with which inbound shipments of product are scheduled, but decreasing the lead times and size of these shipments. Web-based businesses that adopt the JIT model often reduce the number of suppliers and transport companies with which they must deal and select suppliers which are close to their regional distribution centers enabling delivery of shipments with short lead times. In addition, each regional distribution center has only a portion of the Web site's total stock, so it is a simple task to shelve all received product directly into the pick area.

Another reason for choosing this distribution model is that many Web-based businesses want to give their customers reasonably priced next day delivery or 2nd day delivery. To do this could require the Web site to place inventory in numerous regional centers, thereby increasing its inventory holding costs. However, that increase could be balanced by a decrease in overall shipping costs and an increase in customer satisfaction.

Here's how it works. Normally a business would have one distribution center in (let's say) Nashville, Tennessee and a customer in Oregon places an order that could be shipped for delivery within the 2 day time period. But, what if there is a problem (which happens frequently), now the business has to ship "next day" at additional cost (which it has to "eat") to meet the 2 day time limitation. Now take that same scenario but the business has its inventory in 4 regional distribution centers. The Oregon customer's order is sent to a regional distribution center in Utah; and, even if there is a mix-up which causes a delay in shipping the product, it can avoid the "extra cost" next-day shipping method due to the proximity of the distribution center to the customer. In other words, with strategically located distribution centers throughout the country a Web site can promise 2nd day delivery with more certainty due to the proximity of the product to the customer.

It isn't always absolutely necessary to increase inventory. With the right technology running behind the scenes, a Web-based business can maximize its normal inventory levels. Take the same scenario: the Oregon customer's order is sent to the Utah distribution center, but that center is out of stock and cannot fill the order. The fulfillment system can seamlessly transmit the order to another distribution center and still meet the 2nd day delivery deadline by using the more expensive "next day" shipping option. The Web-based business did not carry extra inventory, but because of its data network it could still adopt the just-in-time model. Using this system, there would still be the premium shipping charges to meet the 2nd day delivery deadline, but not in every instance, every day.

The FSP Models
The average FSP offers everything a Web-based business might need for its fulfillment processes. They will take the ordered products from the warehouse shelves, pack them, and hand them to shippers. Then they will follow by sending an automated e-mail response with the Web site's branding to the customer to let them know the package is in transit. Many will also handle credit-card processing, supply current inventory levels to the Web site, reorder products, offer call-center services, send notices of shipping, and handle returns. There are literally thousands of these companies to choose from, but the best way to find one that suits a specific Web site's needs is by referral.

Some FSPs offer everything from soup to nuts: Web design and hosting, order capturing, shopping cart tools, credit card processing, merchant accounts, picking and packing of the product, shipping, invoice generation, inventory management, return/exchange logistics, and customer service. Plus some will, for an additional fee, provide extra services such as wrapping gifts and packing catalogues or other promotional items in with each shipped package.

It sounds good, but remember some of these areas may not be among the FSP's core competencies and may not be the best solution for a Web-based business. Carefully evaluate the company and the offerings, then pick and choose.

Most FSPs will let a Web-based business mix and match the fulfillment services it needs. For example, if a Web site already has a shopping cart and credit-card function, it can limit its selection to inventory warehousing, pick, pack and ship service, returns processing and customer service support. Web-based businesses may want to use a combination of fulfillment options. It may be more cost effective to handle the processing of small items in-house and only outsource the bulkier items. Or it may have some of its products handled by drop-ship methods and others by the FSP. There are many combination of options that a Web-based business might want to discuss with potential FSPs, until it finds a provider and a solution that fits its specific needs.

Should a Web-based business choose a small or larger FSP? Each offers advantages and disadvantages. A small local FSP may be best, especially if it would make it easier for quick replenishment of inventory or because it offers more personalized service. Or, choose a larger national FSP, which can give a nervous startup the confidence that its customers will be adequately served throughout the United States.

Another, good reason for opting for the smaller FSP is that a Web-based business could have its fulfillment services in numerous regional locations allowing it to emulate the JIT model discussed earlier in this chapter. Having more than one FSP also can alleviate concerns about relying on a single fulfillment resource (i.e., redundancy).

Where and how can you find fulfillment service providers? These three Web sites should give you a good start.

For the first listing check out www.lycos.com > Business and Careers > Business Services > Distribution and Logistics > Distribution > Internet Order Fulfillment.

Another comprehensive listing can be found at www.digitrends.net/digitrends/dtonline/features/sections/fulfillment/listing1 or go to www.digitrends.net, on the left hand side of the site you will see a Search Site link, click it, then type in "E-Fulfillment Directory," click, and then use any of the links that say "listing" except the top one.

And, of course, there is Yahoo! (www.yahoo.com) > Business and Economy > Business to Business > Marketing and Advertising > Fulfillment. There are 58 companies listed, of which at least 40 are relevant.

Drop-Ship

In a perfect world the drop-ship model would be the way all Web sites would want to go. If everything worked flawlessly, the Web site would concentrate on sales and therefore sell more products, which in turn benefits both the Web site and the drop shipper. The Web site does not have inventory cost and the drop shipper does not have the marketing costs; this enables both to make more money by reducing the retail price. But it's not a perfect world.

Many Web sites find that drop shippers often don't have in stock all the products that their customer ordered. To offset this, the best practice is to maintain relationships with more than one drop shipper for the same products. This allows you to not only get the best price but also to ensure that the products can be shipped as promised to the customer.

Although many small and home-based Web sites may go with the 100% drop-ship model when first opening shop, most gradually move into a hybrid solution — they still have relationships with drop-ship manufacturers and distributors but they also have begun to amass an inventory and to deal with in-house fulfillment processes. As explained earlier in this chapter, a Web site that opts to use the drop-ship model takes orders and payment for product and forwards its orders to the drop shipper who will "drop-ship" products directly to the Web site's customers. When using a 100% drop-ship model, the Web site does realize some advantage from delegating the physical labor of the entire fulfillment process — from the order and stocking of product through the picking and shipping of the products to the customers — although the Web site does not totally avoid fulfillment expenses.

Any Web site working with drop shippers must diligently keep a firm hand on the entire fulfillment process. If not, the Web site will loose control over the fulfillment process. As it is, the Web site will have difficulty in knowing when the product will be shipped, how the product will be shipped including number of packages, shipper, method (2nd day, ground, etc.). However, with the proper attention to detail, the Web site can usually get the drop shipper to provide current (not real-time) inventory information and insist that it and its customers are provided with real-time tracking or shipping information (this is relatively easy to obtain from the drop-shipper).

When using drop shipping, insist that the Web site's brand be on the products outer package, the shipping labels and the packing list. It would be nice if the drop-shipper would remain anonymous but that is usually not possible. However, if the Web site is persistent, it is possible to have the Web site's brand along side the drop shipper's brand on most products.

Although a Web site using the drop-ship model doesn't incur inventory overhead, it most certainly does incur fulfillment expense since it is compelled to be particularly diligent to guarantee that the fulfillment process is completed to the customer's satisfaction.

Another challenge that Web site's face when dealing with drop shippers is managing, synchronizing and consolidating a customer's order so that all packages comprising that one order arrives at his/her door on the same day by the same shipper. But, with these reservations in mind, if a Web site can manage to keep a firm hand on its drop shippers, it does have a reasonable chance of building and maintaining a satisfied and loyal customer base.

For help with drop-ship oversight look at Mercantec's (www.mercantec.com/licensing) SoftCart Lite and SoftCart Pro that can be upgraded for drop shipping through the SoftCart Drop Ship Module. This allows Web sites to automatically deliver shipping instructions to drop shippers when a purchase is made online. It collects the shopper's product information, compares the SKUs to the drop shipper's database, and creates a unique mail message for every drop shipper involved in the current order. The message contains all of the products and information that the drop shipper needs to complete the shipping/fulfillment process. Plus it offers custom message formatting by vendor/warehouse including EDI X.12 850.

"Drop Shipping News" provides handbooks on drop shipping and directories of drop-shipping sources, for a fee.

Outsourcing Plan

Nothing succeeds without a plan — this time it's an outsourcing plan, written as an addendum to the logistics plan. First, determine the services the Web site business needs and expects from a fulfillment provider and what they will need to know about the Web site — for example, its expected order volume, its business' terms, and whether it'll pay handling on a per-piece-picked basis or on a package-shipped basis.

FSPs differ widely on the variety of options they provide and the type of client they serve. Finding the right fit for a Web-based business requires in-depth research, which includes asking for referrals. Once the research is completed and the information compiled, it will be possible to price out the most cost effective and efficient method of getting the products to the customer while maintaining an adequate profit margin.

It's not an easy decision. The first step to take in trying to solve the dilemma is to look at your carefully drawn up logistics and outsourcing plan. If the solution is still unclear, consider the following while keeping in mind that fulfillment is the last form of customer contact. Take into account that if a Web site fails to embrace order fulfillment with the same vigor as it embraced online selling, it will experience not only distribution headaches, but also, customer defection.

The second step is to look at the current volume of orders and project what the volume is expected to be in 6 months, 1 year, 3 years and 5 years. With figures in hand, take a long hard look at the Web site's staff — can they handle the workload. If the Web site takes off and workload exceeds the staff's capacity, its customers won't be happy with the poor service that they may receive from a harassed and overworked staff. The Web-based business may have jeopardized its hard-earned success with the wrong fulfillment decision. Also, consider the Web-based business' core competency, fulfillment may not be one of them. Stay on top of fulfillment issues, and as the business grows, re-evaluate. Before making any rash decision get a pencil and paper out and compare the costs of adding more staff and facilities (including automation) with the cost of delegating the fulfillment process to an outside company.

If the Web site is still in the first growth period and has expectations of a huge growth spurt within the next 6 months — outsource. However, if the growth is projected to increase steadily over time and the in-house staff is still adequately managing the fulfillment process, then there is time to build a proper in-house fulfillment infrastructure that can scale as the order volume increases.

A start-up Web site that expects to handle a substantial volume of orders from the get-go and does not have a warehouse and staff in place might find that in the beginning it could be more cost-effective to outsource its fulfillment processes to a FSP. In that case, the Web-based business should ensure that its back-end is built so that it is scalable enough to accommodate a move to in-house fulfillment processes when the need arises

If a Web site's order volume is low and inventory requirements are not onerous, then it is probably better to handle fulfillment in-house until the volume justifies a more formal order fulfillment procedure.

Your Product: Next, look at the products offered for sale on the Web site — do any require special handling, i.e., fragile, sensitive to temperature changes, or special licensing requirements (alcohol, pharmaceuticals, etc.). Will the majority of the product orders include multiples of different products, making the picking and packing more labor intensive (such as a computer with a printer, monitor and mouse or a modem with a telephone cord and installation disk). If the answer is yes, then a FSP must be found that will accommodate these needs and still allow the Web-based business to earn a profit. If that isn't possible, then there are two solutions, outsource all fulfillment except the products requiring special handling, take care of them in-house. Or, keep all fulfillment processes in-house.

Customer Service: FSPs are well aware of customer service issues and most offer services that integrate well with a Web sites' infrastructure. Some of the customer service issues to be considered when instituting a fulfillment process include:

- Managing inventory (so the customer is confident the product is available and the Web site can cross-sell, if necessary)

- Offering multiple shipping options

- Tracking orders (so the customer can always be kept informed)

- Handling returns and disputes

Control: If a Web site decides to outsource with an FSP, it must become an integral part of the Web-base business' processes. As such, it is important that everyone coordinate their business processes and infrastructure to maximize the benefits of each business' strengths.

Integration: A Web-based business will need to send its customers' orders via e-mail or FTP directly to the FSP's warehouse facility. The optimal FSP is one that offers software to enable a Web site to integrate its systems with the FSP's back-end systems so that there is real-time inventory information. The FSP should offer continuous technical support to assure that the operation runs smoothly from both ends. Bear in mind that the FSP selected will become a partner in the value chain and as such an essential arm of the Web site's operation.

Issues Specific to a Small Web Site

It is possible to find FSPs that cater to the small business, allowing even the busy home-based Web site to take advantage of the latest cost and time saving techniques, such as supply chain software, and orders sent directly to the distribution center floor for picking.

Hence, a small Web-based business that chooses to outsource fulfillment, should select a FSP that specializes in servicing small businesses, especially if it receives fewer than 10 orders per day. Keep in mind that you need to do the due diligence, if the FSP falls down on the job during a peak selling season, a small Web site might not be able to recover and could easily lose its entire business.

To repeat — outsourcing to a FSP makes good financial sense ONLY when the Web-based business has more money than time. When a Web-based business needs every penny, it should handle its fulfillment processes in-house. For the majority of small Web site's the cost per order is significantly increased when an FSP is brought into the picture, but if it has determined that it can over the long haul make a larger profit by outsourcing, then by all means do so.

A series of coordinated steps is required to bridge the gap between (1) a customer clicking the buy button, thus sending the order to the shopping cart software and into the "pipeline" and (2) the customer receiving the products. Ad-hoc solutions to handle the communication with a FSP and/or drop shipper(s) can be put into place that may be sufficient for a Web site with low sales volume and limited inventory. However, if sales increase substantially, then even a small Web site must deal with the lack of standards for data representation and transmission requirements. This means dealing with the API issues or taking the EDI and XML approach (discussed earlier in this chapter) for communication between systems so as to be

Evaluating the Outsourcer

Keep in mind that an outsourcer (FSP and/or drop shipper) will be an integral part of the Web site's operations. Therefore, find an outsourcer that not only offers the services the Web site needs, but also is a comfortable fit in other ways — location(s), technology, mission statement, financial wherewithal, etc. To determine whether a prospective outsourcer meets a Web-based business' needs, ask it how it approaches key fulfillment issues, such as:

- What types of products does the outsourcer currently have in stock for other clients?
- What is the minimum volume the outsourcer will handle?
- Is that minimum per month or averaged over a set period?
- How does it handle the packing?
- What type of packaging materials will be used? How will the box be labeled? In other words, is only the Web site's brand used or also the outsourcer's brand? It's important, that there isn't any dilution of the Web site's brand.
- Determine that the outsourcer does not require an exclusive contract to fill all of the Web site's product orders. The Web-based business may want the flexibility of processing some of its orders in-house and also it may want to hedge its bets with a secondary FSP or additional drop-shippers.
- Is there a setup fee? If so, how much and is it a one-time fee?
- Does the outsourcer offer special services such as gift-wrap or sub-assembly? If so, what are the fees? Will the outsourcer include the Web site's catalogs or other branding materials or special offers in the shipments? If so, is there an extra fees and what is the fee?
- How quickly will orders be filled? Is there a guarantee?
- What volume of orders can the outsourcer reasonably handle and how scalable is its capacity?
- How will the Web site's infrastructure be integrated with the outsourcer's systems? Will special

able to interact with each outsourcer (FSP and/or drop shipper). Eventually, the "string and sticky tape" method will fail and proper integration will become essential.

How Much Does It Cost?

The cost is dependent upon which services the Web-based business requires and the volume of orders it forwards to the outsourcer since many of the fees or commissions are set on a sliding scale based on volume. On the average, you will pay an FSP a monthly fee for warehousing the products of around 3 cents per small item, or $15 for each pallet of products. An Inventory count is usually performed monthly and the fees are assessed on the

hardware and/or software be needed? If so, what and what support does the outsourcer offer for the integration process?

- What credit cards and alternative payment methods does the outsourcer accept?
- How are sales taxes handled?
- How does the Web-based business get paid and how quickly? (drop-ship model)
- How will the Web site and its customers track orders?
- How will the Web-based business be able to monitor and replenish inventory?
- What reports does the outsourcer provide?
- How will returns and disputes be handled?
- Does the outsourcer offer customer service support?
- Does the outsourcer handle international orders? If so, how and are there extra costs involved?
- What shipping arrangements does the outsourcer have, and is there flexibility in that arrangement to allow for the use of other shippers if they have better rates?
- What kind of account servicing does the outsourcer offer?

Be sure to ask for references and a customer list or at least the names of 10 customers. Call all the references and customers. Ask the customers (if you can get away with it) all the questions set out above, but at least ask what kind of products the outsourcer handles for them and how well it delivered on its obligations to them. Ask them if they have any complaints or reservations about the outsourcer and if they are planning on renewing the contract when it comes due. Another reason for wanting the customer list is so you can look it over to determine that there isn't any conflict between the Web-based business' product line and others that the outsourcer handles. The customer list will also alert you to any large clients that may compromise the outsourcer's resources, especially during a busy holiday shopping season.

products the Web-based business has in the FSP's warehouses at that time. The FSP may also charge a handling fee for each package and for incidentals, such as mailing labels, boxes, packing material, and then, of course, shipping.

There are no outright, up-front expenses involved with the drop-ship model. The drop shipper pays the Web site a commission that can range anywhere from 10% to 25%.

The Contract

Once a decision has been made to go with an outsourcer, the next step is to do the due diligence concerning such issues as financial health, union related issues, stability of management, the customer list, references, the physical plant (lease, ownership, condition of building and equipment, etc.). Finally, get the legal eagles to draft a contract that clearly outlines each business' expectations, services to be provided and fees — give them the logistics and outsourcing plan to use as a guide. Keep in mind that both the Web site and the outsourcer want to maximize revenues, so it is important that everyone agrees on a compensation rate that is fair to all. The contract that is ultimately signed should be for a limited term since outsourcing with a specific outsourcer is a choice that will need to be reassessed throughout the business relationship. However, the contract should be a concrete document that defines the services and responsibilities of both the Web site and the outsourcer.

Once everything is signed, the next task is integrating the Web site's systems with the FSP's back-end so that the fulfillment processes are so seamlessly executed that the customers won't know the difference.

Technical Issues

While off-the-shelf solutions exist to solve some pieces of the fulfillment problems — relational databases and shopping-cart applications, for example — no turnkey packages currently exist to provide complete integration with FSPs. Know that the Web site is responsible for setting up product/inventory master synchronization, pricing, inventory status, invoicing, and final reconciliation. There are many challenges that a Web site faces when it builds and manages infrastructures that interact with third parties.

Once the shopping cart software has received the customer order, it sends the order into the "order capture pipeline." From there the Web site must send each product to the correct fulfillment provider(s) (the right FSP(s), the right drop-shipper(s) and maybe even the in-house fulfillment center), who assumes responsibility for delivering the products to the customer. Even if that does sound simple, it's not, the system must contain business rules to determine which fulfillment provider(s) to send what portion of the customer's order to. An example of rules:

- use the same fulfillment provider for all the products, if possible

- use the fulfillment provider that can give the customer the lowest per unit cost

- check in-house inventory before using an outsource solution

Remember, if more than one fulfillment provider is used, then the customer will receive a separate shipment from each (more shipping expense). Sometime during this process (it varies with systems and is dependent upon whether all the fulfillment providers support real-time inventory queries) the Web site composes an XML message and transmits it via secure HTTP to the appropriate outsourcers. If the Web site has out-sourcers that do not support real-time inventory queries then the site will rely on daily supplied inventory profile data.

Now this is where it gets sticky — call in the consultants and programmers. For each of the interactions with the entire system the outsourcer requires mapping data from the Web site's order management system (and pipeline) into messages that can be understood by the fulfillment providers' systems. First the data has to be represented — the way that is handled is dependent upon the outsourcer's systems. For example, it might be EDI X12 format to represent the transaction, then others have proprietary batch-file data formats, and there are the "special" crafted variety with their own key-value-pair grammars to represent information.

The next step is to collect the customer's shipping address and shipping instructions. Depending on decisions made upstream in the pipeline, the available shipment options are determined by the outsourcer(s). If multiple outsourcers are involved, then a shared shipping carrier is usually used to ship the order. If a single outsourcer is involved, then the Web site queries it for current delivery options. Other complications at this stage can include support for multiple ship-to addresses for the same order (for example, Christmas time, Mother's Day, Graduation season, etc.) gift-wrapping and messages.

Now we are at the payment stage where the credit card information is entered or retrieved from the customer database, and the credit card is authorized for the order total. The Web site interacts with a credit-card clearinghouse to validate the credit card and to determine whether there is sufficient credit available. Communicating with a clearinghouse normally requires a dedicated line and transmittal of the requests using the clearinghouse's proprietary protocol.

Once the credit card has been approved and the customer (yes, all of the above should have occurred within seconds) has clicked on the confirmation button, the order is accepted by the Web site's order management system. At this point, a few options exist depending on the site's policy and outsourcer(s) capabilities. If the site offers the customer the opportunity to cancel the order within a specified time frame, the order is not immediately transmitted to the outsourcer(s). If the outsourcer doesn't support a real-time protocol, then the order will be transmitted during the next batch-file generation cycle. If the outsourcer supports real-time order processing, then the site can transmit over secure HTTP (as discussed previously), containing all of the information necessary for an outsourcer to process the order.

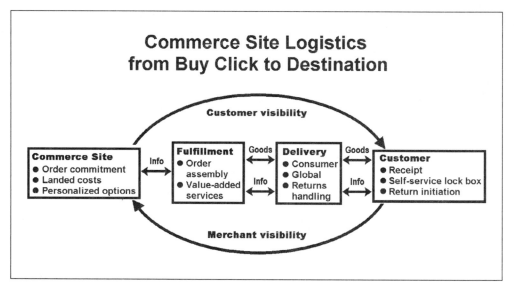

Now it's time for the outsourcer to go to work. If the FSP is handling credit-card settlement for the Web site, then the charge to the customer's credit card is authorized and settled for the order amount. The products are then shipped to the shipping address using the selected carrier. If a product requested by the customer is not available, the customer's order is placed on hold (backorder), until inventory is replenished.

During all of this the customer must be kept informed as to the order status. In addition, it is desirable that the customer be able to go to the Web site and bring up the order history and request a real-time order-status query. If it's supported, the site communicates with the outsourcer via secure HTTP and requests the status. The response message should include details of all shipments, cancellation, backorders, and other transactions that have taken place while processing the order.

Most outsourcers send nightly, via FTP or encrypted email, order status files that describe all of the day's order activity. By law, a Web site can't charge (settle) a customer's credit card until the order has been shipped. So, the order information returned to the Web site by the outsourcer(s) must be verified for accuracy before the credit-card information is processed.

Without valid information, the Web site can't post a shipment invoice to the order management system. Settlement tasks run periodically to process shipment invoices that need collection. The settlement process communicates with the clearinghouse to charge the buyer's credit card (note that when the order was originally placed, funds were only allocated [authorized] but not disbursed). If the site and the outsourcer(s) don't agree on order details, customers may be charged the wrong amount.

Then the information is transferred from the order management system to the Web site's financial system for purchase order generation, accounts payable, and so on.

Once the products are in the customer's hands, the Web site and the outsourcer need to jointly handle any post-purchase activity such as returns or exchanges, and perform transaction reconciliation.

Caveats

Despite the advantages of using a FSP and/or drop shipper, there are a few potential downsides. Putting someone else between a Web site and its customer can be a very risky proposition. And there are significant data integration issues. When sorting through these issues, it pays to see what others have done — get out there and talk to everyone you know that is using or has used an FSP and/or drop shipper.

No matter what outsourcer(s) become the fulfillment partner(s), issues will arise. What happens when the busy and ever important Christmas season arrives and it comes time to decide between shipping an order for a smaller company (maybe like your Web site) or shipping an order for Amazon? Which one is the outsourcer going to choose? It's a given, the big guy will get the most attention.

A smaller Web-based business can protect itself to some degree by establishing a detailed service-level agreement to ensure performance (get the legal eagles involved).

The Internet is a great equalizer. With the right FSP and the right integration between the FSP and the Web-based business, all Web sites can do business on the same playing field with the same type of equipment and the same type of personnel.

INTERNATIONAL ORDERS

Many Web-based businesses don't offer international shipping because of the difficulty of handling the customs and tax issues. To service international customers Web sites need significant expertise in customs clearance, duties and taxes, currency conversion capabilities, and a good relationship with an international shipping company.

If a Web-based business is to have a global customer base, it must take steps to ensure that its back-end systems are designed for international addresses, international currencies, estimating delivery costs and so forth.

Then the Web-based business must tackle shipping. Whatever company it decides to use for its international shipments (and try to make it only one company), that company needs to be able to provide global shipping to virtually any address anywhere and help with customs clearance, duties and taxes payment, and proof of delivery.

Try www.intershipper.com for help with the choice of international shippers.

The United States Postal Service's Express Mail International service offers Global Package Link which establishes a direct link between the Web-based business and the U.S. Postal Service, enabling the post office to handle most of the documentation for international shipments. This is a worthwhile feature for high-volume shippers. Part of the Global Package Link is the Customs Pre-Advisory System (CPAS), which relieves the Web site of paperwork and helps speed its packages through customs. CPAS enables customs agents to review the contents of the shipment prior to its arrival and decide if the parcel requires inspection.

For small international shipments, Global Priority Mail is a good choice. The time in transit is anywhere from four to seven days. The U.S. Postal Service offers two sizes of mailers, which are good for magazines, small books, CDs, and any other small, flat item (as long as the package is less than 4 lbs.). Both mailers have a low flat rate from $7.00 to $9.00, depending on the country to which you are shipping.

CONCLUSION

No matter if a Web-based business is an entrepreneur, a brick-and-mortar, a home-based business, a SME business or a enterprise site, all of the solutions discussed in this chapter do not come without cost. There are capital expenditures and development costs associated with integration and channel conflict in regards to any type of consolidation.

Order processing and fulfillment is a Web site's last form of customer contact. Investing in a logistics strategy is critical to a Web site's continued growth. Whatever the cost and ultimate solution, it is clear that new methods and processes must be utilized for a Web-based business to expect long term survival in the e-commerce arena.

CHAPTER 18

The Future

You can only predict things after they've happened.

Eugene Ionesco

The future is bright for e-commerce. The 20th Century, shaped by the Industrial Revolution, became the age of the automobile and the television. The 21st Century, I believe, will be shaped by the Technological Revolution and it will become the age of the Internet — Global Communication. The Internet already has made a massive impact on all aspects of business. In the 21st century, e-business (the electronic exchange of information including e-commerce) is no longer an option for businesses, it is a necessity.

Today, e-commerce is an ever-expanding consumer industry. For a Web site to succeed it needs to understand its customers' mindset. Customers are generally not looking for a better price, although price is always an issue, it is rarely the primary motivator for buying a product online. They are looking for products they can't find elsewhere. This is why Web sites catering to niche markets are currently prospering. The caveat is to ensure the customer's shopping experience is pleasant and that the overall experience (through the time the package is delivered to the customer's doorstep) isn't marked with too many potholes.

E-commerce for all of its touted success and projected numbers is still in its infancy and needs to be incubated and encouraged. I'm not saying that e-commerce hasn't already had far-reaching impact but there are issues that can hinder its growth.

THE CHALLENGES

Businesses wanting to build or enhance their Web site's capabilities face a multitude of challenges:

- the need for speed and agility

- integrating multiple sales and supply channels

- lack of expertise and facilities

- selecting and integrating multiple technologies

- justifying the investment based on financial return

Few Web sites (even the mega sites) have marketing, customer service, fulfillment, order processing, and inventory working seamlessly. There are many reasons for this but the main one is return on investment. The brick-and-mortars that have made their move to the Web just haven't quite grasped the entire potential of e-commerce. The entrepreneurs have problems understanding the sophisticated technical issues involved in operating a truly mature, successful Web site. The task of implementing full integration through the value chain is a monster. When a Web site's management team initially capitulates to "consider" the need of total integration of its value chain, it usually ends the discussion by shrugging its "corporate shoulders" and deciding such a massive integration effort does not warrant the investment in time, resources and dollars.

Yet, rather than addressing the issue head on, most Web sites choose to experiment with stopgap solutions, although even those require time, resources and dollars. Later, when the matter is revisited — as it must be since it can't be ignored forever — few are willing to take three steps back and admit mistakes. The result is a Web site that is buried under the day-to-day rubble of stopgap "non-solutions." Many Web sites are afraid of putting a large sum of their investors' dollars at risk — integration of the entire value chain is expensive — until the need slaps them in the face. By then the expense in time, resources and dollars is exorbitant due to the need to integrate while filling the burgeoning customers' orders, and doing it all at breakneck speed.

The question of when to integrate services then becomes a matter of timing. Does the Web site wait until critical mass is achieved before investing in integration? Only by taking the time to educate yourselves will you become familiar with the available options and the repercussions of not having them in place.

FACTORS THAT CAN SLOW GROWTH

The Internet, the Web and e-commerce have their peccadilloes. External elements such as the public at large and governments have not yet weighed in regarding this new behemoth. The public's concern about such things as security and the personal information that sites amass must be addressed by the Internet community before the public takes action of its own. In the other arena, a crucial and as yet unresolved factor that could impede the growth of e-commerce is the degree of governmental involvement including regulation, and taxes.

Customers' Security Concerns

The general population doesn't believe the Web is a safe place to conduct transactions — specifically credit card purchases. Slowly this perception is changing as the customer gains more experience on the Web using sites that incorporate digital certificates, SET protocol and SSL. The technology is there — many Web sites use secure servers for online transactions, which encrypt data that is sent over the Internet so that a third party cannot intercept the information. Most consumers will purchase products from a Web site if they can be convinced not only that the technology is in place to safeguard their transactions but that the Web site itself is trustworthy.

Trust and e-commerce are mutually dependent. Although technology, such as using digital certificates, does help in the battle to instill trust, branding is the key. Your brand is the gauge a customer uses to assess quality and reliability. Stand by it and make it a symbol of your contract with the customer to provide not only a product but also service and satisfaction. Would you trust something if American Express said it was OK? Do you trust Lands End? Customers need the reassurance of familiar brands (new, old, traditional, and Web-driven) and assurance that the technology is in place for a secure credit card transaction to build the trust required to take the first steps toward an online purchase.

Privacy Issues

The ability to guarantee the customers' privacy is the most important challenge that e-commerce faces. The extent to which a Web site uses personal information concerns every Internet user. How much does the surfing public want the Web community to know about them?

The growing trend toward personalization on the Web will have a considerable impact on e-commerce. While personalization does not translate into direct sales, it does bring the customer one step closer to a purchase. If you abuse it, you've lost a customer. If handled correctly, your customer may appreciate a familiar relationship that could include the recommendation of additional products or timely notices of sales.

Look, the better you know the customer, the easier it is to know what that customer wants. How you obtain the information necessary for this personalization is the issue. Some Web sites ask for information outright, and then use rules-based filtering systems or adaptive prediction technology that can provide real-time learning of customer likes and dislikes based on mouse clicks. An information exchange is fair game — I answer the questions the Web site gives me a $5 coupon, a 20% discount, a t-shirt, etc. The Web site has literally become a storehouse of my personal information. If my information is passed on to another party to whom I have not given permission, I take issue. This is where the e-commerce community must police themselves or the government will step in to regulate how Web sites use and exchange a customer's personal information.

At the same time, you should bear in mind that the Web site that utilizes personalization tools, if it does it properly, is rewarded as an early innovator. The Web sites that have amassed personalized profiles can get to know their customers over time. The longer a Web sites waits to adopt personalization, the longer their competitors will have to use personalization tools to gain a foothold in the customer base, making it unnecessary for those customers to seek out other sites. Personalization tools lend themselves well to the early adopters who can establish a brand on the Web and who have focused on creating a long-term relationship with their customers.

Impersonalization

Buying products over the Web is convenient for consumers, but it lacks the human contact that comes with traditional shopping. But that is changing. When technology, fulfillment, marketing and customer service stopgaps are replaced by integrated systems then it will be possible for online customer service interaction to become the norm. As a result, overall e-commerce sales will benefit due to increased customer interaction. For example, a customer using the "talk to me" button and getting a CSR with co-browsing (who can point and show products, direct attention to specific features, answer specific questions, and essentially guide the user through the shopping experience) is 50% more likely to buy a product.

Government Regulation

The biggest threat to the growth and freedom of the Internet in the next five years is the various government regulations that might be imposed, especially content regulation. Admittedly, there is troubling content on the Internet, but it should be responded to rather than legislated into the black market.

Most of the Internet, in it's present state (with a few exceptions) would be a better place without governmental involvement. Admittedly, governments have already proposed and even passed a few measures — from privacy to encryption to censorship to taxation and over the next year or so governments will probably try to take bolder steps by introducing legislation that will have a direct impact on censorship, privacy, taxation and encryption. However, on the taxation issue especially, the governments should do nothing. Let the industry incubate. For how long is up for debate — it's a guarantee that governments will ensure that they collect their taxes, they just have to work out how and that does buy e-commerce Web sites a bit of time.

In terms of security, governments are most afraid of the encryption issue. Specifically, the U.S. government has requested that it be entrusted with all private keys for digital certificates due to a fear of having this level of security fall into the wrong hands. Okay, that's fair but why can't governments and private sectors work together, form a joint committee to handle the entire issue. After all is said and done, if a government wants access to private keys for national security purposes, it will get its way.

The role of the governments in the privacy issue is another concern. It does seem like more than 75% of Web sites do ask for some form of personal information, although most only request an e-mail address and a name. Still and all, some do go further, requesting demographic information and even home telephone number and address. Although it is hotly debated as to whether governments have a role in this area, there is a need for something — maybe trust brokers, Truste is a start. Ultimately, the surfing public will decide the issue — they will or will not be comfortable with giving out personal information — Web sites will take notice and it will become a non-issue. No Web site wants to be seen as infringing on its customer's rights. But, at the same time if you offer a chance to win a Porsche by filling in a survey (whether it is in the subway, over the telephone or on the Web), chances are people will give a positive response. Web sites just need to give their potential customers a choice. By giving a choice and leaving the ultimate decision up to them to make, a Web site remains on the right side of the ethical line.

There is one area where the author feels that personal information restrictions should be imposed — age related access to sites and information. However, the Internet community itself should put forth a solution before any government intervention. There must be a technology out there that can limit the amount of personal information that a child can reveal. It should be implemented in such a way that it can be used from site to site.

Everyone agrees that there is a need for standards and cooperation within the Internet community. It just needs planning, direction and time — time to mature.

GLOBALIZATION

The Web is the first wave of a pure global economy. That means opportunity — to take advantage of a rapidly expanding global trade and the ensuing revenue stream. The task is deciding how a specific business can fit into the new global economy.

Many new Web sites receive at least one international order on the first day they are up and running. Amazing proof that e-commerce generates a global customer base. Imagine from just one location, a business can reach a market anywhere in the world, not just in a specific state or country.

One barrier in this rosy picture is the confusion and lack of understanding of worldwide taxes and tariffs. There needs to be a way to make this easier. Integrating enabling modules into a commerce software package could be a first step. Also Web sites need to figure out how to work within the system to keep costs down and ensure fulfillment efficiencies in the areas of tariffs, freight and sales taxes.

Web site's customers have the same questions — "If I buy this product from this site, will I pay a duty on it when it crosses the international border? What are the shipping costs? Can I avoid paying sales taxes?" Devote a Web page to international customers with a complete, easy to understand explanation. From both the customer and Web site perspective, the lack of understanding of all of these issues can create an unnecessary barrier.

WIRELESS AND M-COMMERCE

Research indicates that wireless technology is going to be a big success — and wireless Internet access is a big part of the growth. Wireless is exactly what it sounds like — an Internet connection without the use of phone or cable lines. The industry as a whole is ready to take off...barriers to entry for users are quickly coming down. Small, sleek, apparatuses are available now, (such as, pagers, smart cell phones, and personal digital assistants [PDAs]), network infrastructures are in place, and operating costs are dropping.

Most Web sites have not considered addressing wireless as a business need or priority. It is a question of timing. At this time it is just not possible for most Web sites to replicate the Web experience on the wireless platform. Wireless Web use comes with its own set of restrictions and limitations. So, when should a Web site develop strategies and/or business plans regarding wireless and its apparatuses?

First, as stated throughout this book, most Web sites have to concentrate their resources on getting over the hurtle of full integration of their back-end systems before they can even think about wireless or mobile e-commerce (m-commerce). To accommodate m-commerce a Web site requires another layer of technology to provide scaled down content and navigation since the entire viewable area on most of the current appliances is just four or five lines deep and 18 to 24 characters wide.

For truly successful Internet browsing and m-commerce there needs to be specialized "micro-browsers" to allow users to get the data they need in a wireless environment.

It is a complex and exciting area requiring significant capital resources and technology, and for those who seek the cutting edge of m-commerce: go forth and help define this new frontier.

While the vast majority of Web businesses will not be initially embracing m-commerce, they should do their part to accommodate this future technology. Take downward scalability into account at the beginning of the Web site's design process to ensure a consistent user experience, whether e-commerce or m-commerce.

BANDWIDTH

What will the Internet be like once bandwidth is no longer an issue? When the majority of the surfing public are accessing the Internet through either a Cable, DSL or T-1 connection then Web sites will need to revamp their sites to meet the ever-growing expectations of their customers.

With high bandwidth readily available, the surfing public will become used to viewing streaming video, or having real-time videoconferences where they actually see the person that they are talking to. Dealing with a surfing public with high bandwidth access is somewhat like black and white television program producers that had to upgrade their equipment, mindset and even physical plant to accommodate the technology of color. It's happening and it can't be ignored. Those who don't plan for it will be left behind.

SCANNERS

Tiny digital devices such as pens, palm pilots, etc. could revolutionize the way the buying public shops and gets information and I'm not talking about their connection to the Web. Such devices will soon have scanning technology built into them. Then your customers will go out in the real world and with scanner in hand read bar codes or UPC numbers on almost any product — just like the scanners at the grocery checkout counter.

Just think, a public that can shop anywhere — scanning away in the homes, in the offices, in other people's homes (eek!). Then when they sit down at a computer, they can easily upload to the Internet the information obtained through their scanners and effortlessly make their purchases. No more searching blindly through the maze of Web sites trying to find the right product.

PlanetRx became the first known e-commerce business to sell and use such technology. It is only a matter of time before other e-commerce businesses follow suit. Online grocers are a natural fit for this technology. It's a great way to create a shopping list — just open the cupboard and scan away.

THE XML REVOLUTION

A relatively new standard for e-commerce is eXtensible Markup Language (XML). XML defines a universal method for structuring and communicating data via the Internet and between software applications. XML will become a key enabler for conducting e-commerce and will ease the burden of systems integration. It was formally recommended by the World Wide Web Consortium as a standard in February 1998. Since then, a number of industry leaders, including IBM, Microsoft, Oracle, and Sun Microsystems have announced support for XML.

Unlike HTML (the standard currently used in most Internet applications), XML permits data to be coded for content rather than solely for presentation. With XML, descriptive tags are attached to each piece of data so applications can understand the meaning of the data and process it accordingly. This coding difference allows applications to examine and manipulate data contained in a document. It eliminates the need for both re-keying data and customized programs to translate and format information sent and received across the Internet.

THE NEW KID — ASP

I've touched on ASPs in various sections of this book. As businesses use the Internet for more of their commerce and information exchange, their investment in systems and the technical support necessary to provide functionality and reliability increases. Savvy entrepreneurs saw a need for Internet application outsourcing services — and along came the application service provider (ASP).

For a monthly fee, an ASP will provide its clients with almost any functionality they require. On top of that its clients get agreed-upon levels of reliability and scalability through the ASP's established, sophisticated technical infrastructure and staff. The ASP runs software applications for its clients on closely monitored, centralized facilities equipped with software to manage site capacity and backup communication lines and power. By using an outsourced service such as an ASP, a Web-based business can improve its time-to-market without making the substantial initial and ongoing investment in technology and support staff necessary to support a technology-enabled business process.

LAST THOUGHTS

So, dear readers, go out there and fight the good battle. The Internet and the Web have an investment community and others who realize their value and governments who right now aren't sure what to do with them. However, time is running out. Everyone wants a piece of the pie. Make your plan and carve out a piece of the Web — it's your future.

APPENDIX

WHAT IS A COMPUTER

The components that make up a computer are situated in a chassis:

The **motherboard** is a circuit board that everything plugs into and therefore provides the actual physical connection between the different components that make up the computer.

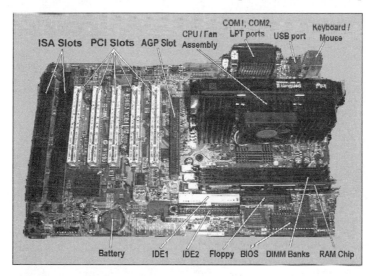

A **system bus** connects the components on the motherboard and enables the CPU to communicate with all of the components. The motherboard consists of:

Memory (RAM or Random Access Memory) chips installed on single in-line memory modules (SIMMs) are a temporary high speed holding area for data and applications for fast access by the CPU

CPU (Central Processing Unit) is a programmable device that can process digital information.

Chipset is a collection of semiconductor chips that are the interface between the CPU and the rest of the computer, and instructs the computer how to organize and transmit data.

The chipset will typically include such features as the system memory controller, the PCI controller and the AGP controller.

A Special **graphics chip** to speed processing due to the complexity of graphics files.

Connected to the motherboard by cables are:

- The **hard drive(s)** which offer large data storage capacity and store most applications, including the operating system.

- **Floppy drive(s)** which are primarily used to load applications, and to retain and transport small data files.

- **CD-ROM drive** (Compact Disc/Read Only Memory) can store larger applications and more data. The faster your CD-ROM the faster your software will load.

Plugged into the Motherboard via **AGP** (Accelerated Graphics Port), **ISA** (Industry Standard Architecture) and **PCI** (Peripheral Component Interconnect) **expansion slots** are various **adapter cards** that allow you to customize the computer, such as:

- sound card (makes sound)

- video card (show graphics and pictures)

- modem (to connect to the Internet) is an acronym for MOdulator/DEModulator. It sends digital info through analog telephone lines.

- network card (to connect to other computers)

A special memory chip, the **L2 cache**, performs certain tasks more quickly than SDRAM.

AGP Bus provides graphics processors with a dedicated pathway to the main memory of a computer.

PCI Bus is the data highway inside a computer along which hard drives, graphics cards and other internal devices send data to each other.

ISA Bus is the data highway inside a computer along which modems, networking cards and other devices send data to each other.

Parallel Port transmits and receives data eight bits at a time, over eight wires and is faster than a serial port. It connects devices such as scanners, printers, external drives, etc. to a computer

Serial Port transmits and receives data one bit at a time through one wire in a series and is slower than a parallel port. It connects printers, mouses and other devices to a computer.

USB Port (Universal Serial Bus) connects devices such as CD drives, zip drives, scanners, printers, mice, keyboards and speakers to a computer.

Power Supply converts the AC voltage from the wall socket to DC voltage that powers the computer circuits.

CMOS battery is what provides the power to a special battery powered memory — **CMOS** (Complementary Metal-Oxide Semiconductor technology) — that a computer uses to keep track of its particular configuration along with the date and time.

There are several competing "mass" storage technologies that allow users to record as well as read data, including removable hard drives, high-capacity diskettes, cartridges, tape drives, writeable CD's, DVD ROMS, and other numerous other devices, all designed to make your life easier.

CPU

Understanding how computers actually work begins with an understanding how the **Central Processing Unit (CPU)** affects the performance of a computer. The CPU (also "microprocessor" or "processor") is a vital component that is:

Central — it is the center of computer's data processing.

Processor — it processes (moves and calculates) data.

Unit — it is a chip, which contains millions of transistors.

The CPU is the silicon chip (also "silicon wafer"), or processor that makes everything work together. Without the CPU, there would be no Personal Computer (PC). The CPU is the "chip" that performs data manipulation in your computer. A CPU is the brain of the computer. It has millions of switches that control the flow of data. Data is coded by the switches in bits. One bit corresponds to a switch inside the computer that can be "on" or "off". The switches are controlled by computer programs called "software."

CPUs are continually undergoing development and for years have doubled their performance about every 18 months. There is no indication that this trend will stop.

CPUs came into being around 1971, when a then unknown company, Intel, combined multiple transistors to form a central processing unit. It was not until years later that the first personal computers came into being. Personal computers are now built using different makes and models of CPUs and although Intel dominates the market, it is certainly not the only company making them. The first CPUs could only work with whole numbers, but once the CPUs reached the Pentium level a mathematical co-processor, called the Floating-Point Unit (FPU), was added to the CPUs architecture for better math processing. Some current CPUs are the Pentium (including the MMX, Pro, II and III), the Cyrix 6X86 and 6x86MX, the AMD K5 (and K6, K6-2, K6-3, K7 Athlon), the IDT WinChip C6 (and the WinChip2 3D), the Celeron, the Xeon, and the Merced.

The CPU is situated on the computer's motherboard and its work is primarily calculations and data transport. Before it can be processed, the data you enter into the computer is transmitted along a path to the CPU called the system bus. The system bus feeds streams of data (consisting of the data itself and instructions on how to handle the data) to the CPU. You've probably heard of program code. That's what the instructions are — program code! Data is what you input via a mouse or a keyboard, i.e., a letter to the telephone company. When you print that letter you are actually using "program code" by sending a print instruction to the CPU.

Your computer's CPU is, in all probability, "8086 compatible" which means that your computer's various programs communicate with the CPU in a specific family of instructions which were written for the Intel 8086 processor. This is also known as "the IBM compatible PC." All IBM compatible processors, no matter how advanced handle the "8086 instruction format."

Many of the older CPUs had a Complex Instruction Set Computer (CISC), which means the computer could understand many complex instructions. However, Reduced Instruction Set Computer (RISC) is used in most newer CPUs. RISC is exactly what it says — the instructions are brief and the same length (for example 32 bit long) processing much faster than the CISC instructions.

You now understand that a CPU is a data processing gadget, mounted on a printed circuit board, called the motherboard. You know that most of the data processing takes place inside the CPU and that the data is transported via the system bus. However, we have not addressed what determines the speed of the CPU. For example, in the Pentium III, "500 MHz" is the clock frequency. What this means is that a small crystal located on the motherboard constantly ticks to the CPU at a steady number of clock ticks per second and at a "tick" something happens in the CPU. Thus, the more ticks per second (frequency) — the more data that is processed per second.

One problem with high clock frequencies is that the computer's other electronic components must keep pace. When the frequency gets too high it becomes an expensive proposition to design equipment that can keep pace. Our manufacturing geniuses came up the solution — split the clock frequency in two, this is called clock doubling. Clock doubling uses a high internal clock frequency for the CPU and a lower external clock frequency for the system bus which is where the CPU exchanges data with the RAM and the Input/Output (I/O) units — keyboards, mouses, printers, monitors, disk drives, etc.

Memory

The next important component of a computer is the chips where data is stored called memory. There are many kinds of memory necessary for the operation of a computer, such as **ROM** (read only memory) PROM (programmable read only memory), Flash Memory which is a type of PROM and cache Memory. The only memory you will need to make any decision about is the **RAM** and cache. The CPU can access data in any of the RAM cell locations in any order and it writes to the memory in any order. If you add additional RAM to a computer, you can increase its ability to process programs and applications at a faster speed. There are several types of RAM, but you only need to remember one — SDRAM or whatever is the most recent incarnation. Forget the others when considering server configuration.

Remember that more is better. In discussing RAM, the size of memory is measured in bytes and each byte has its own address. 1 byte is 8 bits (remember the switches in the CPU is a bit), so a kilobyte ("KB") is 1,024 bytes, megabyte ("MB") is 1,048,576 bytes, gigabyte ("GB") is about a billion bytes and there is even a terabyte which is about one trillion bytes.

Cache

CPUs run much faster than everything else in the computer, which means that a computer is designed to ensure that the processor is not slowed down by the devices it works with. Slowdowns mean wasted processor cycles, where the CPU can't do anything because it is sitting and waiting for data. There is a special kind of fast RAM, like SRAM, that a CPU needs; it is usually referred to as the cache. The cache holds the data that is likely to be needed next by the CPU. The cache operates somewhat as a buffer between the very fast CPU and the slow system RAM (memory) — it's not really slow, the CPU is just very fast.

There are different types of cache in a computer, all acting as a buffer for often-used data to enhance the computer's performance. Each layer is closer to the CPU and faster than the layer below it and each layer caches the layers below it, due to its increased speed relative to the lower levels. By utilizing this cache system, when the CPU needs something from memory, it gets it as soon as possible. Here is how it works: The CPU gets a data request and it goes to the L1 cache because it's the fastest. If it finds the data there it uses it and there is no performance delay. If not, the CPU goes to the L2 cache and if it finds it there the CPU goes on with little delay. If the CPU doesn't find the needed data, it sends a "read request" to the system RAM where the data may be stored or the system RAM may have to go to a disk (hard, floppy, CD-ROM) to retrieve the data which results in slowing the CPU's performance.

Level 1 (L1) Cache (sometimes referred to as internal cache) consists of high-speed memory built into most CPUs. It is small, generally from 8 KB to 64 KB, but fast, it runs at the same speed as the CPU. By using L1 cache, the CPU can access often-used data more quickly. The amount of L1 varies but is not upgradeable.

Level 2 Cache is also called the L2, the "burst" or the "pipeline" and when cache is referred to without qualifiers or as "system cache" or "external cache", it means the Level 2 cache that is placed between the processor and the system RAM. The L2 is usually separate from the CPU and situated on the Motherboard. It is larger and a little slower than the L1 Cache, the size varies (usually between 512 KB to 2 MB) and, unlike the L1, it is usually upgradeable. The L2 works in conjunction with the CPU's internal cache (L1) to provide maximum performance. This cache is where oft-used data is retained in memory as a way to help the CPU so that it seems to run even faster when this oft-used data is accessed. When considering the L2, "the bigger the better."

Disk cache is the part of the system RAM used to cache reads and writes to a drive (hard or external). It is not the size of disk cache that is important, but the organization of the cache itself ("write/read cache" or "look ahead cache"). Disk cache has the slowest speed since system RAM is slightly slower than the L1 or L2 and the drives themselves are much slower than the system RAM.

Hard Drives

Your next major consideration is the hard drives. Your hard drive is the computer's storage area — the filing cabinet. All of files (operating system, applications and data) are stored on the hard drive. Hard drives are measured in "Gigabytes". The bigger your hard drive is, the more files you can load. The hard drive has a tremendous impact on the computer's overall performance causing delay while data is pulled off the drive. For example, drive access time is measured in milliseconds and RAM in nanoseconds.

The **EIDE** (Enhanced Integrated Drive Electronics) drives allow fast transfers and large capacities. The computer's system RAM is used for storing the drive's firmware (software or BIOS). When the drive powers up, it reads the firmware.

The **SCSI** (Small Computer Serial Interface) drive is the fastest with the largest capacity and the highest transfer rate available on the market. This is not to say that the EIDE drive isn't capable of the same, it's just that high-end drives with high capacity and high performance are built for servers. The power of SCSI is that several devices can use its interface simultaneously and the multi-tasking environment of servers is ideal for SCSI since there is frequent simultaneous access.

The Interface

One of the factors that affect the speed of a hard drive is the interface. Currently there are two common interfaces: EIDE and SCSI. The EIDE controller is integrated with the motherboard. The SCSI requires an extra controller since most motherboards don't have integrated SCSI controllers.

The EIDE interface can connect a total of four devices to a computer bus such as 2 hard drives, a CD-ROM and a DVD.

The SCSI interface can connect up to 15 devices to a computer bus. There are several types of SCSI interfaces — 8-bit, 16-bit and even 32-bit. The transfer rate started at 5 Mbps for the old SCSI 1 evolving in increments up to the 16-bit, 40 Mbps Ultra2 SCSI, then the 16-bit, 80 Mbps Ultra2 Wide SCSI. The latest incarnation is the 32-bit, 160 Mbps Ultra3 SCSI or Ultra1 60. For normal computer operation, the performance of a drive receives only a small boost from the SCSI interface but for a Web site, you should seriously consider the SCSI.

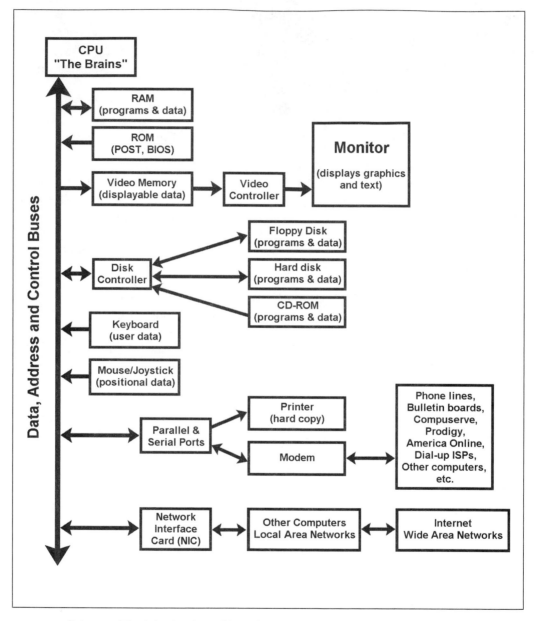

Schema of the infrastructure of typical computer.

GLOSSARY

ACLS (Access Control List Service). Restricts access to computer resources such as files and directories.

Active Server Page (ASP). A dynamically created Web page that employs ActivcX scripting. When a surfer requests an ASP page through their browser, the Web server generates in real-time a page with HTML code, which it then sends to the browser.

Active X. An architecture that lets a program (the Active X control) interact with other programs over a network such as the Internet.

Active X Controls. The interactive objects in a Web page that provides interactive and user-controllable functions.

API (Application Programming Interface). Software that an application uses to request and carry out lower-level services performed by a computer's operation system. In short, an API is a hook into software. An API is a set of standard software interrupts, calls and data formats that applications use to initiate contact with network services, mainframe communication programs, etc. Applications use APIs to call services that transport data across a network.

Applet. Small software programs that can be downloaded quickly and used by any computer equipped with a Java-capable browser. (See Java)

Application. A software program that does some type of task. MSWord, Netscape, Winzip, anti-virus programs are some examples of an application.

Application Service Provider (ASP). A third party that manages and distributes software-based services and solutions to its customers from a centralized server base.

Architecture. Refers to the overall organizational structure of a given system, i.e., processor architecture or proprietary architecture. Central to an architecture is the decision about the selection of structural elements and their behavior, as defined by collaborations of larger subsystems, therefore the architectural style is the definitive guide for the system.

Autoresponders. A mail utility that automatically sends a reply to an e-mail message. They are used to send back boilerplate information on a topic without having the requester do anything more than e-mail a particular address. They are also used to send a confirmation that the message has been received.

ASP. See Active Server Page and Application Service Provider.

Backbone. See Internet Backbone.

Bit. The smallest unit of information a computer can process and the basic unit in data communications. Bits compose a byte.

Bot. See Spider.

Bus. All computers use buses — a collection of wires through which data is transmitted from one part of a computer to another. There are two common buses inside a PC — the older ISA bus, capable of transmitting only five megabytes per second and the newer PCI bus, capable of transmitting up to 132 megabytes per second.

Business Rules. A conceptual description of an organization's policies and practices enabling them to automate their polices and practices, and to increase consistency and timeliness of their business processing.

Byte. A set of bits of a specific length that represent a value, in a computer coding scheme. A byte is to a bit what a word is to a character.

C. A very powerful programming language which operates under Unix, MS-DOS, Windows (all flavors) and other operating systems.

Cache. To store data on a disk for quick and easy retrieval instead of retrieving it each time it is requested. In order to conserve bandwidth, large ISPs will cache popular Web pages.

Cells. The smallest component of a table. In a table, a row contains one or more cells.

CGI (Common Gateway Interface). A predefined way in which CGI programs or scripts communicate with a Web server.

CGI bin. A directory on a Web server in which CGI programs (scripts) are stored.

CGI Script. A program consisting of small but highly potent bits of computer code that is usually executed on a Web server so as to provide interactivity to Web pages.

Chargen (CHARacter GENerator). A utility that provides an approximate speed for a computer's Internet connection in characters per second (with compression taken into account).

CISC (Complex Instruction Set Computer). A microprocessor architecture that favors robustness of the instruction set over the speed with which individual instructions are executed.

Client/Server. The client is a PC or program "served" by another networked computing device in an integrated network which provides a single system image. The server can be one or more computers with numerous storage devices.

Cluster. A group of computers and storage devices that function as a single system sharing one or more panel runs and working in a fault-resilient manner, allowing increased effectiveness and efficiency of security, administration and performance.

Comment Tag. Used to insert comments in an HTML document. Comment tags are ignored by browsers (example: <!-- text --> or <Comment>text</comment>).

Connectivity. The property of a network that allows dissimilar devices to communicate with each other. It also refers to a program's or device's ability to link with other programs and devices.

Cookie. An HTTP header that contains a string that a browser stores in a small text file in the Windows/Cookies directory (for Microsoft Internet Explorer) or in the Users folder (for Netscape Navigator) on a computer's hard drive. Cookies store information supplied by a user to be accessed at a later period in time but it is important to note that a cookie can't interact with other data on a computer's hard drive.

CPE (Customer Premises Equipment or Customer Provided Equipment). Refers to equipment on the customer's premises which had been bought from a vendor.

CPU (Central Processing Unit). A programmable device that can process digital information.

Crawler. See Spider.

Cross-selling. Offering a product similar to the one the customer is interested in if the chosen product is unavailable.

CSU/DSU. See DSU/CSU.

CTR (Click-Through-Rate). The ratio of impressions to click-throughs.

Database Publishing. Allows businesses to leverage existing data and data management assets. Many of today's database applications can create files usable by electronic publishing software. By establishing communication the database can continue managing data, and the publishing system can be used as an information synthesis tool to gather data from a variety of sources (databases, graphics, and text) and present it in a single, cohesive document.

DBMS (DataBase Management System). Software that controls the organization, storage, retrieval, security and integrity of data in a database. It accepts requests from the application and instructs the operating system to transfer the appropriate data.

Digital Certificate. A small piece of unique data used by encryption and authentication software. A digital-based ID that contains a user's information. It accomplishes this by attaching a small file containing the certificate owner's name, the name of its issuer and a public encryption key to the information that is transmitted over the Internet.

Directories. A directory is basically a manual entry database system for which a URL is submitted along with a descriptive title and summary for the web site.

Disk Pack. An assembly of magnetic disks that can be removed from a disk drive along with the container from which the assembly must be separated when operating.

Domain name. Unique address of a Web site. The address that gets you to a Web site, and consists of a hierarchical sequence of names separated by dots (periods). Also known as a Web address. It can identify one or more IP addresses. See URL.

DSU/CSU (Digital or Data Service Unit/Channel Service Unit). Communication devices that connect an in-house line to an external digital circuit, such as a T1, DDS, etc. and is similar to a modem, although they connect a digital circuit rather than an analog one.

Dynamic Web page. The dynamic change in the contents of a Web page through the use of a separate file wherein the current contents of that file is displayed on all pages connected to the underlying database whenever a browser requests a Web page.

ECML (Electric Commerce Modeling Language). A universal format for online checkout form data fields. ECML provides a simple set of guidelines that automate the exchange of information between consumers and Web-based merchants.

Echo. A command in a software program that sends data to another computer which "echoes" it back to the user's screen display, allowing the user to visually check if the other computer received the data accurately.

E-Commerce. Buying and/or selling electronically over a telecommunications system. In doing so every facet of the business process is transformed: Pre-sales, updating the catalog and prices, billing and payment processing, supplier and inventory management, and shipment. By using e-commerce a business is able to rapidly process orders, produce and deliver a product/service at a competitive price and at the same time minimize costs.

EDI (Electronic Data Interchange). A series of standards which provide a computer-to-computer exchange of business documents between different companies' computers over the Internet (and phone lines). EDI allows for the transmission of purchase orders, shipping documents, invoices, invoice payments, etc. between a Web-based business and its trading partners. EDI standards are supported by virtually every computer company and packet switched data communications company.

EIDE (Enhanced Integrated Drive Electronics). A hard drive that allows fast transfers and large storage capacities. The computer's system RAM is used for storing the drive's firmware (software or BIOS). When the drive powers up, it reads the firmware.

EJB (Enterprise JavaBeans). A Java API developed by Sun Microsystems that defines a component architecture for multi-tier client/server systems.

Encryption. A system of using encoding algorithms to construct an overall mechanism for sharing sensitive data. The translation of data into a secret code.

ERP (Enterprise Resource Planning). A business management system that integrates all aspects of a business, such as, product planning, manufacturing, purchasing, inventory, sales, and marketing. ERP is generally supported by multi-module application software that helps to manage the system and interact with suppliers, customer service, and shippers, etc.

Extranet. A private, TCP/IP-based network that allows qualified users from the outside to access an internal network.

Ferroresonant transformer. A transformer that regulates the output voltage by the principle of ferroresonance. This occurs when an iron-core inductor is part of an LC circuit and it is driven into saturation, causing its inductive reactance to increase to equal the capacitive reactance of the circuit.

Finger. A standard protocol. A program implementing this protocol lists who is currently logged in on another host. It is a computer command that displays information about people using a particular computer, such as their names and their identification numbers. (Integrated finger is a common Unix network function that reports information relating to a user after entering his or her e-mail address.)

Firewall. Hardware and/or software that sit between two networks, such as an internal network and an Internet service provider. It protects the network by refusing access by unauthorized users. It can even block messages to specific recipients outside the network.

Firmware. Software which is constantly called upon by a computer so it is stored in semi-permanent memory called PROM (Programmable Read Only Memory) or EPROM (Electrical PROM) where it cannot be "forgotten" when the power is shut off. It is used in conjunction with hardware and software and shares the characteristics of both.

FPU (Floating Point Unit). A formal term for the math coprocessors found in many computers. The modern computer has the FPU integrated with the CPU.

Frames. A programming device that divides Web pages into multiple, scrollable regions. This is done by building each section of a Web page as a separate HTML file and having one master HTML file identify all of the sections.

Frame Relay. A packet-switching protocol for connecting devices on a Wide Area Network (WAN). Frame Relay supports data transfer rates at T-1 (1.544 Mbps) and T-3 (45 Mbps) speeds.

Framesets. See Frames.

F-Secure SSH. Provides for secure UNIX shell logins. SSH creates encrypted connections that protect confidential information, such as passwords, from exposure to network eavesdroppers.

FTP (File Transfer Protocol and File Transfer Program). Allows users to quickly transfer files to and from a distant or local computer, list directors, delete and rename files on the distant computer. FTP the program is a MS-DOS program that enables transfers over the Internet between two computers.

Gateway. An electronic repeater device that intercepts and steers electrical signals from one network to another. In data networks, gateways are typically a node that connects two otherwise incompatible networks and often perform code and protocol conversion processes.

GIF (Graphics Interface Format). A format for encoding images into bits so a computer can read the file and display the image on a computer screen.

gTLD (generic Top Level Domain). A small set of top-level domains that do not carry a national identifier, but denote the intended function of that portion of the domain space. For example, .com was established for commercial users and .org for not-for-profit organizations.

GUI (Graphical User Interface) pronounced "gooey". A program with a graphical interface that can take advantage of a computer's graphics capabilities thereby making the program easier to use.

Hacker. An unauthorized person who breaks into a computer system to steal or corrupt data.

Hardware. Objects that go with the computing environment that can be touched. For example, modems, interface cards, floppy disks, hard drives, monitors, keyboards, printers, motherboards, memory chips, etc.

Home page. The main page of a Web site, usually serving as an index or table of contents to other documents stored on the Web server.

HTML (HyperText Markup Language). Used to create documents on the World Wide Web by defining the structure and layout of a Web document through the use of tags and attributes thereby determining how documents are formatted and displayed.

HTTP (HyperText Transfer Protocol). Defines how messages are formatted and transmitted over the World Wide Web, and what actions Web servers and browsers should take in response to various commands.

Hypertext. A type of system in which objects, whether they are text, graphic files, sound files, programs, etc., can be creatively linked to each other.

Image Map or Imagemap. Clickable images. The image is a normal Web image (usually in GIF or JPEG format). The map data set is a description of the mapped regions within the image. The host entry is HTML code that positions the image within the Web page and designates the image as having map functionality.

Infrastructure. The interconnecting hardware and software that supports the flow and processing of information.

Input/Output (I/O) Unit. Any operation, program, or device that transfers data to or from a computer, such as disks (floppy, hard, or writable CD-ROMs, etc.). I/O units can also consist of single function operations such as Input-only devices such as keyboards and mouses and output-only devices such as printers.

Intranet. An internal TCP/IP-based network behind a firewall that allows only users within a specific enterprise to access it.

Internet. A public global network of computers that exchange data.

Internet Backbone. The worldwide structure of cables, routers and gateways that form a super-fast network. It is provided by number of ISPs that use high-speed connections (T-3s, OCs) linked at specific interconnection points (national access points).

Internet Address. A registered IP address assigned by the InterNIC Registration Service.

IP Address. A unique identification consisting of a series of four numbers between 0 and 255, with each number separated by a period, for a computer or network device on a TCP/IP network.

Java. A high-level object-oriented programming language similar to C++ from Sun Microsystems designed primarily for writing software to leave on Web sites which is often downloadable over the Internet. Java is basically a new virtual machine and interpretive dynamic language and environment.

Java Applet. Small Java applications that can be downloaded from a Web server and run on a user's PC by a Java-compatible Web browser.

Java Script. An open source scripting language developed by Netscape (independent of Sun's Java) that enables interactive Web sites by interacting with HTML source code.

JDBC (Java DataBase Connectivity). A Java API that enables Java programs to execute SQL statements similar to ODBC.

JPEG (Joint Photographic Experts Group) also JPG. A compression technique used in editing still images, color faxes, desktop publishing, graphic arts and medical imaging. Although it can reduce image files to approximately 5% of their normal size, some detail is lost in the compression.

Kerberos. A security system that authenticates users but doesn't provide authorization to services or databases, although it does establish identity at log-on.

Keyword. In database management, a keyword is an index entry that identifies a specific record or document. In programming, keywords (sometimes called reserved names) can be commands or parameters, which are reserved by a program because they have special meaning. On the World Wide Web keywords are the terms that you enter into the search field of a search engine or directory.

LAN (Local Area Network). A short distance data communications network consisting of both hardware and software and typically residing inside one building or between buildings adjacent each other — thus allowing all networked devices to share each other's resources.

Link. On the World Wide Web, a link is a reference to another Web site or Web page or document and it takes you to the other Web site, Web page or document when you click on it.

Macros. Small simple programs written to automate specific tasks.

Mail List. A program that allows a discussion group based on the e-mail system.

MAN (Metropolitan Area Network). Two or more LANs links together so resources between the LANs can be shared.

Merchant Account. A business account at a financial institution that functions as a clearing account for credit card transactions.

Meta Tags. HTML code between the <HEAD> and </HEAD> section of a Web page. Meta Tags are accessed by a search engine's spider and used by search engines to describe your entire Web site and individual web pages. Meta Tags are either in the form of keywords or a descriptive phrase.

Micropayments. A business transaction type, which specializes in the sub-dollar range. Although each transaction is a small amount, it can add up to a sizable market because of global access of the Internet.

Motherboard. A circuit board that everything (adapter cards, CPU, RAM, etc.) plugs into and therefore provides the actual physical connection between the different components that make up the computer.

Navigation. Traveling from place to place on a Web page, a Web site or the Web, from information to information. It can also mean to search for information from a menu hierarchy or hypertext. Navigation in a hypertext environment (the Web) is a physical experience of scrolling, scanning and clicking, moving over the text with your mouse pointer and actively clicking on hyperlinks.

Netstat. A utility that provides statistics on the network components, i.e., it shows the network status. It displays the contents of various network-related data structures in vari-

ous formats. For example, it displays: all connections and listening ports (server connections are normally not shown), ethernet statistics, addresses and port numbers in numerical form (rather than attempting name look-ups), per-protocol statistics (shows connections for the protocol specified by protocol), and the contents of the routing table.

ODBC (Open DataBase Connectivity). A standard database access method developed by Microsoft Corporation that allows databases such as dBASE, Microsoft Access, FoxPro and Oracle to be accessed by a common interface independent of the database file format.

ODBMS. See OODBMS.

OODBMS (Object-Oriented DataBase Management System aka ODBMS). A database management system (a program that lets one or more users simultaneously create and access data in a database) that supports the modeling and creation of data as an object.

Packet. A bundle that contains data and certain control information including a destination address which is transmitted on a network.

PC (Personal Computer). A computer designed for use by a single person versus simultaneous use by more than one person.

PERL (Practical Extraction and Report Language). An interpreted scripting programming language which is used in writing CGI scripts.

Ping (Packet InterNet Groper). A program used to test whether a particular network destination on the Internet is online by repeatedly bouncing a "signal" off a specified address and seeing how long that signal takes to complete the round trip. A common Unix network function that reports on whether another computer is currently up and running on the Internet as well as how long the ping takes to reach the computer.

Plug-ins. Software modules that run on the viewers' local machine and add to the functionality of an application, such as a browser.

Pop-up Window. A second browser window that "pops up" when called by a link, a button or an action.

Processor Architecture. The over all organizational structure of the processor. The main elements of any processor architecture are the selection and behavior of the structural elements and the selected collaborations that form larger subsystems that guide the workings of the entire processor.

Protocol. A set of rules governing the format of messages that are exchanged between computers and people.

Proxy Server. A server that rests between the client and the server to monitor and filter the traffic traveling between them. It can boost Web browser response time by storing copies of frequently accessed Web pages.

Rack Unit. A vertical shelving system to mount servers.

RAID (Redundant Array of Independent (or Inexpensive) Disks). A system designed to link the capacity of two or more hard drives that are then viewed as a single large virtual drive by the RAID management system. This allows for improved data storage reliability and fault tolerance.

RAM (Random Access Memory). Computer data storage that comes in the form of chips that can be accessed randomly, i.e., any byte of a chip can be accessed without touching the preceding bytes. RAM is the most common memory found in computers, printers, etc.

RDBMS (Relational DataBase Management System). A program that enables one or more people to simultaneously create, update and administer a relational database.

Real-Time. Occurring immediately (as opposed to simultaneously as in real time). The data is processed the moment it enters a computer, as opposed to BATCH processing, where the information enters the system, is stored and is operated on at a later time.

RISC (Reduced Instruction Set Computer). A microprocessor that is designed to favor the speed at which individual instructions execute over the robustness of the instructions; i.e., it performs a smaller simpler set of operating commands so that the computer can operate at a higher speed.

Router. A high intelligent device that connects like and unlike LANs (Local Area Networks), MANs (Metropolitan Area Networks) and WANS (Wide Area Networks), which are protocol sensitive and which can forward packets between the connected networks. As software, it is a system level function that directs a call to an application.

SCSI (Small Computer System Interface) pronounced "scuzzy". A standard for a bus (with its own controller and microprocessor) and interface that allows faster communication between the input/output devices and the computer's main processor and daisy chaining of up to 7 different devices.

Script. A type of computer code that can be directly executed by a program that understands the language in which the script is written.

Search engine. A database system designed to index Internet addresses via a schema that allows submission of a URL and through a defined process the search engine includes the submitted URL into its index.

Server. A computer that manages network resources. For example, a Web server has a very fast permanent connection to the Internet and subsystems to protect against power outages, hackers and system crashes. A database server manages and processes the database and database queries.

Server cabinet. A metal cabinet designed to house rack-mounted servers (some also house tower configured systems). The cabinet will usually have a slotted front door, perforated steel rear door and top panel, with room for fans or blowers, and lift off side panels.

SET (Secured Electronic Transactions). A standard that enables secure credit card transactions on the Internet thereby making the theft of credit card numbers via the Internet much more difficult.

SMTP (Simple Mail Transfer Protocol). A TCP/IP protocol for sending e-mail between servers. The majority of the e-mail systems in use today send mail use SMTP to send mail via the Internet.

SNMP (Simple Network Management Protocol). A network monitoring and control protocol. Data is passed from SNMP agents that are hardware and/or software processes reporting activity in a network device such as a hub, router, bridge, etc. to the computer administering the network. The SNMP agents return information contained in a MIB (Management Information Base), which is a data structure that defines what is obtainable from the device and what can be controlled, i.e., turned off, on, etc.

Software. Computer instructions or data — anything that can be stored electronically is software.

SPARC. Sun Microsystems' open RISC-based architecture for microprocessors. SPARC is the basis for Sun's own computer platforms and it's licensed to third parties.

Spider. A special program (also referred to as "bot" or "crawler") utilized by search engines to index Web sites. There are two spider classes — deep and shallow. The deep spider drills through the entire Web site and then either finds the URL and copies the file or finds a single directory within the URL and copies the file. A shallow spider can do one of two things, it can either spider the URL given and stop, or only spider those URLs it finds within a single level of directories.

SQL (Structured Query Language) pronounced "sequel". A database language used for creating, maintaining and viewing database data.

SSL (Secure Socket Layer). A transport level technology developed by Netscape for authentication and data encryption between a Web server and a Web browser.

SSL Server Certificate. Also known as a Digital Certificate, it is a small piece of unique data used by encryption and authentication software which enables SSL encryption on a Web Server. This allows a Web site to accept credit card orders securely.

Storyboard. The pictorial representation of the screen elements and their operations for every Web page, which taken as a whole, constitutes a Web site.

Systat. A program owned by SPSS that provides powerful statistical techniques through its convenience in handling data, selecting and defining procedures to use, and formatting output.

Tables. A collection of data arranged in rows and columns and in which each item is arranged in relation to the other items.

Targeted text link. Text you can click on that will transport you to a specific section of a Web site.

Tcl Scripting Language (pronounced "tickle"). An open-source tool command scripting language that can be embedded within existing C++ code. As such, Tcl is used in the development of many Web sites.

TCP (Transmission Control Protocol). A transport layer, connection-oriented, end-to-end protocol that provides reliable, sequenced and unduplicated delivery of bytes to a remote or local user.

TCP/IP (Transmission Control Protocol/Internet Protocol). A networking protocol (the Internet's protocol) that provides communication across interconnected networks, between computers with diverse hardware architectures and various operating systems.

Telnet. A terminal-remote host protocol. A program that lets one computer connect to another computer on the Internet.

Text-only Browser. A browser that cannot handle hypermedia files. For example, Lynx is a text-only browser that lets you travel from one link on the Web to the next, in sequential order. Lynx gives access to all of the information that the graphical browsers can, just without the pictures or sounds. Netscape and Internet Explorer are graphical browsers that let you see pictures and hear sound.

TLD (Top Level Domain). Domains of which .com, .net and .org are the most common.

Traceroute. Software to help you analyze what's happening on an Internet connection by showing the full connection path between one Web site and another Internet address. A common Unix network function that reports the number of hops, or intermediate routers, between a computer and a remote server.

Traffic Allowance. Refers to how many bytes can be transferred from a Web site per month, i.e., number of megabytes sent to a Web site's visitors' browsers.

UPS (Uninterruptible Power Supply). Generally a device that allows a system to maintain operation when changes to the power supply would otherwise interrupt the function of that system. They can range from a 9 Volt battery backup to a generator.

Up-selling. Offering customers additional recommendations when they are placing an order.

URL (Uniform Resource Locator). The global address of resources on the Internet. The first part of the address indicates what protocol to use, and the second part specifies the IP address or the domain name where the resource is located.

VPN (Virtual Private Network). A secure, encrypted connection between two points across the Internet. It can act as an intranet or extranet, but uses the Internet as the networking connection. Most VPNs are built and run by Internet service providers.

WAN (Wide Area Network). A network that is geographically scattered with a broader structure than a LAN. It can be privately owned or leased, but the term usually implies public networks.

Web. A subset of the Internet that in today's world is accessed via a Web browser.

Web address. See Domain Name.

Web hosting service. A third party that leases space on its Web servers and use of its other hardware such as UPS, backup, its technical staff, etc., so the lessee's Web site can be accessed over the Internet.

Web page editor. A plain text editor, such as Notepad for Windows offers a place to type in your HTML code so that you can post the file on your Web site. A more complicated editor can do just about everything for you (so there is no need to know HTML) just drag and drop text, images, etc. onto your page, and the editor writes the code.

Web Server. A computer with data and specific software to operate a Web site.

Web Site. Data residing on a computer which has software running on it that allows the download and presentation of the data to another computer that is permanently connected to the Internet.

Whois. A common Unix network function that queries databases for information about domain names, IP address assignments, and individual names.

WYSIWYG (What You See Is What You Get) pronounced wiz-e-wig. An application that enables you to see on the computer monitor exactly what will appear when the document is printed.

XML (eXtensible Markup Language). A system for organizing and tagging elements of a document specifically designed for Web documents. It enables designers to create their own customized tags to provide functionality not available with HTML. XML also has the ability to enable the structured exchange of data between computers attached to the Web, thus allowing one Web server to talk to another Web server. This means manufacturers and merchants can begin to quickly swap data, such as pricing, stock-keeping numbers, transaction terms and product descriptions.

INDEX

WEB SITES